'RACE' AND COMMUNITY CARE

'RACE', HEALTH AND SOCIAL CARE

Series editors:

Dr Waqar I. U. Ahmad, Head of Research Unit on Ethnicity and Social Policy, Department of Social and Economic Studies, University of Bradford.

Professor Charles Husband, Professor of Social Analysis and Associate Head, Research Unit on Ethnicity and Social Policy, Department of Social and Economic Studies, University of Bradford.

Minority ethnic groups now constitute over 5 per cent of the UK population. While research literature has mushroomed on the one hand in race and ethnic relations generally, and on the other in clinical and epidemiological studies of differences in conditions and use of health and social services, there remains a dearth of credible social scientific literature on the health and social care of minority ethnic communities. Social researchers have hitherto largely neglected issues of 'race' and ethnicity, while acknowledging the importance of gender, class and, more recently, (dis)ability in both the construction of and provision for health and social care needs. Consequently the available social science texts on health and social care largely reflect the experiences of the white population and have been criticized for marginalizing black people.

This series aims to provide an authoritative source of policy relevant texts which specifically address issues of health and social care in contemporary multi-ethnic Britain. Given the rate of change in the structure of health and social care services, demography and the political context of state welfare there is a need for a critical appraisal of the health and social care needs of, and provision for, the minority ethnic communities in Britain. By the nature of the issues we will address, this series will draw upon a wide range of professional and academic expertise, thus enabling a deliberate and necessary integration of theory and practice in these fields. The books will be inter-disciplinary and written in clear, non-technical language which will appeal to a broad range of students, academics and professionals with a common interest in 'race', health and social care.

Current and forthcoming titles

'RACE' AND COMMUNITY CARE

Edited by
Waqar I. U. Ahmad and Karl Atkin

Open University Press
Buckingham · Philadelphia

Open University Press
Celtic Court
22 Ballmoor
Buckingham
MK18 1XW

and
1900 Frost Road, Suite 101
Bristol, PA 19007, USA

First Published 1996

A catalogue record of this book is available from the British Library

ISBN   0 335 19462 1 (pb)   0 335 19463 X (hb)

Library of Congress Cataloging-in-Publication Data
Race and community care / edited by Waqar I. U. Ahmad and Karl Atkin.
    p.   cm. — (Race, health, and social care)
    Includes bibliographical references and index.
    ISBN 0–335–19462–1 (pb). — ISBN 0–335–19463–X (hb)
    1. Minorities—Services for—Great Britain.   2. Social work with minorities—Great Britain.   3. Community health services—Great Britain.   4. Race discrimination—Great Britain.   I. Ahmad, W. I. U. (Waqar Ihsan Ullah), 1957-   .   II. Atkin, Karl.   III. Series.
HV3177.G7R33   1996
362.84′00941—dc20   95–50908
                                                                CIP

Typeset by Graphicraft Typesetters Ltd, Hong Kong
Printed in Great Britain by Biddles Ltd, Guildford and King's Lynn

Contents

Series editors' preface

Minority ethnic groups now constitute over 5 per cent of the UK population. While research literature has mushroomed on the one hand in 'race' and ethnic relations generally, and on the other in clinical and epidemiological studies of differences in conditions and use of health and social services, there remains a dearth of credible social scientific literature on the health and social care of minority ethnic communities. Social researchers have hitherto largely neglected issues of 'race' and ethnicity, while acknowledging the importance of gender, class and, more recently, (dis)ability in both the construction of and provision for health and social care needs. Consequently the available social science texts on health and social care largely reflect the experiences of the white population and can be criticized for marginalizing minority ethnic people.

This book edited by Ahmad and Atkin not only offers a wide-ranging introduction to contemporary issues surrounding the health care needs of members of minority ethnic communities within the framework of community care; it also introduces a new book series. The texts in this series will recognize the very particular political and professional processes and interests which interact in determining the health care needs, and health care delivery, experienced by minority ethnic communities in Britain. By taking as its prime focus and concern the experience of health and social care of minority ethnic communities in Britain, this series will routinely be interdisciplinary in the way it draws on social and political sciences in contextualizing the issues of service definition and provision it addresses. It will recognize, but challenge, professional boundaries in the ways in which it examines the recognition of health and care needs, and the mobilization of resources to meet them. It must in the broadest sense allow its authors to be 'political' as they make explicit the social bases of health and social care needs and the power relations inherent in the mobilization of the political will and economic and human resources to respond to these needs.

However, the series will not, and cannot, be a platform for the expression of a uniform political agenda, or for a pre-existing programmatic model of health and social care delivery systems. The series editors have no wish to assume such an awesome, and improbable, omnipotence. Indeed, the relatively recent willingness of some policy analysts and health care professionals to address the health care needs of minority ethnic communities has not generated a sufficient body of analysis or professional innovation for such a consensus to have emerged, or be given any credence. The diversity of experience represented within ethnic communities and between communities guarantees complexity; and the politics of the British national and local government system provide a sufficient basis for contested definitions of health care needs and health care delivery. For these reasons at least this series will inevitably address contentious issues, air contradictory analyses and range from wide macro-analyses to quite specific policy issues. This first book is itself an exemplar of this style.

In trying to reveal the differing processes underlying the legitimate expression of ethnic identity and the inexcusable defence of racial exclusion, the texts in this series will of necessity require some sophistication of their authors – and their readers. In accepting ethnic diversity as a demographic *de facto* reality in contemporary Britain, the series takes the equitable recognition of difference to be an essential defining feature of contemporary caring professions. Where specific profiles of health and welfare need are linked to discriminatory social practices which replicate privilege and disadvantage between different categories of citizen, universalist assumptions about the means of meeting the apparently equivalent needs of 'clients' will of necessity be challenged. And where normative expectations regarding the ethics of social care are critically exposed by differing personal moralities of obligation to one's own kin or community, the philosophical basis for state intervention into caring cannot be left unexamined. Additionally, the generic features of health care systems in Britain will be explored to reveal their particular impact upon services to minority ethnic communities. And the autonomous capacities of these communities to define and meet their needs will be examined in relation to generic systems of provision. The equitable recognition of difference in identity and need is an essential starting point for a policy debate around the appropriate means of guaranteeing an equitable and sensitive system for providing appropriate diversity and flexibility in service delivery: something which is recognized in this text.

This series will provide an authoritative source of policy-relevant texts which specifically address issues of health and social care in contemporary multi-ethnic Britain. Given the rate of change in the structure of health and social care services, demography and the political context of state welfare, there is a need for a critical appraisal of the health and social care needs of, and provision for, the minority ethnic communities in Britain. By the nature of the issues to be addressed, this series will draw upon a wide range of professional and academic expertise, thus enabling a deliberate and necessary integration of theory and practice in these fields, and establish its relevance for a broad range of academic courses, as well as practitioners and policy-makers.

Waqar I. U. Ahmad and Charles Husband

Notes on contributors

Waqar I. U. Ahmad is Head of the Research Unit on Ethnicity and Social Policy, Department of Social and Economic Studies, University of Bradford.

Karl Atkin is Senior Research Fellow at the Research Unit on Ethnicity and Social Policy Research, University of Bradford.

Gary Craig is Professor of Social Policy at the University of Humberside

Charles Husband is Professor of Social Analysis and Associate Head, Research Unit on Ethnicity and Social Policy, Department of Social and Economic Studies, University of Bradford.

Dhanwant K. Rai is an independent researcher and was previously a Researcher at the National Institute for Social Work.

Janet Rollings is a counsellor at the University of York and was previously a Research Fellow at the Social Policy Research Unit, University of York.

Ossie Stuart was a Research Fellow at the Social Policy Research Unit, University of York and is now an independent researcher and lecturer.

Charles Watters is a Lecturer at the Tizard Centre, University of Kent.

Fiona Williams is Professor of Social Policy at the School of Sociology and Social Policy, University of Leeds.

Acknowledgements

Charles Husband discussed the format of the book at length with us, and, as joint series editor, read the full manuscript before submission. We are most grateful to him for his support and detailed feedback. Our thanks go to Jenny Bowes for transforming chapters submitted in different formats into a coherent manuscript at great speed. Finally, we thank Jacinta Evans, Joan Malherbe and other colleagues at the Open University Press for their help and patience.

1

'Race' and community care: an introduction

Waqar I. U. Ahmad and Karl Atkin

Community care is a vital plank of public policy. Reflecting this, literature on community care has mushroomed over the past few years and includes descriptions and analysis of the policy (Wistow *et al.* 1994), issues in implementation (Malin 1994), critiques of community care from a number of perspectives (Dalley 1988; Morris 1991) and the importance of family obligations to the care for the sick or elderly in their own homes (Finch and Groves 1983; Qureshi and Walker 1989; Finch and Mason 1993). There remains, however, a dearth of research and debate on community care for people of minority ethnic communities. This book is a contribution to this neglected area.

The origins of community care

Community care re-emerged as a prominent feature of public policy in the mid-1980s. The Social Services Committee Report was instrumental in placing community care on the policy agenda. Subsequent reports by the Audit Commission and Sir Roy Griffiths ensured that it remained high on the policy agenda (House of Commons Social Services Committee 1985; Audit Commission 1986; Griffiths 1988). The concept's attractiveness to politicians across political divides, policy-makers and practitioners seems to owe much to its convenient vagueness and ability to encompass a range of meaning. As Parker (1990: 7) notes, 'community care can be and has been used to refer both to policy goals or ideals and to a variety of practical measures – the provision of welfare and personal social services for example – designed to further that ideal.'

Community care is not, however, a recent policy development. For example, the 1908 Royal Commission on the Care of the Feeble Minded advocated guidance and supervision in the community, where appropriate (Jones 1960). Despite the growth in large segregated institutions during the first half of the century the emphasis on community care was gradually strengthened by successive policy documentation and legislation (e.g. the 1929 report of the Wood Committee and the 1927 Mental Health Act). The real impetus for the present policies of care in the community began in the late 1950s (Cmnd 169). Since then successive governments have sought to shift the care of older and disabled people away from institutions to care in their own homes. Although originally concerned with relocating people from long-stay hospitals to 'the community', the policy has since been widened to include the provision of health and social care to people in their own homes. The assumptions underpinning community care remain reasonably unchallenged: that living outside large-scale segregated institutions is in the best interests of disabled people and is in accordance with their own wishes and those of their family. None the less, as this book demonstrates, community care, both as a concept and as policy and practice, is characterized by complexities. In particular the current restructuring of welfare provision raises the possibility of a fundamental transformation in the management and delivery of community care in the UK.

The new community care

Community health and social services are undergoing the most substantial changes since the beginning of the post-war welfare state (Wistow *et al.* 1994). Specifically, the idea that market efficacy – rather than collective planning mechanisms – is the best way of ensuring efficiency, accountability and choice in community care is at the heart of government health care policy. To achieve this, the 1990 NHS and Community Care Act introduced the separation of purchasing and providing functions in health and social care agencies. Notions such as the 'quasi-market' and the 'mixed economy of care' have begun to inform the organization of community care services.

Two concerns – one financial and the other organizational – inform these general changes. First, the government, under pressure to control growing public spending on health and social care, was concerned with using existing budgets more 'efficiently'. Consequently, 'value for money' and the prevention of waste and inappropriate targeting of resources, identified by various reports (Audit Commission 1986), emerged as central aspects of government policy. Second, government policy had questioned the responsiveness and accessibility of community care services. Griffiths's agenda for action on community care, for example, argued that community service delivery was poorly related to need (Griffiths 1988). This echoed the concerns of the earlier Audit Commission report, which emphasized the importance of 'a flexible service response' that offered a wider range of options. The report concluded by calling for 'the adjustment of services to meet the needs of people rather than the adjustment of people to meet the needs of services' (Audit Commission 1986). Ensuring that provision was tailored to more systematically assessed needs and preferences of individual users and their carers became a fundamental policy goal for future community care services. Ideals such as citizenship, consumerism, participation and choice have emerged as key objectives in attempts to empower recipients of health and social services (Cmnd 849; Cmnd 1599).

Within this context, the policy guidance and reviews associated with the 1990 NHS and Community Care Act argue that 'good community care' must recognize the circumstances of minority communities, be sensitive to their needs and be planned in consultation with them (Cmnd 849; Department of Health 1990; Audit Commission 1992a, b). The present restructuring of community care and some recognition of the multiracial nature of British society provides opportunities to improve provision to black and ethnic minorities. The introduction of needs-led care, the opening of consultation and planning processes to direct local influence and a new awareness of carers' needs are all potentially helpful developments. These opportunities, however, arise in the context of resource constraints and existing demands – community care for minority ethnic communities fits into this broader context (Butt 1994).

The introduction of the current community care reforms cannot be divorced from the existing disadvantages facing minority ethnic communities, especially since empirical evidence suggests that community services do not adequately recognize and respond to the needs of people from ethnic minorities (Dominelli 1989; Atkin and Rollings 1993a, b; Butt 1994; Walker and Ahmad 1994). Problems of access to, and appropriateness of, community health and social services have been well documented. Three themes emerge as significant and their impact is evident throughout the book.

First, community service provision often ignores the needs of black and minority ethnic groups. For example, structural barriers to access are not taken into account when in the organization of services. Often service managers will say that services are 'open to all' regardless of ethnic background. Yet racial inequalities and poverty disadvantage minority ethnic people and can create additional barriers to gaining service support; and the dietary, linguistic and caring needs of minority ethnic communities are often disregarded because services are organized to white norms (Atkin and Rollings 1993a, b). Examples include the inability of health and social services to provide support for people who do not speak English or, more specifically, the unavailability of vegetarian food or halal meat in day care and domiciliary services. 'Specialist services', a popular response to these problems, although often beneficial, are too often a euphemism for short-term and inadequately funded provision (Patel 1990; Butt 1994). Yet, at the same time, mainstream services use the existence of specialist services to absolve themselves of responsibility for ensuring access and appropriateness of services (Atkin and Rollings 1993a, b). It should also be remembered that 'special provision' often leads to internal divisions within the minority ethnic communities who compete with each other on the basis of 'culturally distinctive needs' (Walker and Ahmad 1994; see also Chapters 3 and 7, this volume).

Second, community care services often misrepresent the needs of ethnic minorities because of a preoccupation with cultural differences (Ahmad 1993). The emphasis on cultural practices means that many service organizations blame the potential client group for either experiencing specific problems or not making 'appropriate' use of services, rather than examine the relevance of the service being provided. The onus for change is thus on minority groups rather than purchasers and providers of services. For example, minority ethnic communities are frequently characterized as being in some way to blame for their own needs because of their supposedly deviant and unsatisfactory lifestyles (Cameron *et al.* 1989). Indeed, there is a history of defining health and social problems faced by minority ethnic communities in terms of cultural deficits where a shift towards a 'Western' lifestyle is offered as the main solution to their problems (see Ahmad 1993: Chapter 3 for discussion). More recently, a variety of congenital malformations as well as higher deaths among Pakistani babies are being attributed to consanguineous marriages (Ahmad 1996). Reductionist approaches to minority cultures abound, and although their simplicity and rigidity hinders rather than helps service delivery, they remain popular with professionals (Bowler 1993).

Third, racist attitudes on the part of service providers have been reported in a number of studies in health and social services (e.g. Cameron *et al.* 1989; Ahmad *et al.* 1991; Bowler 1993). Health and social service professionals exercise considerable discretion and their views about users and carers can influence the nature of service provision (Twigg and Atkin 1994). Local authorities often list black people as 'high risk' clients, 'uncooperative' and 'difficult to work with' (Cameron *et al.* 1989). Similarly, stereotypes of minority ethnic group patients, as 'calling out doctors unnecessarily', 'being trivial complainers' and 'time wasters', are common (Ahmad *et al.* 1991; Bowler 1993). These racist attitudes deprive minority ethnic communities of their full and equal rights to services.

Despite the current restructuring of community care provision, there remains widespread uncertainty, puzzlement and ignorance about what should be done to meet the community care needs of minority ethnic communities (Butt 1994; Walker and Ahmad 1994). Policy remains underdeveloped, comprising little more than bland statements in support of racial equality, while the mechanisms that might achieve race equality, and the principles that underlie them, remain unexplored. Devices such as the internal market, the separation of purchaser and provider roles, the mixed economy of care and the enabling role of social services do little to acknowledge, let alone alter, the unequal structuring of opportunities and are, therefore, unlikely to deal with the fundamental disadvantage faced by ethnic minorities.

None the less, it is important not to lose sight of the opportunities created by the 'new community care'. The critical emphasis of the literature

is understandable and has successfully highlighted racism, marginalization and unequal treatment. By focusing on disadvantage there is a danger,
however, of adopting a 'victim-orientated' perspective that undervalues the
significance and contributions of the struggle of minority ethnic people and
their organizations. Change can be pushed through by community action,
as shown for services for sickle cell disorders and thalassaemia. As Walker
and Ahmad (1994) have argued, community care offers a potential win-
dow of opportunity, although exploiting this opportunity requires resources
and organization, which many minority community groups lack. On the
part of purchasers and providers, more appropriate approaches to needs
assessment and community consultation may facilitate improved purchasing and contracting, and the increasingly fashionable ethnic monitoring may
also prove a useful tool for monitoring progress. Future work in this area
needs to acknowledge the possibility for change rather than merely describe
the problems faced by black and ethnic minorities.

Anti-racism and multiculturalism

Besides empowerment, wider debates on anti-racism and multiculturalism
are pertinent to community care. Much of the debate on 'race', health and
social care, in explaining differences between the majority white population and minority black population, conceptualizes the issue in terms
of cultural pluralism and ethnic diversity (see Ahmad 1993; Atkin and
Rollings 1993a, b). This approach also finds expression in a number of
policy areas, including education (Rattansi 1992) and social work (for
critiques see Dominelli 1989; CCETSW 1991a, b). According to multicultural orthodoxies, diversity in language, religion, cultural norms and
expectations prevents effective communication and creates misunderstand-
ings between the majority and minorities. Overcoming the linguistic and
cultural barriers that cause misunderstanding and promoting understanding of the other's culture should result in more sensitive and responsive
services (see Husband 1991; see also Chapter 3, this volume).
    There are several problems with this view, notably that the relation-
ship between ethnically distinct minorities and the majority white society
is seen exclusively in terms of cultural practices. Within this largely uncrit-
ical framework the outcome is to present 'white' culture as the norm. This
diverts attention from the wider power relationships within society and in
particular fails to recognize that the dominant white culture and the minority cultures do not meet on equal terms (Ahmad 1996). The situation of
black people cannot be solely understood in terms of culture – the political, social and economic positions of black people, related to historical
legacies of colonialism and post-colonial relationships, are equally important. Consequently 'anti-racist' approaches, emphasizing the importance of
structural disadvantage in understanding the experience of racialized minorities, challenged the multicultural orthodoxies (Dominelli 1989; CCETSW

1991a, b; Ahmad 1993; Atkin and Rollings 1993a, b). In privileging structural, historical and international considerations, anti-racist approaches
have tended to dismiss the emphasis on cultural difference as a surrogate
form of racism. This is significant as contemporary forms of racism are
increasingly articulated through the language of culture, lineage, belonging
and identity (see Husband 1991; Ahmad 1996). Anti-racist critiques have
been successful in highlighting the disadvantage and racism facing minority ethnic groups.

People from minority ethnic communities are, however, more than the
product of the racism they experience and their forms of resistance and
engagement have often utilized cultural and religious resources. Yet in
orthodox anti-racism cultural identities become buried under the rhetoric
of oppression, resistance and political alliances (Gilroy 1990) – some argue
that, gaining its roots and sustenance from the black American civil rights
movement, orthodox anti-racism privileged Afro-Caribbean perspectives
to the detriment of Asians (Modood 1988). More recently, the symbolic
as well as the practical significance of religious and cultural identities in
mobilization and resistance have been confirmed in Muslim protests (see,
for example, Samad 1992; Ahmad and Husband 1993).

A challenge for academics and practitioners alike, including in relation
to community care, is to recognize the context of black people's lives, to
which their cultural norms, values and resources and racialized oppression
and marginalization are equally pertinent. In drawing together themes and
contributions for this volume, we have been conscious of encompassing
both structural as well as cultural factors in minority ethnic users' interaction with community care.

About the book

Health and social care provision to minority ethnic communities can only
be made sense of in the context of debates around 'race', citizenship and
welfare and racialized constructions of community. Part I, 'Community,
citizenship and welfare', considers these debates in two chapters. Fiona
Williams (Chapter 2) examines the historical relationship between 'race'
and welfare in the first half of the twentieth century by considering three
significant developments. First, in relation to the construction of state
welfare, she notes that ideas of the nation and citizenship went hand-in-
hand with exclusion from welfare of those who were regarded as not
belonging: this continues to have implications for black as well as white
(e.g. the Irish) minority ethnic communities. Racist exclusion from state
welfare, of course, goes back, at least, to the times of Elizabeth I, who
ordered expulsion of black people from the country so that they would
not scrounge on the 'relief' which was the citizenship right of the (white)
nation. Second, Williams draws parallels between different 'race', class,
sexuality, gender and (dis)ability based ideologies of oppression that were

brought together in the eugenics movement. The eugenics movement allowed a neutralization of racist discourses by claiming a scientific basis, and justified differential access to state provision: more control of their presumed dangerousness and out of control sexuality, and less relief of poverty. Third, she considers the reconstruction of the historical legacy of racism in the shape of the pathologization of the black family which accompanied the recruitment of black people to the British labour market in 1940s and 1950s. The migration process, for many, led to the break down of the black (especially Afro-Caribbean) family, which only confirmed the presumed deviance of black family life against the normality of white middle-class families. However, Williams stresses that neither racisms nor resistances against these are post-war phenomena.

Charles Husband (Chapter 3) elaborates on many of the issues raised by Williams. For Husband, to speak of 'community' is to invoke a principle of connectedness and cohesion between people which goes beyond privileging the individual. However, he argues that 'Ethnic communities are psychological *and* political constructions in which personal identities are both reproduced and given collective focus through the socio-political context in which people live.' Three popular meanings of the term 'community' are considered by Husband: community in terms of descriptive notions of territoriality or identity; community of value; and the notion of the 'active' community. Although all three definitions are contested, they are, none the less, antithetical to the individualistic conceptions of human relations. For Husband, in the state's desire to manage community diversity, it privileged or constructed conceptions of ethnic communities which made their management easier. In policy terms, for example, ethnic diversity is acknowledged but then translated into a politics of 'special needs', without challenging practice and organization of services that such acknowledgement demands. Husband also argues that notions of community are closely tied to ideas about nationality, citizenship and deservingness: 'The exclusion of those who do not belong defines those who do.'

Together, Williams and Husband provide the necessary context of a politics of nation, citizenship and exclusion in which state welfare is located and in which black people live their lives and engage with state welfare.

Community care, to a significant extent, rests upon assumptions of willing and available care in the family. Although the literature on caring in the past decade has contributed much to our understanding of the nature and negotiation of caring relationships, relatively little has been written on caring and minority ethnic communities. In Part II, 'Family, obligations and community care', Ahmad, and Atkin and Rollings explore family obligations and family based care.

Ahmad (Chapter 4) notes that although there is an increasing and rich literature on family obligations and the white population, there is a dearth of information on minority ethnic communities. He draws together disparate literature on Asian communities to assess the nature of obligations and processes of continuity and change. He argues that the process of migration itself rests heavily on family-based systems of obligations, and ideas about appropriate behaviour are vital to people's moral and social identities. Material obligations have a particular significance in the lives of migrants and Ahmad looks at these as well as the importance of family support to the social and economic survival and success of Asian communities. However, as noted by Finch (1989), social norms provide only flexible guidelines for behaviour; the negotiation of behaviour is related to, among other factors, personal and moral identities, histories of relationship, closeness of ties, class, gender and place in the family hierarchy. In the second half of the chapter, Ahmad considers the processes of continuity and change, arguing that change rarely implies wholesale rejection of parental values and expectations. He acknowledges, however, that the available evidence on family obligations among Asians (and especially smaller minority ethnic communities) remains limited and highlights the need for work in this area.

Atkin and Rollings (Chapter 5) discuss care-giving in Asian and Afro-Caribbean families. Based on small-scale descriptive studies, the chapter considers physical, emotional and material aspects of caring. Good quality research literature is especially lacking on physical and emotional consequences of caring, where, like the dominant perspective in mainstream literature, the emphasis is on stresses and strains of caring rather than coping strategies and support, which families and disabled people find helpful. Following the rapid growth in the caring literature, it is argued that further research is not required (e.g. Twigg 1992). However, caring among minority ethnic communities remains an under-researched area where high-quality research will add appreciably to knowledge and facilitate improvements in policy and practice.

The literature on 'race' and health has largely ignored issues of chronic illness or disability. Although little is heard about black disabled people, even less is heard *from* black disabled people. However, the past few years have witnessed the emergence of a black disability movement, which is articulating a critique of disablism, racism and other oppressions as experienced by black disabled people. In the opening chapter (Chapter 6) of Part III of the book, 'Case studies in community care', Ossie Stuart, a leading member of the black disability movement, offers a polemic on ethnicity, disability and community care. For Stuart, definitions of disability are central to defining disabled people's needs and the ways of meeting these needs. Whereas the medical and individualistic definitions have been rightly criticized, for Stuart the social model of disability has also tended to homogenize the experiences of all disabled people. For certain black critics, this homogeneity has privileged white perspectives on disability, and Stuart argues for the incorporation of a politics of difference into a fuller understanding of black disabled people's experiences and engagement with oppressions. For these reasons, he is critical of the notion of double discrimination, or the more popular idea of simultaneous oppression: for Stuart both these conceptualizations assume 'the subordination and singularity of black disabled people's experience'. Stuart's arguments challenge the comforting certainties of crude forms of anti-racism and disability politics, and a consideration of these arguments is important for development in both research and practice in this area.

In contrast to disability, there is no shortage of research on ethnicity and mental ill-health. Racism in psychiatry is legendary, both historically and in contemporary practice (Littlewood and Lipsedge 1989). Findings of differential diagnosis of schizophrenia and routes into psychiatric services, differences in treatment regimens, as well as differential outcomes of psychiatric treatment, and breakdown of traditional filters to psychiatric care are well known (Cochrane and Sashidharan 1996). However, relatively little is written on ethnicity and mental health in relation to community care. Charles Watters (Chapter 7) provides a rapid review of some of these findings before considering the relevance of care management and care programme approaches to service provision. However, as Watters notes, both these approaches deal with people who are already within the psychiatric system and are not concerned with issues of access. In relation to access, Watters considers the consequences of the break down of the traditional filters to psychiatric care – from community to GPs, to specialist referral and hospitalization. For Watters, stereotypes of black patients hamper in the normal functioning of these filters. Based on his own empirical work, he also considers the value of specialist projects. Like Cochrane and Sashidharan (1996), Watters is concerned about the effects of 'specialist provision' in terms of mainstream services abdicating responsibility for sensitivity or appropriateness. This relates to Husband's (Chapter 3) point about the management of ethnic diversity through the construction of a culture of special needs, often sustained through funding to the voluntary sector.

A discussion of 'cash' is important for community care for two broad reasons. First, material considerations are important in disabled people's ability to purchase independent care or their families' ability to provide care. Second, social security payments include a 'cash for care' component for those in need of community care or their carers. In Chapter 8, Gary Craig and Dhanwant Rai review the evidence on poverty among minority ethnic communities, consider the role of cash benefits within community care, provide a brief overview of minority ethnic people's experiences of using the social security system and take a critical look at the research findings and the research process in the area of social security. The picture to emerge is one of low entitlements, low information, low access, low uptake and experiences of racism. The responses from the social security system have emphasized scrounging and fraud among minority ethnic communities rather than the abusive exclusion of black people from rights to welfare as citizens. The social security system has, of course, often acted as a second line of immigration control, with its policies of checking residence and entitlement credentials, which brings us back full circle to the relationship between the emergence of the welfare state and racist exclusion of black people from welfare services as discussed by Williams (Chapter 2).

The voluntary sector, as Atkin (Chapter 9) discusses, is an important element in the mixed economy of care. Atkin considers the role of the black voluntary sector in the mixed economy of care. The black voluntary sector is less well resourced, in personnel as well as financial terms, less experienced and considerably younger than the mainstream voluntary sector. This gives it many advantages in terms of flexibility and sensitivity; many of these black voluntary organizations emerged in response to the failure of the statutory and mainstream voluntary services to meet the needs of minority ethnic groups. However, Atkin fears that the requirements of the contract culture may result in the black voluntary sector being either squeezed out of competition or forced to collaborate with larger white organizations. Either way, it is in danger of becoming marginalized and losing autonomy. He does, however, offer a message of hope in the remarkable achievements of the black voluntary housing sector. These are testing times for the black voluntary sector and purchasers, providers and users of community care services. Community care provision will be much poorer if means of meaningful participation of the black voluntary sector in the mixed economy of care are not established.

A note on terminology

Terminology in 'race relations' is contested from both theoretical and political positions (e.g. Modood, 1988; Mason, 1990; Ahmad and Sheldon 1993; Cole 1993). In this volume, diverse terms are used to describe members of minority ethnic communities; for example, 'black', 'ethnic minorities', 'minority ethnic groups'. Recognizing the often politically and theoretically significant choice of terminology, we as editors have felt it inappropriate to impose our own preferences on to other contributors.

Annotated bibliography

Atkin, K. and Rollings, J. (1992) *Community Care in a Multi-racial Britain: a Critical Review of the Literature.* London: HMSO.
A comprehensive literature review exploring the organization of community care in a multiracial Britain. The authors discuss the experience of care-giving and disability in minority ethnic communities: their use of health and social services; the organization and delivery of community health and social care services to people from black and ethnic minorities; and the role of voluntary provision.

Walker, R. and Ahmad, W. I. U. (1994) Windows of opportunity in rotting frames: care providers' perspectives on community care and black communities, *Critical Social Policy*, 40, 46–69.
This is one of the few empirical articles to examine the impact of the NHS and

Community Care Act on service delivery to black and ethnic minorities. The paper explores the perspectives of statutory and voluntary service providers, as they attempt to provide services for black and ethnic minorities within the context of the mixed economy of care.

Wistow, G., Knapp, M., Hardy, B. and Allen, C. (1994) *Social Care in a Mixed Economy of Care*. Buckingham: Open University Press.
This book describes the mixed economy of community care in England. The authors do not deal explicitly with the issue of ethnicity, but provide a useful introduction to the difficulties faced by local authorities in implementing the NHS and Community Care Act.

In addition to the works described above, there are a series of 'official' publications that provide a good introduction to community care policy. The 1986 Audit Commission Report, *Making a Reality of Community Care* (London, HMSO), is one of the first sustained critiques of care in the community and convinced the government of the need for a more considered policy response. As part of this response, Sir Roy Griffiths was commissioned to examine the organization of community care services. His 1988 report, *Community Care: an Agenda for Action* (London: HMSO), is a useful starting point to current policy initiatives on community care, offering specific recommendations on improving community care provision. The White Paper *Caring for People* (Cmnd 849, 1989, London: HMSO) addressed many of the issues raised by Griffiths and also included reference to the 'particular care needs' of minority communities. Examples of recent policy guidance include the Department of Health publication, *Community Care in the Next Decade and Beyond* (1990, London: HMSO), and two Audit Commission reports, *Community Care: Managing the Cascade of Change* (1992, London: HMSO) and *The Community Revolution: Personal Social Services and Community Care* (1994, London: HMSO).

Part I

COMMUNITY, CITIZENSHIP AND WELFARE

2

'Race', welfare and community care: a historical perspective

Fiona Williams

Introduction

The aim of this chapter is to provide a historical understanding of the issues of 'race' and racism as well as the development of state welfare, with specific reference to the area now called 'community care'. As such it is also concerned with providing some conceptual tools to enable us to understand some of the complexities in the historical relationship between 'race' and welfare in the first half of the twentieth century. The chapter starts with a brief introduction to some of these conceptual issues and then uses three historical moments to explore key aspects of 'race' and welfare. The first is the relationship between the construction of the nation, citizenship and the welfare state in the first two decades of the century, focusing in particular on the processes of exclusion from social rights to welfare. The second is the impact of the eugenics movement in the 1920s and 1930s on the construction of certain social groups as pathological and requiring incarceration and segregation from mainstream society. It examines how the discourses involved in this movement were racialized, and how this racialization also overlapped with notions of class, gender, disability and sexuality. The third moment is the immediate post-war period from the late 1940s, which is characterized by the recruitment of black men and women from the Commonwealth to work in those services and industries, including the public welfare services, which were experiencing a shortage of labour. In this section, I examine some of the ways the historical legacy of racism reconstituted itself, especially in relation to the pathologization of black family life.

The history of 'race' and welfare: some conceptual issues

There are three popular misrepresentations in discussions on 'race' and racism in welfare. The first is that racism in welfare is predominantly a post-war phenomenon associated with the greater presence of black people in Britain and the expansion of the welfare state. The second is that resistance against racism is a relatively *new* political development – a *new* social movement. And the third is that racism constitutes a form of outdated prejudice by uneducated individuals, a failure to accept cultural diversity and/or a divide-and-rule tactic by the capitalist state. None of these claims is *wrong*, but they are partial and therefore misleading.

To begin with, I suggest that the discourses of 'race' and racism are historically embedded in some of the earliest forms of state welfare, especially in the inscription of *eligibility* to state benefits. For example, in the 1834 Poor Law the cost of poor relief was the responsibility of the parish from which a claimant originated. Workers moving from one area to another in search of work were often, when they became unemployed, ill or aged, sent back to their parish of origin. This practice hit Irish immigrants most, for many had arrived in Britain to escape starvation from the Irish potato famine. If they subsequently applied for poor relief they risked deportation. If they didn't it made them vulnerable to destitution or exploitation. Nevertheless, one of the key defences against the argument that the Poor Law inhibited the movement of labour was that to change it would make Irish labourers eligible to relief (Rose 1971: 193). Such clear exclusionary practices need to be understood in the context of widespread anti-Irish sentiments which had their legacy in the anti-Catholicism of the Reformation, but which by the early nineteenth century found their expression in the fear by the state of Irish political agitation and a fear by the trade union movement of wage-cutting Irish labour. These sentiments fed into a developing discourse of a hierarchy of 'races', of which one aspect was the assumption of the superiority of industrialized over rural societies. This discourse also developed a number of different racialized facets, as subsequent sections in this chapter illustrate. At the same time the definition of eligibility to social rights became increasingly, by the turn of the century, tied to the construction of the nation state and associatedly to nationhood and to the boundaries of nationality expressed through citizenship (see also Chapter 3 this volume). This is explored below, but the point here is that the early development of the nation state and the welfare state drew the lines of inclusion in and exclusion from both, and set in motion the practices and forms of knowledge which regulated and excluded along racialized (and other) lines. In this way, members of the black Commonwealth who arrived in the 1950s and 1960s stepped into a situation heavy with the legacy of racisms.

What the example of the Poor Law also shows is that the construction of 'race' and the processes of racism operate differently over time and place. Although there is considerable debate about which groups might be said to constitute racialized 'others' (see, for example, Anthias and Yuval-Davis 1993; Miles 1992; Mason 1994), I extend the concepts to include, at different points in time, in Britain, the subordination and the marginalization of Irish people, Jews and people from Africa, South-East

Asia and the Caribbean. This is not to deny racism experienced by people from say, Turkey, the Middle East or China, but my main references are to the racialization of these first groups. Again, the point is that the construction of 'race' and the operation of racisms need to be set far wider than the experiences of Asian and Afro-Caribbean immigrants in the post-war period. By the same token, the forms of resistance also need to be given a historical dimension. While it is true that the rise of new social emancipatory movements around specific aspects of oppression – in gender, 'race', sexuality or disability – is a particular feature of political life from the late 1960s onwards in Britain and the USA especially, it is also the case that individual and collective resistance is also part of the history of 'race' and racism. The forms this resistance has taken have also changed over time: sometimes subsumed under anti-imperialist or anti-fascist movements, sometimes expressed through spontaneous political agitation, at other times through the establishment of self-help initiatives and so on.

For all these reasons I prefer not to understand racism as operating through a single or main cause or route (prejudice, the capitalist state). Instead I present racisms (and resistances) as operating in different ways, on different sites, changing in form and degree over time and place. Sometimes 'race' and racism articulate closely with class, gender or sexuality; at other times they appear to follow a separate logic, only then to be disrupted by the shifting relations of power. Similarly, the discourses of 'race' and racism have no overall coherence or outcome: they operate unevenly and with contradictions. Sometimes it is the contradictions and unevenness which provide the space for contestation; at other times forms of resistance expose the unevenness.

To connect this understanding of 'race' and racism to the history of community care is no easy task. If we understand community care to be the current organization for the social care and support given to particular groups in society – frail older people, disabled people, people with learning difficulties, people with mental health problems, people living with chronic or terminal illnesses or with drug or alcohol induced dependencies – then this history is as complex and varied as it is under-explored. At a simple level, from the perspective of *policy* we can, within this century, point to a development of institutionalization – the incarceration and segregation of those groups deemed unfit for either paid work or motherhood – and then to its gradual dismantling from the 1950s (Scull 1984; Busfield 1992). From the perspective of *politics* we can point to the different and conflicting interest groups involved in the creation of and resistance to these policies – from political, professional, trade union and gender, 'race' and disability-based groups (see, for example, Jones 1986). From the perspective of those whose lives were and are influenced by these policies, then, historically we have very few accounts. Indeed, it is only in the past five years that there has been any major attempt to record an oral history of the lives of those who were affected by policies for incarceration and segregation (see, for example, Potts and Fido 1990). But there are very few specific histories of those who were cared for in the community (for an exception see Bayley 1973), and the issue of why some people were incarcerated and others were not still remains relatively unexplored. Furthermore, any attempt to explore these histories of institutional or community care in terms which highlight gender or 'race' has not received much specific attention (see Baxter 1989b and Williams 1992 on people with learning difficulties). In the following sections I look at three historical moments which reveal significant aspects either of the general relationship between 'race' and racism and the history of welfare or of the specific historical intersection of the politics of 'race' with the politics of institutionalized or community care. The issues I explore (nationality, citizenship and exclusion, 1905–1925; the influence of the eugenics movement, 1913–1939; the pathologization of the black family in the 1950s and 1960s) should not be seen as discrete to these time periods, but simply as time-specific illustrations of the construction of 'race' in the development of welfare.

Nationality, citizenship and exclusion, 1905–1925

In the period 1905 to 1918 a whole range of welfare benefits and services were introduced in Britain, as in many other industrialized countries. These included the first old age pensions, national insurance, school meals for the needy, services for mothers and babies and the development of municipal housing. While at one level these measures can be seen as important concessions to improve the lives of the working class, at another level it needs to be remembered that during the same period the Aliens Act (1905) – the first state control on immigration – was passed amid abusive anti-semitism, as was the 1913 Mental Deficiency Act, which gave powers to central and local government to detain, if necessary indefinitely, 'idiots, imbeciles, moral imbeciles and the feeble minded'. Behind the passing of these different reforms three interrelated processes were being played out. The first concerned the development of industrial capitalism. An increasingly militant working class, the challenge to Britain's industrial supremacy from the USA and Japan, a rivalling of imperial power by Germany, the poor health of recruits in the Boer War and a decline in the birth rate all pushed towards policies aimed at conceding to working-class demands but also at producing workers and soldiers of sufficient fitness and ability to defend Britain's economic and imperial power.

The second process concerned family life and the separation of the (male) public sphere of paid work from the (female) private sphere of the family. Policies for women focused upon their roles as wives and mothers rather than workers and, while they met many women's needs, they also seemed to consolidate an image of woman's place in the home. The discourse of motherhood raised it to a new dignity and responsibility: women were seen as contributing to the quality of the 'imperial race' for national efficiency, and to its quantity for the imperial army. Motherhood represented not only women's destiny, her duty and her dependency, but also her desert, for various measures sought to train, regulate and select the fit mothers from the unfit. If such policies elevated motherhood, they also tied women's role in the family to the development of the 'race' and the nation and, in addition, restricted women from the public sphere of paid work and the social rights that went with it. For example, women were excluded from some of the first national insurance and unemployment benefits: in the health insurance scheme of the 1911 National Insurance Act women were only eligible for three-quarters of the rate and were penalized by not being insured for time taken off for childbirth.

Policies for insurance and income maintenance also marked the popular acceptance that eligibility to social rights should, like other forms of citizenship such as the right to vote, be defined in terms of *nationality*. This represented the third significant process in the background to the development of the welfare state: the consolidation of the nation state and national identity, during which the boundaries of nationhood were given greater economic, social, legal political and ideological meaning. In other words, the introduction of some of the first forms of social welfare rights and provisions took place within a context where the boundaries of citizenship were becoming more circumscribed and its social geology in terms of differentiations around gender, 'race', age and disability more complexly layered. One example of this connection was the simultaneous introduction of the first effective forms of immigration controls with the first major forms of social insurance. Campaigns for immigration controls to limit Jewish refugees from East Europe and Russia were supported by all the major political parties and significant parts of the trade union movement. These campaigns often gave vent to and legitimated anti-semitism and imperialist jingoism. In 1905 the Aliens Act imposed immigration controls and, among other things, demanded that any person who could not support herself or himself, or who might need welfare provision, should not be allowed entry into the country, and that anyone who within twelve months of entry was homeless, living in overcrowded conditions or living off poor relief, should be deported. Following this, the 1908 Pensions Act denied a pension to anyone who had not been both a resident *and* a British subject for twenty years. In the health insurance scheme of the 1911 National Insurance Act non-British residents who had not been resident for five years received lower rates of benefits (seven-ninths) even though they paid full contributions.

The translation of the politics of welfare and of nationality into the practices of racism was a short step. During periods of moral panic about foreigners it became commonplace for the authorities to threaten so-called 'aliens' who turned to public funds with deportation, to deny access to social rights on the basis of nationality (which, in practice, meant white, Christian and English-speaking) or to use welfare agencies to police immigrants. In 1918 the increases in mass unemployment led initially to more generous 'as of right' benefits. However, in some cases the government was explicit about the restriction of such rights. For example, in 1919 the Ministry of Labour refused to grant the 'out of work donation' – a non-contributory, non-means tested and relatively generous unemployment benefit – to black seamen who were eligible for it, and sent secret instructions to labour exchange managers that the seamen should be kept ignorant of their rights (Fryer 1984: 299). In 1919 the Aliens Act was tightened and Jewish aliens had to carry identity cards, inform the authorities of any absences from home of over two weeks and stay out of designated areas. The police were also given powers to raid and close down clubs and restaurants frequented by aliens (Cohen 1985: 87). When, in 1920, the Aliens Order tightened up illegal immigration, it was, interestingly, the Special Irish Branch of the police that was given the task. Such institutional powers and practices compounded popular racist fears. In 1919 there was a spate of racist attacks upon long-standing black communities in Liverpool, Cardiff and South Tyneside. A South Wales newspaper described one such attack: 'Always "the black man" was their quarry, and whenever one was rooted out by the police . . . the mob rushed upon him' (Fryer 1984: 306).

Originally immigration controls were introduced on the basis of the costs of immigration. However, very soon these costs were deemed to include the rights to welfare provisions and to a contracting labour market so that immigration controls became synonymous with protecting welfare provisions and the labour market for the white male working class. They also legitimated the strategy of deportation or repatriation as a solution to perceived 'scroungerism'. The threat of deportation was common, as this account from a long-standing black resident of Butetown in Cardiff shows. It recalls her experience of applying for poor relief for her aged mother when her own husband was out of work:

> Well, we went back again with my mother [for poor relief], and he said 'We'll have to deport her.' I said 'Deport her? Where are you going to deport her to? She only lives up the valley . . . I wouldn't bring her to you if I could keep her.'
>
> (Open University 1993)

One of the forms of resistance to these exclusionary policies was self-help (see also Chapters 3 and 9, this volume). An interesting example of this is Lara Marks's study of the development of the Jewish Maternity Home and Sick Room Helps Society, established in 1895 as part of a wider system of Jewish self-help (Marks 1990). One earlier charitable institution was the Jewish Board of Guardians, which was set up by the established middle-class Jewish community to provide medical aid and welfare relief for the working-class Jewish community in the East End of London. The Jewish refugees who arrived at the end of the nineteenth century faced considerable deprivation, ill-health and poverty. They were often forced into the lowest paid casual labour and worst housing and denied the forms of welfare provision and benefits described earlier. Even though many of the services aimed at promoting the good health of mothers and children had been set up in the East End, they often ignored the language needs of Jewish mothers or were insensitive to cultural differences in rituals of birth, death and diet. One response was the setting up of the Sick Room Helps Society (SRHS) and later the Jewish Maternity Home. The SRHS provided home helps to Jewish women just before and after childbirth. The home helps were provided, organized and paid for by the Jewish community and the source was Jewish widows who might otherwise have been in receipt of poor relief. Such a scheme ran counter to the conventions of nursing care at the time, which were eager to distinguish between the vocationalism of the paid trained nurse, the unpaid middle-class charity volunteer and the casual paid domestic worker. The home help was usually a local Jewish working-class woman, neither 'called' to her job nor charitable in her exercise of it. Nevertheless, the creation of the SRHS is thought to be a major factor contributing to the lower infant mortality rate within the Jewish East End community compared with the surrounding Gentile communities (Marks 1990). Ironically, medical officers at the time often put the better health of Jewish infants down to stereotyped views of the behaviour of Jewish mothers: they were seen to be 'good' mothers: they often did not do paid work outside the home, they breastfed, they did not drink alcohol and they were fond of children. While such characteristics may have helped, it is more likely that the organization of home helps was more significant (Marks 1990). Indeed, in the 1920s some local authorities introduced home help support services based on the model of the Jewish SRHS.

This example of self-help needs to be seen as a reaction to the exclusionary practices which were inherent in welfare policies and flowed from, on the one hand, the attempts to control and limit immigration, and, on the other, the establishment of the social rights attached to citizenship, which itself was becoming increasingly defined by a particular form of British national identity. The discourses that underpinned this national identity were also, as the next section shows, fed by particular notions of national and racial supremacy.

The influence of the eugenics movement 1913–1939

The point at which the discourses of 'race' and racism meet the history of community care is in the influence of the eugenics movement during the first three decades of the century. It is also at this intersection, and especially in policies for segregation and incarceration, that it is possible to see the complex interplay of the social relations of class, gender, race, disability, age and sexuality and the influence of these upon the construction of social problems.

The Eugenics Society was founded in 1907 and, with the National Association for the Care of the Feeble Minded, campaigned for the passing of the 1913 Mental Deficiency Act. This Act gave local authorities the right to detain 'mental deficients' in institutions or colonies and to grade and classify them as 'idiots', 'imbeciles' or 'feeble minded'. Institutionalization was not a new method of social care: workhouses, orphanages and asylums had, during the eighteenth and nineteenth centuries, played an important role in providing minimal protection and care for those – old, sick, mentally and physically disabled, young – who were neither able to earn an independent wage nor able to be dependent on a wage-earner. (To some extent the demands on labour in industrial capitalism for speed, numeracy and literacy also excluded more groups and numbers of people.) Neither was detention new as a form of punishment and deterrence against crime or pauperism. What was significant, however, and this is what the 1913 Mental Deficiency Act marked, was the use of institutionalization and segregation not as a method of protecting the vulnerable from society, but as a strategy to *protect society from the corrupting influence of the 'deficient'*. Such a strategy was understood and justified in terms of the supposedly scientific truths underpinning the theory of eugenics. These claimed, first, that degeneracy was hereditary and, second, that the social problems of society were concentrated among the 'feeble minded'. More specifically, eugenicists claimed that according to the scientific laws of heredity, human characteristics are inherited, that the characteristics of degeneration could be identified through diagnosis and classification, and that policies of birth control, regulation of marriage, sterilization and segregation could improve 'race quality' by preventing the fertility of degenerates and encouraging the regeneration of desirable groups. However, accompanying these claims were beliefs that the incidence of deficiency and degeneracy was greater among certain social groups – in particular, the poor and unskilled working class – and among immigrant groups. Support for ideas of racial inferiority came from the use of crude ethnocentric intelligence tests given to immigrants entering the USA (Italians, Russians, Poles, Jews) in the first two decades of the century (Gould 1984). These beliefs were reinforced by Darwinian-influenced ideas about a supposed hierarchy of 'races', with white (imperialist) 'races' at the top and black (colonized) 'races' at the bottom. Gender and sexuality also permeated these strategies to protect society from these social, moral and racial threats. W. E. Fernald, a superintendent of an American institution for the feeble minded, whose views were influential, wrote in 1912:

> Feeble-minded women are almost invariably immoral and if at large usually become carriers of disease or give birth to children who are as defective as themselves. The feeble-minded woman who marries is twice as prolific as the normal woman.
>
> (Quoted in Abbott and Sapsford 1987: 25)

Discourses of feeblemindedness presented images of women as immoral, carriers of venereal disease, over-fertile, promiscuous and a cause of potential social, economic and moral decline, and these dominated official policy. Indeed, the Eugenics Society counted many famous social reformers and cultural figureheads among its supporters: the Cadburys, Beatrice and Sydney Webb, George Bernard Shaw, J. M. Keynes, Dr Barnardo, William Beveridge. Its influence reflected the support it had from many powerful groups: the Fabian socialists, Conservatives, Liberals, voluntary organizations, scientists, social workers and the medical profession. Medical discourses of women reinforced such characterizations. The study by Ehrenreich and English of medical practice in the early twentieth century in the USA and Britain shows how doctors viewed different social groups of women in different ways (Ehrenreich and English 1976). Upper-class women were often seen as weak, inherently sick, given to hysteria and capable of only leisurely pursuits. Poor, working-class, black and immigrant women were seen as strong and robust but also as contagious, harbouring disease, over-breeding and constituting a threat to the 'race'. Unsurprisingly, the target for segregation and incarceration by local authorities was more often women – young, single mothers in particular (Williams 1992: 153).

What the Mental Deficiency Act did was thread together notions of institutionalized care and protection of the vulnerable with discourses of social problems, social progress and social reform which were themselves profoundly gendered, racialized and classed. The debates that the Act and its implementation generated – about intelligence, segregation and sterilization – though often contested, formed a firm seam of thinking which was to surface from time to time in the post-war education and health care experiences of black women and children.

The policies for detention and segregation were also significant for the pattern they set in identifying and pathologizing certain social groups as the cause of social problems. While these ideas competed, or sometimes accompanied, more structural explanations for social problems, the processes of using expert or scientific forms of knowledge to justify attempts to classify and control particular social groups became a key element in twentieth-century welfare provision. These policies also helped to magnify or reconstitute images of 'otherness' projected on to groups already marginalized through the inequalities of class, gender, 'race', disability and sexuality. The contradictory characteristics which identified people as sub-human, diseased, simple-minded, innocent, dangerous, sexually menacing, the objects of pity, ridicule and dread and the burden of charity were as flexible in their application to certain social groups as they were fixed in the public imagination (see Baxter 1989b). Such characteristics were applied to the very poor, to 'unfit' mothers, to 'aliens', to the Irish, to physically and mentally disabled people, among others. This, then, was a rich and complex legacy of 'race', racism and welfare into which the newly arrived black migrants from the Commonwealth stepped in the 1950s. However, this is not to imply that the ideas of the eugenics movement were carried unchanged into post-war welfare politics. In fact, by the 1940s the influence of the eugenics movement itself had waned dramatically, although its concerns – population decline, IQ testing, maintenance of 'racial standards' – still picked their way through post-war reconstructions. But mass unemployment of the 1930s and the Second World War disrupted hopes of achieving progress through social engineering. More positive universal strategies, such as family allowances, won out over selective sterilization strategies, as a means of encouraging population enhancement. The disorganized working class presented less of an imagined threat than it had before the defeat of the General Strike in 1926, and the rise of fascism in Nazi Germany (where racial hygiene was pushed to its logical and horrifying conclusion) and of Stalinism in Russia revealed a darker side to modernity's belief in technological and social progress. Nevertheless, eugenics was the intellectual and scientific pinhead of knowledge upon which a wide range of twentieth-century welfare discourses danced.

Meanwhile, by the end of the Second World War, the policy of institutionalizing those in need of care and support also, slowly, came under attack from quite different quarters, even though the full implementation of deinstitutionalization took some fifty years to set in motion. As early as 1951, the National Council of Civil Liberties in a pamphlet entitled *50,000 Outside the Law* campaigned for the release of people wrongfully detained in institutions and colonies. In addition, the development of drugs technology, the turn by some parts of the medical profession to a more therapeutic approach to mental illness, the shift from seeing 'mental handicap' as a medical condition to seeing it as an intellectual or educational impairment, the provision of forms of income maintenance for people without access to an independent wage and, increasingly, the high cost of institutional care and a shortage of unskilled labour, all contributed to the pressure for community care. By the 1970s the question of welfare costs combined with a political commitment for families and communities to be (re)instated as the 'natural' sites of care, and, with the civil rights campaigns by disabled people, these very different forces tipped the balance in favour of deinstitutionalization.

The pathologization of black family life in post-war Britain

The previous two sections of this chapter have looked at the relationship between 'race', welfare and citizenship and at the way social problems became racialized in the first half of the century. The reconstruction of post-war Britain through the creation of a Keynsian welfare state represented in many ways a major break with the past. At the same time, many aspects of pre-war Britain – especially the unequal relations of class, 'race', gender and disability – reconstituted themselves on different political, economic and cultural terrains. The Beveridge Report, for example, advocated marriage and motherhood as the white woman's personal and national duty, and captured, in its new programme of social insurance, the ideal of women's dependency upon a male breadwinner. However, the creation of National Assistance (now Income Support) did unintentionally give women without husbands (widows, lone mothers) but with dependants some safety net of independent income, albeit at poverty level. The issue of 'race', citizenship rights and welfare was just as contradictory.

One of the major problems facing the British government in the late 1940s was the shortage of labour in both manufacturing industries and the developing welfare state. There were two solutions to this: to use married women in the workforce or to draw on migrant labour, either from the poorer parts of Southern Europe or from the colonies. The first strategy ran counter to the ideology of the male breadwinner family and would involve the socialization of child care. To pull in European workers would entail complicated problems with time-limited work permits, whereas workers from the Commonwealth were, by virtue of Britain's imperial model of citizenship, automatically British citizens. On the other hand, the government was concerned with problems of assimilation and whether the new immigrants would be of good enough 'human stock' (1949 Royal Commission; see Williams 1989). The decision to recruit migrant workers from the black Commonwealth was, then, from the start ambivalent and begrudging. Their cultural and 'racial' differences were seen as a problem, but their labour as a solution, and their status as British subjects as administratively expedient. They were seen primarily as units of easily accessible labour and little consideration was given to their needs for housing, health care, schooling and so on, or to the anticipated racism they were to face.

As British citizens, the new migrants should have been able to exercise their social rights to welfare provisions, but different processes of direct and indirect racism excluded them. Ironically, one of these processes was inherent in the very essence of the post-war welfare state – its universalism. The provision of universalist systems of education, health care and national insurance contained in principle a commitment to egalitarianism. In practice this meant treating everyone the same regardless of 'class, colour or creed'. However, not only did this apparent egalitarianism serve to ignore many of the specific needs immigrant workers (or indeed any other minority groups) had – for example, for immediate access to low-cost housing which did not involve a residency qualification, as most council housing waiting lists did, or for translation services – it also reinforced a particular view of normalcy, especially of gender relations and of family life. The white, Christian, heterosexual, male breadwinner family represented the universal norm. In so far as black workers and their families deviated from this norm – whether for cultural or material reasons – this increasingly fed into a pathological view of black family life. One example of this process can be seen in the situation of Afro-Caribbean women in the 1950s and 1960s. Many Afro-Caribbean women who came to Britain were self-supporting and were recruited to work in full-time jobs, with low pay and long hours (often in the welfare services). Sometimes this meant leaving their children behind with relatives in the Caribbean until they had accommodation and resources to provide for them in Britain. Otherwise it meant bringing children into a situation where there was little formal child care provision for working mothers. Either way, the situation these women found themselves in ran counter to the familial ideology of the time, which warned against the separation of mothers from their children and the harm that full-time working mothers might inflict upon their children. The conditions imposed upon them as migrant workers meant they were seen to be failing as mothers. In this way, notions of the inadequacies of black family life entered the discourses of welfare professionals. Some evidence of this began to emerge in the 1980s, showing that disproportionate numbers of black children had been taken into care in the previous two decades (ABSWAP 1983).

Another example of both the pathologizing of black family life and the reformulation of old ideas about 'race' and intelligence can be drawn from the experiences of black children and schooling in the 1950s and 1960s. Black children entered a system which was already operating to control and select children for a hierarchically structured labour market along class and gender lines. These processes took on a racialized dimension. Working-class failure at school was explained in terms of the inadequacy of working-class culture. Asian and Afro-Caribbean under-achievement became attributed to the inadequacies of black cultures or family life. In fact, from the very start, black children were seen as a problem. In 1965 a DES circular recommended a 30 per cent limit of immigrant children in any one school and the 'bussing' of surplus children to other schools. Racist discourses and ideas of subnormality converged and a disproportionate number of black children were labelled as 'ESN' (educationally sub-normal). An account of this from the point of view of Afro-Caribbean mothers is given in *The Heart of the Race* (Bryan *et al.* 1985: 64–5):

It was the attitude of the teachers that did the most lasting damage. They were to interpret black children's disorientation and bewilderment as a sign of stupidity. Their concepts of us as simple-minded, happy folk, lacking in sophistication or sensitivity became readily accepted definitions. Theories about us, put forward by Jenson in America and endorsed by Eysenck here in the late sixties gave such views a spurious credibility by popularising the idea that race and intelligence are linked in some inherent way.

None of these processes went uncontested. To begin with, pressure groups and voluntary organizations, such as the National Council for Commonwealth Migrants and local groups such as the Colonial People's Defence Committee in Liverpool, attempted to meet needs and inform people of their rights. In the early 1970s black professionals and parents exposed and campaigned against the labelling of black children as ESN, and in some areas Saturday schools were set up, run by and for black teachers and children. Within the women's movement's campaigns for reproductive rights, black feminists highlighted the use of abortion, sterilization and long-lasting contraception on black, Third World, disabled and poor women, exposing the legacy of fears about the fertility of specific social groups and concepts of fit and unfit motherhood.

Conclusion

This chapter has used three historical periods to explore the complex and changing relationship between 'race', racism and welfare in the first half of the twentieth century. In the first period, the relationship between the emerging definitions of nationality and citizenship at the beginning of the century on the one hand, and the creation of a state system of welfare on the other, were examined in terms of the formal and informal denial of social rights to people deemed to be 'aliens'. This relationship laid the basis for some of the exclusionary aspects of what is termed welfare citizenship, that is, access by right to welfare benefits and services. In the second period, the 1920s and 1930s, I looked at the way the discourses of welfare – especially in the construction of social problems, social reform and social progress – were racialized. One of the key areas of influence, both in this process of racialization and in the policies of institutionalization, was the eugenics movement. This movement inscribed social and moral degeneracy with the inequalities of class, 'race', gender and disability. The third period was that of the immediate post-war reconstruction, in which notions of welfare citizenship and pathology were reconstituted around the recruitment and arrival of black migrant workers and their families. Through these different historical issues the aim has been to explore the backcloth to the issue of 'race' and racism, its relation to class, gender and disability, its forms of resistance and the history of welfare before the formal implementation of community care.

Annotated bibliography

The material in this chapter has been drawn from a variety of academic sources, so the texts I recommend are those that provide a good analysis of, first, the history of community care, second, the influence of social Darwinism and eugenics in the first half of the century and, third, the history of 'race' and welfare.

Abbott, P. and Sapsford, R. (1987) *Community Care for Mentally Handicapped Children*. Milton Keynes: The Open University.
The first half of this short book contains a succinct but comprehensive history of the processes of institutionalization of people with learning difficulties from the end of the seventeenth century and de-institutionalization from the 1950s. The second half explores the experience of community care through the eyes of mothers of children with learning difficulties.

Jones, G. (1986) *Social Hygiene in Twentieth Century Britain*. Beckenham: Croom Helm.
This is a fascinating historical analysis of the discourses of 'social hygiene' in

professional and political organizations from the early twentieth century to the Second World War. It argues that ideas about improvement of the quality of the population, to eliminate the unfit and improve efficiency among the working classes, were central to health and welfare policies, and to social categorization.

Neither of these two books look specifically at 'race' or ethnicity, so for a general historical analysis of the relationship between the development of state welfare and 'race', gender and class relations, turn to Williams, F. (1989) *Social Policy: a Critical Introduction. Issues of Race, Gender and Class.* Cambridge: Polity Press, revised update due in 1997. However, for an excellent and much more specific historical account of Black people's lives in Britain, you should read *Staying Power: the History of Black People in Britain* (1984), London: Pluto Press.

3

Defining and containing diversity: community, ethnicity and citizenship

Charles Husband

Introduction

Conceptualizing 'the community' is a famously fraught task and generations of students in social science and social work courses have unkindly been set the task of generating a calculus which might contain this confusion. The confusion is real enough. Modernity's transformation of traditional lifestyles and cognitive maps has unevenly impacted upon different nations and unevenly changed the lived experience of members of these same nations, and this change has itself been understood differently by members of similar social strata. And in the latter part of the twentieth century we have a globally uneven transformation of the capitalist project that has led to a fascination with globalization and an invitation to speak of a post-modern era (Featherstone 1990). Simultaneously there are those who advance a perspective on the world which is 'post-modernist', which asserts that the conceptual certainties of time, space and identity that were defining features of modernity have now lost their legitimacy and relevance. However, as Turner (1994) has pointed out, the extent of the material shift towards a post-modern social structure is an empirical issue which is contested, while the post-modernist conceptual paradigm is an epistemological stance that may be seen as independent of the verifiable transition in the social structure of the contemporary world.

In blunter terms the material world in which people exist and survive has undergone uneven global change over the past four centuries. The sense of territory, geography, locality and dwelling space has undergone dramatic transformation; the individual and family have found their rootedness, stability and connectedness to the physical world changing in consequence. The concept of community is properly ambiguous because there are sound reasons for its diversity as it has been developed in relation to different material relations, such as a fifteenth-century French village, nineteenth-century Manchester or the late twentieth-century urban Los

Angeles. And the paradigmatic contestation between political philosophies prioritizing the autonomous individual and those asserting the necessary sociality of the human condition have sustained opposed vantage points for accounting for the form of social relations in specific social settings.

To speak of a community is to claim a comprehension of the relation of people to each other, and to their physical environment, and implicitly at least to invoke a principle of cohesion which has political significance for the legitimate administration of their connectedness. The aboriginal connectedness to the land, the nation's definition of its territorial boundaries or a neighbourhood's assertion of a finite urban patch all link identity, territory and claims to pre-eminent authority in that area. Yet ethnicity, gender, religion or occupation may equally offer the basis of identity and claims to communal interests and rights, in which territory is not necessarily fundamental; although often it becomes invoked as a potent focus for the politicization of such interest communities. Thus we have further reasons to anticipate difficulties in resolving all the diversity that must be contained in the concept of community.

This chapter will seek to explore the implications of the complexity of defining community, with particular relevance to its application in multi-ethnic Britain. In following one attempt to unravel the potential defining elements of community it will be argued that the conceptualization and co-option of the concept of community in relation to social policy has an inherently political significance. Different perspectives on the nature of human beings' social nature inform approaches to examining the individual's location in a social context; and consequently generate alternative policy implications. When into this already contested conception of community we attempt to integrate contemporary understandings of the multidimensional and variable nature of ethnic identities, the challenge to those invoking 'community' as a principle of social organization and policy formulation is amplified. It will be argued that such policy debates take place within a political context in which state institutions are significant forces in defining and managing ethnic diversity. Not least among these processes is the struggle to sustain a dominant definition of British identity and the regulation of citizenship as a critical element in policing legitimate identities. Consequently this chapter will pay particular attention to the politics of diversity as it impacts upon attempts to mobilize resources around minority ethnic communities' interests (see also Chapter 7, this volume, for a discussion of community in relation to community care of people with mental health problems).

We now examine one attempt at defining the concept of community, as a means of moving this analysis forward.

Community and ethnicity

Community in the descriptive sense

Butcher (1993) approaches the conceptualization of community by differentiating three distinct, though interrelated, senses of the term: these are defined as the 'descriptive', 'value' and 'active' senses of community. Noting that the use of community has social referents, in relation to the form of social relations that establishes the connectedness of members of a community, and psychological referents, in that members of a community routinely have a sense of belonging, Butcher moves on to distinguish two types of descriptive community. The distinction is made between *territorial communities*, in which what people have in common is their geographical location, such as neighbourhood, village, town or place, and *interest communities*, which are based on something *other* than physical proximity, such as ethnicity, occupation, or religion (Butcher 1993: 12–13). Thus this typology asserts the necessity of distinguishing between physical–spatial bases of community and psychological affiliations based upon common category membership (see, for example, Turner 1987). Equally, it allows for the possibility of simple and complex interactions between these two principles of community.

This has obvious implications for any attempt to discuss minority ethnic communities in Britain. At the psychological level the notion of ethnicity as a single and permanent defining feature of an individual is not tenable. Ethnicity is at one level a psychological 'consciousness of kind'; but this is a consciousness that is subject to a variety of moderating influences. Individuals do not pass through each day as a unidimensional and ever self-conscious and focused Afro-Caribbean, Latino or Jew. Ethnicity has been described as being situational: it becomes relevant in particular contexts and with particular others (Wallman 1986). Ethnicity is not usually experienced or expressed as a single autonomous and self-sufficient category of identity. The writings of black feminists have, for example, very fully illuminated the interactions between gender and ethnic identities (Grewal *et al.* 1988; hooks 1991; Mohanty *et al.* 1991; Bhavnani and Phoenix 1994). Thus communities of interest based on ethnicity are not the simple summation of persons having 'the same ethnicity'. Ethnic communities are psychological and political constructions in which personal identities are both reproduced and given collective focus through the socio-political context in which individuals live. As we shall see below, the politics of state provision for communities in Britain may privilege one form of identity over another.

Equally, minority ethnic communities *may* have a territorial identity in the sense that persons with a common ethnic identity may, through processes of, for example, employment, housing or legal restraint, find themselves concentrated in relatively narrowly demarcated localities. The ghetto is one such instance, just as the depiction of certain bourgeois areas of England as 'the White Highlands' indicates another. The ethnic demography of Britain indicates a number of areas of relative concentration of ethnic communities; England, Scotland, Ireland and Wales being the largest, and perhaps least obvious to some. Yet this example illustrates one problematic feature of the territorial bases of community; namely the embedding of one territory within another. As a consequence of demography one may live in a national territory that promotes the identity of English, in a town that promotes the identity of Bradfordian, in a district that promotes the identity Pakistani and in a neighbourhood that promotes the identity Mirpuri, and one may live in a street that promotes a sense of being 'Asian' because of the concentrated impact of racist exclusion. And metropolitan community policy may facilitate the recognition of some of these identities and spatial territories more easily than others.

Thus a descriptive identification of communities in terms of territoriality or interests is helpful, but points to the necessarily complex relationship between proximity and territorial affiliation on one hand, and processes of personal and collective identity on the other, in shaping community aspirations and politics. Hesse (1993), for example, has pointed to the danger of assuming a common cognitive mapping of space and time shared by all residents in Britain. Speaking of the dispersed locations in which ethnic minority communities have settled in Britain, he notes the different historical trajectories and processes of migration, which have been defining features of different communities' emergence. Thus, regarding the long-established ethnic minority communities of Liverpool or Cardiff as identical to the African-Caribbean and South Asian communities of Birmingham, Leicester, Bradford or Bristol, as identical to the refugee communities of Somalis in Sheffield or Latin Americans in London – since they are all ethnic minority communities in urban contexts in Britain – is a denial of the distinctly different experience and consciousness of their own dislocation and settlement. As human geographers are increasingly arguing, time and space are not abstract processes which determine us, but rather are social constructs which we reproduce in interaction with one another (Jackson and Penrose 1993; Keith and Pile 1993). A community's consciousness of its past and current identity defines its relation to its 'spatiality' and its relation to a time frame in a unique and creative dynamic (Keith and Pile 1993). Majority and minority communities are not situated, preformed and unambiguously defined into a static and universal framework of time and space. Particularly is this so when it can be argued that Western modernity, and its association with slavery, colonialism and imperial domination, has constructed a shared modelling of time as a continuous unfolding of a history of progress across a stable geographic world; whereas, for the peoples of Africa, Asia and Australasia, their history is fractured by discontinuities of misappropriation from their space, a denial of their origin claims, with their temporal anchoring of a people in their own history, and a succession of massive global translocations of their people into an ongoing diaspora (Gilroy 1993a, b; Hesse 1993). Thus at a fundamental level we may need to be careful to see the spatial and territorial environment of inter-ethnic contact as itself a contested social construction which has different imaginative and experiential sources in different communities of interest.

Community as value

If we return now to the second of Butcher's senses of usage of the term community, we encounter *community as value*. In his words,

> Our approach is to suggest that what defines community initiatives and policies is their attempt to embrace, and find a practical expression for, particular community values. We will stress three in particular, identifying them as the principle of solidarity, participation and coherence.
>
> (Butcher 1993: 14)

Here Butcher is asserting a moral and emotional element, perhaps essence, that is to be found in the usage and conception of the notion of community. Thus *social solidarity*, he argues, is an expression of sentiments of attachment in terms of for example, 'fraternity, trust, selflessness, "sisterhood" and loyalty', and is expressed through acts of mutuality and cooperation. It follows from this that participation in actions directed at common interests is an engagement with the supra-individual; it is an expression of individual agency informed by a sense of collective purpose and benefit. Such participation is inherently a behavioural denial of simple individualism and self-interest. Finally, the fusion of solidarity and participation can be seen as having a cognitive consequence, in that through praxis guided by these values the individual achieves a more *coherent* sense of the relation of self to others and their situation. In Butcher's words, 'Cultural, religious and ethnic communities operate particularly powerfully in offering "meaning" to their members' lives, but all communities provide some sense of coherence that would not otherwise be available' (Butcher 1993: 17).

Clearly, in constructing this 'value' dimension of the conceptualization of community, Butcher is providing a model which is antithetical to an individualistic conception of social relations. Indeed, he points explicitly to the communitarian credentials of his model: the emphasis on solidarity is a rejection of the self-centred egoism and possessive individualism associated with aspects of contemporary society (see e.g. Jessop *et al.* 1988; Husband 1994); the participative essence of this conception of community represents a critique of contemporary privatism and of the exclusion of the individual from meaningful engagement in civil society. The significance of the source of coherence in this model is that it asserts the essential sociality of individuals in their relation to society. Such a model has a number of implications for the analysis of 'community' in contemporary multi-ethnic Britain. First, yet again it underlines the fundamental politicization of community as a concept and a domain of social policy. In an era that has seen the assertion by a head of state, Margaret Thatcher, that there is no such thing as society, and the willing exacerbation of social inequalities through the implementation of radical liberalism, this is clearly a conception of community that is politically contested. Nor, as we look at the current flirtation with communitarian perspectives by segments of the left in Britain, and the critiques this has attracted as feminists among others have exposed its potential for being a vehicle for repressive and retrograde policies, can we assume that communitarian analysis is homogeneous or unproblematic.

Communitarianism has at its core an assertion of the fundamental social nature of human kind, whose very being is generated through interaction in society. From this perspective the individual cannot exist outside of society and *choose* to enter into it on the basis of rational self-interest. Communitarians stress the essential associativeness of human beings, and there is consequently a sense in which humans are invested with a moral sensibility of their relation to others. Clearly, in the context of the social anxieties of contemporary Britain, with its experience of the consequences of the ideology of possessive individualism promoted by over a decade of Thatcherism (Jessop *et al.* 1988), with the challenge to the family as indicated by the high rate of divorce in Britain and with the increasingly limited capacity of the welfare state raising questions about the adequacy of informal social care, communitarian values have a receptive audience. However, as Gray (1995) observed,

> what does the idea of community mean for public policy? A notable feature of the recent vogue for communitarianism has been its lack of concrete policy proposals, and its reliance on a moralistic and sometimes reactionary rhetoric of personal responsibility. There is little in the literature that focuses on the economic sources of the decay of communities.

Thus, as Gray points out, a narrow focus upon the moral core of communitarianism can facilitate 'a fundamentalist agenda for the restoration of the "traditional" family' as a moral crusade against the perceived degeneracy of contemporary social values. Moral crusades in the absence of a coherent analysis of the economic and political determinants of the challenges facing the contemporary family, neighbourhood or 'community' facilitate a blaming of the victim as morally inadequate. Thus, for example, the apparent interest of members of the Labour Party in the analysis of Amitai Etzioni (1995), the American communitarian theorist, attracted concerned attention. If, as Butcher points out, there is a value dimension to the community, then we may assume that these values will be contested, or if agreed may be rendered ambiguous through being inflected with differing political philosophies.

Second, as Butcher asserts in relation to his model, the identification of 'ideal type' elements within the conceptualization of community cannot be allowed to slip into a naive assumption of their existence or significant impact in any particular community. Thus it becomes an empirical task to reveal the precise articulation of values within a community, their relative salience and the nature of their interaction. In multi-ethnic societies this raises a further challenge: namely the possible degree of miscomprehension of the way in which an observer from one culture may identify the values in another. There is the initial task of identifying significant values at the descriptive level; and the subsequent challenge of establishing that these survive cross-cultural application. And there is the difficulty in comprehending their range of relevance and the domain of behavioural impact which may be attributed to a particular value. Critical analyses have done much to reveal how the consciousness of the colonizer remains as a current impediment to the dominant white understanding of the contemporary multi-ethnic world (Young 1986; Bernal 1987; Sharabi 1990). Others have revealed how the specific impact of past experience of personal and cultural oppression, and resistance to it, continue to impact on contemporary minority ethnic communities (Gilroy 1993a, b; West 1993). Acknowledgement of this contemporary impact of past relations must lead to caution in the analysis of current social policy, and in the planning of health and welfare initiatives through institutions still redolent of the interests and consciousness of the white and dominant ethnic communities.

Equally, this knowledge should not be allowed to justify inertia or personal and professional seizure in the face of the complex reality. There is now a long history of the ethnographic examination of minority ethnic communities which has generated a strong critique of the 'ethnic school of race relations' (Bourne 1980; Lawrence 1982a, b). At the core of this critique was a condemnation of the analytic reduction of ethnic communities to a culturally essentialist definition, exclusively in terms of 'their ethnicity'. There were at least two critical aspects of this critique. One followed the argument above and challenged the right and competence of the oppressor to define the identity and culture of the oppressed. The other was to expose the political function of abstracting communities from their political, economic and socio-historical context in order to portray them solely as 'cultural' beings. This process removed the possibility of locating these same people in relation to the framework of their relation to the labour market, their experience of racism, their political marginalization and a plethora of other variables. Consequently this analysis was only capable of explaining the disadvantage of minority ethnic communities in terms of *their* malignant cultural deficits. It facilitated blaming the victim (Ryan 1971; see also Ahmad 1993: Chapter 2).

This necessary criticism generated a defensive anxiety among some academics and a confusion about the appropriate use of information regarding cultural difference in relation to policy issues among many in the caring professions. Indeed, at one point a variant of anti-racist theory appeared to assert that any concern with cultural difference was reductionist and anathema to those opposing racism. Fortunately the necessity of recognizing and comprehending the relevance of culture as a crucial variable in the understanding of ethnic communities' concerns and the development of strategies to challenge racism has become widely accepted, although it remains problematic. For anti-racist initiatives in social care it has been seen that a refusal to engage with cultural difference can be a dangerous 'radical' form of a 'colour blind' approach which treats all persons' experience of oppression and marginalization as equivalent. Attempts are now being made to enable those working in health and social care to confront racism, both personal and institutional, by seeking to acknowledge the significance of cultural difference while placing processes of exclusion and oppression in a wider socio-political framework (see, for example, CCETSW 1991a, b; Husband 1994, 1995). At the same time, scholars and intellectuals within minority ethnic communities are actively interrogating the contemporary nature and relevance of their communities' history and culture (e.g. Modood 1992; Gilroy 1993a, b), and there is a considerable academic industry which is engaged in the analysis of ethnic diversity in Britain from a range of perspectives (Afshar and Maynard 1994; Ballard 1994; Bhavnani and Phoenix 1994). For those who wish to address the needs of minority ethnic communities this literature is a resource, but certainly not a prescriptive basis of policy or personal practice. If minority ethnic communities are to be seen as more than the fortunate and passive beneficiaries of the benign intervention of statutory or mainstream institutional structures, practitioners must seek to interrogate their own personal and professional assumptions, and accept the challenge posed by the complexity of contemporary ethnic relations.

The active community

This brings us to the last element of Butcher's conceptualization of community. This third meaning of community is that of the 'active' community.

> This is the idea of community that public policy makers often have in mind when they seek to promote initiatives that draw upon, or seek to develop, community strengths and capacities . . . We recognise an 'active' community, therefore, through evidence of the diversity and vitality of the groups and organisations that play a role within it, the extent to which those groups and organisations are engaged in purposive action, and the extent to which community members are seen to be committed to their goals and activities, roles and functions.
> (Butcher 1993: 17–18)

This notion of the active community clearly draws upon the earlier elements of a community as having a capacity for self-definition and values of solidarity, which may result in collective participation towards a common goal. This active community is a necessary prerequisite for *community development* policies, which have been defined by Glen (1993: 24) as having three main elements: enabling the community to define its own needs and make provision for them; employing processes which foster creative and cooperative networks of people and groups in communities; and, possibly, putting in place a community practitioner facilitating these aims through non-directive skills. The community development strategies seek to enable and facilitate a self-conscious community in achieving existing aspirations in relation to known needs. This approach is therefore predisposed to recognize the existing integrity of a community and to develop self-help strategies on a neighbourhood or other territorial basis.

However, Glen (1993: 28ff) notes an alternative policy response to community need in which the political powerlessness of the community is seen as a central feature of its existence, and a fundamental focus for change. Thus he depicts *community action* strategies as involving organizing for power around concrete issues, employing conflictual strategies and tactics and frequently employing activist organizers, who may be paid professionals. An aspect of this approach is the inherent politicization of the issue in focus, as it is characterized by an examination of relations of power in specific resource allocation, and in society in general. It is also feasible within this approach to depict a community as having an inadequate or weak conception of the extent of its disadvantage and needs, and consequently part of the process of community action would be the conscientization of members of the community. Exactly who within, or without, the community has the privileged access to this truth must of necessity be open to disputation and political definition. There is a long-running debate in community development about what constitutes authentic participation: at one level this is defined as bottom-up or spontaneous participation, yet in reality it seldom seems to happen without the involvement of external paid workers.

Thus again we find the elements of Butcher's conception of community enabling descriptive clarity while generating practical complexity. The active community may be invoked by active parties to policy initiatives, who have distinctly different orientations to facilitating the community. In both the examples here, whoever has the power to define the identity of the community, and claims to represent its 'authentic' interests, claims an authority in relation to defining and meeting that community's needs.

The definition and management of diversity

The central state, and the local state, have been keenly interested in policing the 'active community' and those who would facilitate its needs. The question of who shall speak for minority ethnic communities, and through what channels they might speak to each other and the state, was an early concern of British 'race relations'. The emergence of community relations councils in the 1960s and after has been regarded by some as a mechanism for defusing community politicization and for co-opting elements of community leadership (see Issacharoff and Hill 1971). Indeed, successive governments have sought to defuse and defocus the formulation of policy *by* minority ethnic communities through promoting ever-changing, but ambiguous, policies *for* minority ethnic communities. In discussing British educational policy, Kirp (1979) noted that unlike the United States, Britain has consciously adopted a policy of 'racial inexplicitness' in education. In other words, British policies have been premised on a desire to diffuse the significance of 'race' in the determination of policy by embedding racial issues in broader 'educational' contexts. The 'needs' of minority children therefore have been subsumed under a plethora of racially inexplicit categories: language, urban deprivation, educational disadvantage, cultural adjustment and so on.

(Cited in Dorn and Troyna 1982: 182)

However, Kirp's 'racial inexplicitness' was not unique to education, and was matched in other areas by what Young (1986) called 'programme ambiguity'. For example, when the 1968 Urban Programme was introduced, it was carefully phrased in generic terms as being designed to meet: 'Those areas of special need including but *not exclusively aimed at* those areas with a relatively high immigrant or black population' (emphasis added). And later, with the introduction of the Inner Urban Areas Act of 1978, it was argued that since ethnic minorities experienced the same disadvantage as other people living in urban areas,

They should benefit directly through measures taken to improve conditions, for example, in housing, education and jobs . . . However, the attack on the specific problem of racial discrimination and the resultant disadvantages must be primarily through the new anti-discrimination legislation and the work of the Commission for Racial Equality.

It is regrettable, if not entirely surprising, that the potential of that legislation has been fundamentally undermined by the judicial and institutional apparatus which should have implemented it (Lustgarten 1987). At the same time the political refusal to confront the racist basis of ethnic inequalities in service delivery and resource allocation has served to force minority ethnic community policies to compete within broadly framed policy agendas, with significant consequences for their community development and community action strategies, and for issues of inter-ethnic collaboration and competition. One of the benefits to the state of racially inexplicit programmes has been the denial to the majority populations of the consequences of their racism, and a disguising of the cost to the state of their attempts at containing the political consequences of such racism. Where, as in the state's response to the cataclysmic civil disturbances of the early 1980s, there have been policies explicitly addressing the needs of marginalized minority ethnic communities there has been a potent counter-reaction within the government and an orchestrated populist backlash. The successful pillorying of 'loony-left' local government policies (epitomized by the Greater London Council) and its linkage with an onslaught on anti-racist policies most effectively demonstrated the limited political platform for explicitly addressing the needs of disadvantaged ethnic minority communities (see Murray and Searle 1989; Searle 1989; Husband 1994). And as Anthias and Yuval-Davis (1993) have illustrated, the operation of 'race relations', community and equal opportunities policies have additionally had serious consequences for those who would advance the interests of the active ethnic community.

The state has not been the only player in making the 'managing of diversity' an issue in social policy in general, and community provision in particular. Not only has post-modernism as an epistemology promoted a 'decentring of the subject', with a consequent introduction of diversity in identity as a dominant characteristic of post-modern conceptions of the social world (see Howe 1994; Rattansi 1994; Taylor-Gooby 1994), but additionally there has been through the past decade and more a reflection of the fracturing of dominant stable identities by the expression within community politics of a multiplicity of identities through the *politics of difference*. Meekosha points to one aspect of this phenomenon:

> The interconnection of race, sexuality and gender provokes a pol-
> itics of identity often resulting in opposition between and inside dif-
> ferent minorities and within feminist politics. These dimensions of
> 'difference' have generated overwhelming issues for practitioners in
> the 1990s . . .
> The surfacing of essentialist politics – claiming that solidarity with
> the identity group transcends all other competing claims to loyalty –
> simplifies complex layers of interacting oppressions into crude dicho-
> tomies or polarities: black/white, gay/straight, male/female, disability/
> ablebodiedness. The politics of difference, diversity and identity have
> given a new edge to demands for equality and social justice.
> (Meekosha 1993: 172)

The implications of Meekosha's statement are profound; for it indicates that while one positive aspect of post-modernist analysis has been to
stress the complexity, uniqueness and situational contingency of individual
identity, in opposition to the simple mapping of the immutable 'great
narratives' of class, sex or nationality on to the individual, this conceptual fluidity and complexity has been undermined in its political expression. For example, the black critique of white feminism (e.g. hooks 1991),
the challenge to heterosexual definitions of 'Blackness' (Lorde 1984) and
challenges to the adequacy of 'Black' as a viable collective categorization
(Modood 1992) have all promoted a more sensitive comprehension of the
multiple personal identities and experiences that may be expressed through
a shared ethnicity. Thus ethnicity becomes heavily nuanced through its
unique expression in any individual's life. The ethnic label becomes just one
vector shaping the direction of a person's experience, rather than a sole
determining characteristic of his or her being. For example, my 'Englishness' can only be understood in relation to my gender, age, regional identity,
sexual orientation and skin colour; among other things. That is true sub-
jectively for my experience of being English, and consequently frames the
route to anyone's attempt to understand Englishness by taking me as an

example. This contemporary, 'post-modern', concern with challenging the objectification of identities by revealing the social forces which attribute fixed identities to others, and by exposing the fragility and complexity of identity, has done a great service to all practitioners in the caring professions. In terms of professional practice it has taken us beyond the critique of 'the ethnic school of race relations', and its identification of the misuse of ethnicity, to point to a positive means of conceptualizing and responding to lived ethnic diversity. In this it challenges simple nostrums which offer cross-cultural competence through pre-packaged and formulaic techniques. It is a challenge to practice.

However, as Meekosha has indicated, the intellectual and emotional openness to difference which is inherent in this approach has been in many instances inverted into a myopic and exclusionary politics of difference, where 'The political debates about identity and difference have often led to a one-dimensional symbolisation of the complex needs of people – the multiplicity of categories brings in turn a reduction to crude equivalence between "groups" and "needs": women need child care, disabled people need access, and so on' (Meekosha 1993: 184). Here the imaginative refusal to entrap the individual within an over-determining single identity, through the assertion of diversity and complexity, becomes brutally focused in the committed assertion of 'this difference' in the face of the collective provision for a broader 'community'. The politics of difference can thus represent a critique of the assumed solidarity of any such community, and a denial of territorial propinquity as an adequate basis for defining identity or needs. Thus this manifestation of the politics of difference has posed a challenge to the 'ambiguous programmes' and 'racial inexplicitness' of service provision. One response to this challenge has been for an institutional recognition of difference through a strategy in which the 'specificity' of particular groups' demands are defined as special needs and then incorporated into the generic programme.

This strategy has the potential of demonstrating a formal recognition of diversity of experience and need, while effectively denying the reality of that difference through a refusal to contemplate the challenge to 'normal practice' such a recognition demands. In effect a token adjustment in service delivery is negotiated within the existing institutional framework. Signs in the hospital go up in 'Asian' languages to direct 'Asian' patients to an unchanged treatment regimen; or ethnic minority staff are recruited in order to be isolated and marginalized in the social work, or community, location (see Rooney 1987). There is of course also the complementary strategy in which 'special needs' are recognized and special provision is made, *outside* of the mainstream services. Such special initiatives isolate the mainstream services from change and shelter them from having to confront the ethnocentrism of the current practice. Additionally, as the history of Section II funding in Britain has demonstrated, such special provision can leave ethnic minority staff vulnerable and whole programmes subject to continued external surveillance and potential precipitate closure.

Where the recognition of diversity fails to challenge and change the practice and values of mainstream services it racializes service by rendering non-mainstream users aberrant and problematic. *Their* difference is seen to exclude them from 'normal' provision. Consequently, not only may such persons be directed to services predominantly in an under-funded voluntary sector, or to programmes that are ambiguously sustainable over time, but in addition *they* may attract bitter resentment from the majority because of their 'special treatment'. In Britain, the meshing of the tradition of universal service delivery to the particularity of user needs is not an easy accommodation.

Additionally it has been argued (Anthias and Yuval-Davis 1993) that through the 1970s and 1980s in Britain local government moved towards an equal opportunities rhetoric in which community policies were directed to those marginalized identities who had previously been excluded from the imagined homogeneous community. Both Meekosha (1993) and Anthias and Yuval-Davis (1993) provide powerful insights into the consequences of this conflation of equal opportunities and community policies. Not least of the consequences of those processes was the impact of the criteria for being recognized as an appropriate object of funding; and of having to compete for limited 'community' funding.

> The funding process has also played a major role in the categorization or naming of groups, and the criteria for designing groups in terms of race, colour, oppression, deprived, not only are imposed from outside, but are both opportunistic and contradictory. A grouping would have to emphasize its members' deprivation and marginality in order to claim funding. This then leads to ghettoization of 'needs groups'. It is in this way that minorities indirectly become defined and constructed by the state and their 'empowerment' can be of a very limited and specific nature.
>
> (Anthias and Yuval-Davis 1993: 182)

The interface between the pursuit of the narrow self-interest of the politics of difference and the state's strategies in managing diversity has promoted divisiveness within territorially defined urban communities, and competition between the marginalized communities of interest defined through their exclusive claims as communities of identity. During a period when there has been an increasing isolation and rejection of the 'enemy within' (Jessop *et al.* 1988), including the poor, the gay, the unemployed and ethnic minorities, this fragmentation of the disadvantaged has undermined possible united political opposition to the contraction of state provision and the promotion of a divided, two-nation (the haves and the have nots) Britain. These forces have also increasingly seen the shifting of responsibility for a wide range of social provision on to the voluntary sector. And, as we have seen above, the fracturing of the voluntary sector around difference of identity has made it particularly vulnerable to state coercion through funding and regulation.

Ethnicity, nationality, citizenship

The politics of difference and, within Britain, the challenge to the inclusive identity and politics of Blackness have not emerged in a vacuum. As
has been suggested above, the state has had a continuing interest in the
management of diversity, and it is notable how early in the modern experience of labour migration into Britain a 'race relations' infrastructure was
developed. The attempt to regulate 'community relations' has historically
been developed simultaneously with an attempt to regulate immigration
into Britain (see Chapter 2, this volume, for a historical perspective).
Britain's positive self-image as a tolerant society has been threatened by
the explicit, and widespread, racist response to the arrival and settlement
of 'non-white' migrant labour. From the late 1950s this racist response had
an articulate voice within party politics, and certainly from 1964 it became
a bi-party issue as the Labour and Conservative Parties entered into an
escalating competition to respond to the populist racist sentiments in a
spiral of anti-immigrant legislation. Successive Immigration Acts fed the
racist sentiments they sought to placate (Solomos 1989; Husband 1991).
However, the racist excesses this strategy promoted brought the rule of law
into question, fuelled extremist politics which threatened the electoral
security of the established political parties and generated urban unrest that
politicized black communities (Hall *et al.* 1978; Husband 1987). Such
xenophobic and racist excess was dysfunctional to the state and the community relations legislation of 1968 and 1976 was intended to challenge
racist *behaviour* and reassert the rhetoric of tolerance. As has already been
noted above (Lustgarten 1987), the implementation of this strategy through
existing dominant institutions may have facilitated its rhetorical function,
but seriously neutralized its behavioural impact. The success of the former
may be judged from the unambiguous posturing of British civil servants at
a variety of European conferences as the possessors of the definitive experience in effectively promoting 'harmonious community relations'. They were
of course building upon an imperial administrative repertoire in which the
administration of ethnic difference was a highly developed political art.
    Attempts to promote harmonious community relations while pursu-
ing draconian immigration policies are contradictory. Those whom the
state defines as a threat to be excluded are the kin and potential marriage
partners of minority ethnic British citizens already living in Britain (see
Chapter 4, this volume, for a discussion of the impact of immigration
policies on family-based obligations). The exclusion of those who do not
belong defines those who do; and the xenophobic and racist ethos of the
TREVI agreement, of the Schengen group and of the European Union's
border policies have served to define a privileged European identity (Pieterse
1991; Husband 1994: Chapter 8). Within that 'European' context Britain
has throughout the period of Thatcherism pursued a highly orchestrated
programme of racialized nationalism in which neo-conservative values have
been linked to neo-liberal economic policies. The nation, that imagined

community of 'we Britons' (see Anderson 1991; Colley 1992), has progressively been defined in terms of English ethnicity. The Educational Reform Act has sought to reassert the primacy of *English* culture and Christian religion in the national curriculum, and Norman Tebbit's cricket test has indicated how even leisure pursuits may be occasions of treason.

With this history, and this present, minority ethnic communities are routinely defined as outside the national community. And, as we have observed above, in the pursuit of resources it has often been through the explicit assertion of their marginality that they best succeeded. Thus one basis for the emergence of a politics of difference can be found in the exclusion of persons with ethnic minority identities from normative citizenship status.

Bottomore (1992) usefully distinguished between 'formal' and 'substantive' citizenship, with the former being defined as 'membership' in a 'nation state' and the latter as 'an array of civil, political, and especially social rights, involving also some kind of participation in the business of government'. This is a distinction which has considerable significance for understanding the situation of minority ethnic communities in Britain, for as Brubaker has observed,

> That which constitutes citizenship – the array of rights or the pattern of participation – is not necessarily tied to formal state-membership. Formal citizenship is neither a sufficient nor a necessary condition for substantive citizenship ... That it is not a sufficient condition is clear: one can possess formal state-membership yet be excluded (in law or in fact) from certain political, civil, or social rights ... That formal citizenship is not a necessary condition of substantive citizenship is perhaps less evident ... Often social rights, for example, are accessible to citizens and legally resident non-citizens on virtually identical terms.
>
> (Quoted in Bottomore 1992)

The issue here is that within contemporary Britain the majority of ethnic minority persons in the country enjoy formal citizenship in law; yet as we have seen they are denied equivalence as members of the 'nation'. Thus the institutions of the state and the agents of the state may treat them differentially. This may include noting *their difference* in order to assert that 'we treat everyone the same': a colour blind form of universal provision which asserts the dominant communities' mores and needs as normative. This must lead to the denial of a range of distinctive needs and a provision of inappropriate services. Of course, the recognition of difference may result in intentional racist discrimination, with a consequent denial of rights. And the recognition of difference may generate an exaggerated sense of the 'specificity' of needs, such that adequate generic services are not offered. All these instances point to the possible slippage between formal citizenship rights and substantive citizenship in terms of provision and treatment.

However, not all persons who have ethnic minority identities enjoy formal citizenship status. Cohen (1994) has distinguished between citizens, denizens and helots. Denizens he defines as privileged aliens who have a right of residence or domicile but do not possess citizenship in a country. Many would be persons having distinct skills and occupying well paid jobs. Helots are defined as including people who have illegally entered the country, or overstayed their visa, or who may be asylum-seekers who have not been recognized under the international conventions. Clearly these categories confuse the simple stereotypical labelling of people in terms of their apparent ethnicity. Denizens may, for example, be wealthy and internationally mobile and have little interest in participating in any indigenous community. Helots may be well integrated into a 'community' yet be subject to summary dismissal from the country if identified as such by 'the authorities'. Additionally, the neurotic concerns of the state with policing entry into the country has meant that policies aimed at identifying and regulating helots have impinged upon the substantive rights of citizens and denizens.

Citizenship in Britain is a legal status that exists in relation to a highly politicized definition of the nation. And regrettably, despite the naive hopes of pluralists, the state is not a neutral administrative vehicle which services and regulates citizens. The state is the contested resource in an ethnic struggle between those who would assert their dominance over the definition of the nation and those who would contest it (Brass 1985). Thus within Britain the definition of communities in terms of ethnicity has been an expression of a contemporary nationalistic project which has sought to contain the significance of the real change in the demography of British society. The legal status of citizenship enjoyed by the majority of British minority ethnic persons provides a basis for leverage within state institutions in pursuing appropriate resourcing of their needs. And the high profile of ethnic difference as a basis for competition within the state and in civil society has acted to suppress other agendas and modes of mobilization around, for example, class and broader heterogeneous territorial communities (see also Chapter 2, this volume).

We therefore have a situation in which 'the community' is a subject of conceptual disputation. And in its political expression the community has been transformed and generated by the opposed strategies of state institutions seeking to manage diversity and communities of interest investing heavily in the effective coherence provided by the finite boundaries of identity politics. Not surprisingly the community is elusive. Yet I would claim to live in one, and belong to several.

Conclusion

The discussion above has attempted to open up for examination the problematic nature of the concept of community as it is applied in multi-ethnic Britain. A concept which is in itself famously ambiguous has been shown to be inherently politicized in its usage in relation to contemporary social policy. The language of 'community' is everywhere co-opted into discourses of inner-city and urban policy and of wider political agendas. At the same time that the policies of neo-liberal economics pursued a market individualism which exacerbated global shifts in the labour market, and weakened the safety net of the welfare state, thus eroding the material infrastructure of the 'community' and 'family', Thatcherite neo-conservative rhetoric invoked a back-to-basics appeal to 'traditional' values and a racialized imagery of British community life. And in their demographically specific locations in British cities, in which ethnic minority communities experienced their racial oppression and economic marginalization, the politics of resistance for contemporary and historical reasons found the 'community' a meaningful site of mobilization (Gilroy 1993a, b; Hesse 1993). This focus has paralleled a movement from a predominantly class-based framework for critical social theory to a more diffuse politics of difference reflecting contemporary movements which have predominantly been associated with identity struggles, around, for example, sexuality, 'race', ethnicity, age, disability or lifestyle. I have tried to indicate above how these politics of difference intersect with social policy through their constituting a contested ground in which the definition and management of difference is a major concern of the state.

At one level the class-based certainties of much community theory and practice of earlier decades have been rendered seemingly naive and oversimplistic as those responsible for service delivery and resource allocation have been required to confront the rich complexity of the identities of service users. One consequence of this challenge has been the ethnicization of practice wherein users' ethnicity has become the primary and sufficient defining feature in determining their needs. An essential feature of this penetration of the politics of difference into social policy is highlighted in Meekosha's insightful analysis:

> The concept of difference has become a substitute for more critical concepts such as privilege, conflict of interest, oppression and subordination. Difference can avoid discussions of power... These differences have challenged the calls for equality, by eroding the clarity of goals espoused in earlier demands and supplanting them by modes of self-affirmation in separate identities: at times the desire to become 'equal' dissolved in the statements of individual uniqueness.
>
> (Meekosha 1993: 180–5)

These statements point to differing aspects of the incorporation of difference into social policy. At one level claims to difference by service users may be incorporated by service providers in ways which abstract the 'ethnic minority user' from their social context. Thus, for example, Ahmad's (1995) critique of the wide application of the concept of consanguinity to *explain* a range of health needs of South Asian patients powerfully indicates how ethnic identity may be prioritized, with the consequence of utterly neglecting the socio-economic determination of ethnic minorities health status.

Meekosha's second statement, however, reminds us of the possibility that ethnic communities' modes of self-mobilization may not fit happily with the analytic framework of those professionals who would espouse their cause. The discussion above has suggested that there is a distinct specificity to the 'spatiality' of ethnic minority settlement in Britain, which may itself be sufficient to cause miscomprehension by health care professionals of their clients' relation to their neighbourhood, and their cognitive mapping of their community. Additionally, the focused programme-related agenda of the professional community worker may have difficulty in relating to some of the more expressive, apparently non-goal directed, activities which may be part of community self-affirmation. The danger then arises that the professionals selectively give representative status to those members of the ethnic minority community whose views are most compatible with their 'professional' perspective. As I have suggested above, the issue of who may speak on behalf of whom is also an issue within all ethnic 'communities', including majority ethnicities (see, for example, Wright 1985; Pettman 1992: Chapter 6).

One consequence of the many expressions of the politics of difference in multi-ethnic Britain is that the dominant white norm is no longer securely invisible. The certitude of collective identity, the stability of an unambiguous shared history and the common virtue of Christian orthodoxy are no longer secure in white British consciousness. The rapid economic and cultural changes associated with globalization and the 'post-modern condition' have themselves changed the lived experience that underpinned the routine assumptions relating to work and lifestyle in 'the British way of life'. The invention and re-invention of tradition cannot seal the cracks in British self-regard (Hobsbawm and Ranger 1983). More pointedly, the *de facto* reality of Britain as a multi-ethnic society has opened up a struggle over British identity; made all the more pointed because, unlike in some other European multi-ethnic countries, the majority of the ethnic minority population are British citizens. Thus the racialized politics of Thatcherism and its attempted reassertion of (white) British identity, in opposition to the 'enemy within' of ethnic minority communities, seeks to fracture the British population in a way which is directly at odds with the implicit universal provision of services to be enjoyed by all citizens. For those working in the caring professions there is a recurrent, and disconcertingly unpredictable, encounter with self as their assumptions, values, behaviour and even professional ethics are suddenly rendered visible and problematic. In, for example, social work, psychiatry, academia and nursing normative professional practice is no protection against charges of ethnocentric or racist behaviour (see, for example, Fernando 1988; CCETSW 1991a, b; Torkington 1991; Husband 1992; Henwood and Phoenix 1996). A self-reflexive openness is more than ever an essential prerequisite for professionals in the caring professions.

The fanciful evocation of 'community' that is inherent in the government's 'care in the community' programme requires an intellectual openness and personal honesty of those operating within its framework. The underpinnings of professional practice have been challenged as being Eurocentric, and unimaginative attempts at embracing ethnic diversity as a professional issue are rapidly identified as tokenistic and inadequate by users and more astute fellow professionals. Additive strategies that reify ethnicity and compartmentalize provision are contributions to a divisive and ultimately unequal system of service delivery. The challenge lies in recognizing the relevance of ethnic identity in relation to other determinants of need and thus determining appropriate services. Ethnic minority communities are themselves actively promoting innovation in service delivery, and in some instances their very success outside mainstream provision raises important questions about the balance between universal and particular provision in response to ethnic diversity (see Chapter 9, this volume). It may be that at present in many areas of service delivery it is easier to identify what is bad practice now than to assert confidently what are templates for good practice in the future. At the level of institutional structures and professional competencies we are currently riding a rapid learning curve. A willingness to sustain self-doubt and professional anxiety may be the most essential and difficult competence we can ask of caring professionals.

Annotated bibliography

Anthias, F. and Yuval-Davis, N. (1992) *Racialised Boundaries: Race, Nation, Gender, Colour and Class and the Anti-racial Struggle.* London: Routledge.
The title says it all. This book sustains a critical examination of the ideologies which frame social divisions. The book provides an exploration of the relation of 'race' and racism in the construction of the nation and national identities. Of particular relevance, in the context of this book, is the examination of the 'race relations industry' and the complex reality of anti-oppressive strategies as they involve, and impact upon, 'the community'.

Butcher, H., Glen, A., Henderson, P. and Smith, J. (1993) *Community and Public Policy.* London: Pluto Press.
This book offers the reader an accessible and wide ranging introduction to the debates surrounding the relationship between public policy and community values. Brought together under the headings of 'Concepts and context, community policy in practice' and 'Critical perspectives', this edited text provides a wide ranging review of concepts and issues.

Rattansi, A. and Westwood, S. (1994) *Racism, Modernity and Identity: on the Western Front.* Cambridge: Polity Press.
To quote the blurb: 'The West has a unique civilization, a powerful "front" – modernity, liberty, democracy, affluence. This volume offers critical perspectives from both "inside" and "outside" the cultural and intellectual frontiers of the Western projects.' The book offers a challenging and rewarding read which examines

racism and the dynamic nature of ethnicities within a European context in which Western modernity is widely declared to be in crisis. Both 'modernity' and 'postmodernity' are critically explored as frameworks for making sense of contemporary global phenomena, and their significance for a Europe which has historically sought to define and regulate its 'non-Western' others.

Wright, W. (1985) *On Living in an Old Country*. London: Verso.
A gem of a book, which gently and subtly exposes the fabric of English ethnicity. The book, through an examination of a wide range of apparently unrelated, almost random events, shows how a sense of history is incorporated into the taken for granted present. In particular the analysis of the heritage industry exposes the invention of tradition which underpins life in Deep England.

Part II

FAMILY, OBLIGATIONS AND COMMUNITY CARE

4

Family obligations and social change among Asian communities

Waqar I. U. Ahmad

Introduction

Community care rests heavily on the family and is negotiated within the context of obligations, reciprocities and people's economic circumstances and moral identities (Qureshi and Walker 1989; Finch and Mason 1993). Inter- and intra-generational relationships within the family remain the most important sources of support and physical care. This is true of social, material and caring obligations, and as true of the majority as of minority communities. While there is an extensive and rich literature on family relationships and norms and negotiation of obligations in the majority white community (e.g. Finch 1989; Qureshi and Walker 1989; Finch and Mason 1993), this contrasts with a dearth of information on minority ethnic groups. Much of what is known of family obligations among minority ethnic communities is a by-product of researchers' substantive interests in migration, settlement and, more broadly, race relations. Yet the stereotypes of virtuous caring families, especially Asian, abound (see Walker and Ahmad 1994). These stereotypes ignore both the diversity of perspectives and behaviour within an ethnic group and the similarities across ethnic groups. Nor do they take account of the importance of demographic and social change among minority ethnic communities, which may affect both norms and behaviour in relation to family obligations.

This chapter, in the first section, draws together this disparate literature from race relations to build a picture of family obligations among Asian communities. In this, I consider the role played by family-based obligations in migration and settlement, before considering the nature and system of obligations among Asian communities. In the second part of the chapter, I consider the processes of social change and how the Asian communities attempt to reproduce cultural values and practices in the second and subsequent generations. Cultural retention is a serious consideration for minority communities but, as in other communities, it does not take place in a

Table 4.1 Regional distribution of all ethnic groups, 1991

Percentage of resident population

Region or metropolitan county	Entire population (millions)	Caribbean	Black African	Other black	Indian	Pakistani	Bangladeshi	Chinese	Other Asian	Other Other
South East	31.4	66.3	83.5	56.6	52.9	29.9	63.1	53.3	72.4	57.9
Greater London	12.2	58.2	77.1	45.2	41.3	18.4	52.7	36.1	57.1	41.7
East Anglia	3.7	1.0	1.1	4.0	0.8	1.2	1.0	2.4	1.9	2.6
South West	8.4	2.5	1.3	3.7	1.3	0.8	1.4	4.3	2.3	4.3
West Midlands	9.4	15.6	2.5	10.5	18.9	20.7	11.9	6.1	5.8	8.4
West Midlands MC	4.6	14.4	1.9	8.8	16.8	18.5	11.1	3.9	4.5	6.5
East Midlands	7.2	4.9	1.6	6.0	11.8	3.7	2.6	4.8	3.7	4.9
Yorks & Humberside	8.8	4.3	2.3	5.7	4.8	19.9	5.1	5.2	3.7	6.2
South Yorkshire	2.3	1.2	0.6	1.4	0.4	2.8	0.7	1.4	0.7	1.6
West Yorkshire	3.7	3.0	1.2	3.7	4.1	16.9	3.7	2.5	2.3	3.6
North West	11.4	4.3	4.4	9.0	6.6	16.2	9.1	11.1	4.5	8.2
Greater Manchester	4.6	3.4	2.5	5.2	3.5	10.4	7.0	5.3	2.5	4.4
Merseyside	2.6	0.4	1.4	2.4	0.3	0.2	0.4	3.6	0.6	1.9
North	5.5	0.2	0.7	1.1	0.9	2.0	2.2	3.2	1.6	1.8
Tyne & Wear	2.0	0.1	0.4	0.5	0.5	0.8	1.7	1.8	0.8	0.9
Wales	5.2	0.7	1.3	1.9	0.8	1.2	2.3	3.1	1.9	2.6
Scotland	9.1	0.7	1.3	1.5	1.2	4.4	0.7	6.7	2.3	3.0

Source: Owen (1993), Table 6

social vacuum. Here, I consider the role of minority institutions in cultural retention and the significance of the immigration process, women's involvement in the labour market and the presumed challenges from (and facing) the second and third generations to social change and continuity. The focus of this chapter is deliberately broad; Atkin and Rollings (Chapter 5) consider the specific issues around family-based physical care and tending.

Migration, obligations and settlement

The system of obligations and reciprocities is central to the migration process. The few 'pioneers' became the major sources of information for their kin and community and even when migration took place in response to recruitment drives in the Caribbean and South Asia, family obligations played an important part in the organization of passage and settlement. While kin and village folk in Britain facilitated intelligence, entry vouchers and work permits, and upon arrival helped with accommodation and jobs, the kin in countries of origin provided support to the migrant's immediate family and children and looked after their business interests. The importance of kin support to the social and economic life of migrants is partly reflected in settlement patterns of different migrant groups (Peach 1984, 1986). Chain migration resulted in clustering of populations from same regions. And, as Werbner (1990a, b) notes, encapsulation was reinforced by positive factors such as kin group, religion, community institutions and ethnic businesses, and negative factors such as outside hostility and fears about loss of cultural values. Table 4.1 shows settlement patterns of the major minority ethnic groups.

However, the diversity of apparently homogeneous populations in terms of regional identity, religion and ethnicity as well as class and caste needs to be noted. For example, Nowikowski and Ward (1978) note three categories of migrants from Pakistan: professional, business bourgeoisie and the urban and rural middle strata. The expense of the passage as well as poor access to information networks has meant that few of the relatively poor have been able to migrate. Werbner (1990b), on the other hand, argues that Pakistani migration was composed of traders, students and workers. The traders were part of the pre-war migration, when pedlars settled in some of the larger cities, like London, Leeds and Glasgow. Even among these traders, differences of 'caste' are significant and most chain migration and support was confined to one's own kin group. The students were members of the Pakistani elite from upper social classes and castes. The workers were migrants largely from villages in Gujarat and Jhelum districts but from a heterogeneous group of different landowning castes as well as some service castes. Their settlement patterns and community networks reflect these class and caste boundaries. At a broader level, ethnic concentrations within Britain are apparent for Pakistanis, Bangladeshis and Afro-Caribbeans, largely organized on sub-ethnic group bases. Such concentrations have relevance for support networks, family obligations and their negotiation.

Family, community and obligations

The 'extended family' is a much used concept in relation to Asian and other minority ethnic communities, but its various definitions and heterogeneity are poorly understood. Ballard (1990: 229) notes the structure of the Punjabi family – the Punjabis constitute up to three-quarters of the population of South Asian origin living in Britain – as of patrilineal descent and patrilocal residence, where

> Each family (*ghar*) – which ideally includes a man, his sons and his sons' sons, together with their wives and unmarried daughters – is a strongly corporate group, whose members are expected to live cooperatively together under the same roof while jointly exploiting their common assets and property. As well as being the arena within which the most intense personal relationships are sustained, such units also provide the basic building blocks for the local social structure. It is above all as members of their families, rather than as lone individuals, that Punjabis participate in the wider world.

This, however, is necessarily a generalization: such families are universal neither in Britain nor in South Asia. Anwar (1979: 52), in a detailed discussion of the 'extended family' in relation to his study of the Pakistani community in Rochdale, notes:

> If by extended family is meant a group of kin of three generations or more with a well defined corporate linear character, involving cooperation in productive activities, common ownership of assets and recognized common responsibilities, such units are almost entirely absent from the modern urban industrial scene. But if extended family means in a very loose sense those extra-familial kin who maintain a relationship of some intimacy with members of a nuclear family, then such groups do persist in fully developed urban conditions.

It was this latter definition by which Finch and Mason (1993) in their study of family obligations conclude that the extended or joint family is alive and well in contemporary Britain. Anwar further elaborates on the variety of family forms that may be defined as joint or extended families. In a non-exhaustive list, these include:

- joint family living together;
- joint family living across cities, countries or continents;
- joint family living together but not pooling income;
- joint family living together and pooling income;
- joint family not living together but pooling income;

- joint family not living together and not pooling income;
- joint family not living together and not pooling income but fulfilling some obligations of material, moral and social support;
- independent nuclear units acting as a joint family.

Although most of these family forms can be seen among Britain's Asian communities, Bhachu argues that in some communities there may be a stronger trend towards nuclear households, with considerable autonomy but reciprocal obligatory relationships between independently resident siblings and parents and children (Bhachu 1985, 1988).

Anwar argues that the two main forms of kin networks and systems of obligations are those based on the family (nuclear or joint/extended) and *biraderi* (although this is a Punjabi term other South Asian groups have similar social organization). A *biraderi* is an endogamous, kinship-based group with reciprocal relationships of moral, financial and social obligations, and is an important source of identity and support. According to Wakil (1970), 'A *biraderi* is an individual's bank, police force, and psychiatrist.' Anwar (1979) and Wakil (1970) differentiate between a *biraderi* of recognition and one of participation. In terms of kin support, the former is of little value whereas the latter is defined by incremental gift exchange, obligations at special occasions – births, marriages, deaths, accidents, promotions, circumcision etc. – and a system of material and social support. Wakil (1970), for example, notes the role of the *biraderi* in relation to births, marriages and deaths in the Pakistani (Punjabi) society. On birth, gifts are exchanged by relatives with the family of the newborn. The child's mother's family plays an important part in this. Their obligations extend to granddaughters and sisters' children. On marriage, various family members have well defined responsibilities towards dowries or *bari* (contributions in the form of clothes, money and household effects from the family of the groom). The bride's maternal grandparents' and uncles' obligations extend to her children, especially daughters. Part of the reason for the focus of obligations on female kin rests in the systems of inheritance in South Asia, where in practice males inherit most of the parental wealth. A generous contribution to the dowries of daughters and granddaughters partially compensates for their limited share in parental wealth. In death, the *biraderi* joins in public displays of grief and sympathy, and provides practical help such as food and accommodation for the bereaved and the wider kin and non-kin who come to pay their respects. Expectations at the level of the *biraderi* depend not just on personal or current family relationships but also on inherited obligations. Thus, for example, migrants from South Asia quite unambiguously expected hospitality and support from those close or distant kin who were already settled in Britain (Anwar 1979; Ballard 1990).

Biraderi relationships are governed by rules of reciprocity related to status in a relationship, gender, age and relative material wealth. Those of equal status attempt to maintain a competitive reciprocal relationship, with incremental exchanges, which also serves as a marker of relative status (Anwar 1979; Werbner 1988, 1990b). The range of tasks with which families helped, in Anwar's study, extended from looking after a relative's children to financial support, help in finding employment and finding suitable marriage partners. Preferential marriage patterns, which reflect the strength of ties between two families, are employed to cement these relationships further.

The system of *biraderi*-based obligations is governed by rules of *vartan bhanji* (give and take):

> *Vartan bhanji* involves exchange of sweets, fruits, foods, money and yards of cloth; extending beyond material things, it includes the exchange of services, favours, like treatment, entertainment and participation in ceremonial events. In its operation this mechanism of exchange involves a wide range of relationships among the *biraderi* and other groups who make the Punjabi society. It is of vital importance to people as a means of achieving *izzet*, prestige.
>
> (Anwar 1979: 68)

The closeness of ties and strength of relationship are important and are expressed in the fulfilment of mutual reciprocities and expectations of kin support. Many argue that the need for kinship support increases in Britain because of the absence of the full *biraderi* (Anwar 1979). Anwar's study shows a hierarchy of preference for family help, from close family to *biraderi*, fellow villagers, friends, neighbours, other Pakistanis and the rest of the society. Services performed by *biraderi* included house repairs, shopping, care of children, advice giving, help after an accident, help with English, loans and so on. Anwar also found some overlap between help from the family and from neighbours (see also Bhachu 1988; Warrier 1988; Westwood 1988).

According to Werbner (1990b), gifts play a central role in reflecting and strengthening kinship bonds. Women play a central part in gift exchange in *biraderi* dealings at two levels. First, appropriate and timely fulfilment of obligations towards kin has greater consequences for the moral identities of women than men (Anwar 1979; Werbner 1990b). However, men's moral as well as masculine and familial identities can also be damaged through insufficient regard to their kin, especially if this is seen to be influenced by their wives. Ballard and Ballard (1977) remind us that conventional forms of *vartan bhanji* were revived only after the wives and children joined the male migrants. Second, Werbner (1990b) notes that many of the ceremonial gift exchanges revolve around monopolistic control of women as daughters or wives. Thus various lifecycle events related to women are 'the nexus of the gift economy, drawing together primary symbolic, economic, personal and communal themes'. Werbner considers the symbolic as well as practical value of gifts to migrant economies in cementing existing relationships and creating new ones, including with non-kin:

Gifting 'totalises' relationships. One type of exchange implies others as well. Through gifting migrants transform persons who are strangers into lifelong friends. Through such exchanges not only men but whole households and extended families are linked, and exchanges initiated on the shopfloor extend into domestic and inter domestic domain.

(Werbner 1990b: 331–2)

Although the *biraderi* and the extended family are predominant forms of social support they are not universal; nor do people utilize these resources at random. Qureshi and Walker (1989) show that there are hierarchies of expectations that relate to closeness of kin ties, which run thus: spouse, relative living in same household, daughter, daughter-in-law, son, other relatives or neighbours. Anwar provides a hierarchy of expectations not dissimilar to this, and Finch and Mason (1993) were struck by similarities between Asian and white respondents in relation to norms of social obligations. One area of difference was the reliance on sons and daughters-in-law as opposed to daughters, reflecting assumptions about daughters joining their husbands' family, and usually the youngest son being responsible for parents. The youngest son also normally inherits the parental house, though this may be changing in the British context.

Obligations are also structured by people's circumstances, and legitimate excuses for failing to discharge obligations in Qureshi and Walker's study included the potential helper's prior commitments to other family members, personal inability of helpers to provide care, and unreasonable behaviour or expectations of the person needing care. An individual's position in the family (relationship, gender, age, relative prosperity, physical health etc.) carries with it a complex of duties, rights, obligations and expectations. For example, whereas unmarried daughters may be expected to tend elderly parents, after marriage their priority would be seen to shift to the well-being of their family of marriage. And because of the gendered expectations regarding employment, there would be the expectation that the sons would be primarily responsible for the material support of their parents: married daughters would rarely make such contributions and would have no strong obligation to do so. Daughters-in-law, rather than sons, would be expected to provide physical care, except perhaps for the personal hygiene of adult males in the family. And whereas the normal flow of material and social obligations may be from the older to the younger generation, as in the white community (Qureshi and Walker 1989), the younger Asian people in the British context may be providing additional reciprocal services, particularly in terms of their knowledge of English and local cultures – the possible impact of this on changing household relations is considered later.

It is also noted that people can be isolated within broad communities. Most support networks remain quite parochial. Ballard (1990) notes that the apparently cohesive, large communities are in fact organized on caste, class, kinship, religion, origin and language basis. Bradford shows the importance of such ties in the way its mosques have developed over time. From few mosques with broad congregations, it now has a large network of mosques organized around ethnic, linguistic or regional allegiances as much as on denominational differences. Singh (1992) shows a similar trend in the development of gurdawaras in Bradford. Conflict and competition is very much characteristic of the smaller *biraderi* or family networks within larger communities, as well as within families and *biraderis*.

It is important not to reify the *biraderi* as a necessarily supportive structure or kinship ties as superseding all other considerations. People's decisions to support kin or family are mediated by a range of personal, material and historical factors (Qureshi and Walker 1989; Finch and Mason 1993). An example from the political arena illustrates this. A dynamic young Asian local politician in a northern city was perceived to have been voted in on the strength of the *biraderi* vote in his local ward. Although he developed as a star in his ruling local administration, he was unhappy about the slow progress towards securing parliamentary candidacy. Following promises of a faster route to parliamentary candidacy, he switched allegiance to the opposition party, to much public condemnation. At the next local election he lost his seat to the replacement candidate (with few or no *biraderi* ties to the electorate) from his previous party. Political allegiance, in this case, was a much stronger factor than *biraderi* obligations to vote for one's own.

More generally, *biraderi* and family relationships are not always harmonious. In the South Asian context, conflicts between mothers-in-law and daughters-in-law are legendary. It is illustrative that in the early 1990s one of the most frequently requested songs on West Yorkshire's Sunrise Radio was about such conflict: the lyrics were about a daughter-in-law expressing her intent to beat up her cruel mother-in-law behind the grain store! Just as legendary is the conflict between people who are *shareek* (or partners in inheritance). Historical vendettas between *shareeks* are common in the Punjab. Even when conflict is not present, healthy (and sometimes unhealthy) competition in areas such as personal and children's achievements, conspicuous consumption including jewellery, clothes, cars and houses, morality and gender identities, business and financial success, timely and conspicuous fulfilment of obligations, status within the family and *biraderi*, is part and parcel of *biraderi* life.

Kin and *biraderi* have played a vital part in the settlement and prosperity of migrant communities. As several commentators have noted, migration rested on a system of family obligations, both in sending countries and in areas of settlement. Newcomers were offered hospitality as well as practical help in securing jobs, accommodation and access to indigenous institutions. Early house purchases were either from personal savings or more often through loans from kin (Ballard and Ballard 1977; Anwar 1979). Interest-free loans for special occasions and for communal projects such as mosques, manders or gurdawaras remain a common means of establishing places of worship and at times acts of considerable generosity are witnessed in this regard.

Class and kinship

Kin relationships and reciprocities, however, are influenced by people's economic position and their other obligations. Anwar (1979) and Werbner (1990a, b) show interesting differences in kin support and family organization between working-class and middle-class Pakistanis. They report that relationships of mutual obligations are more likely to revolve around kin group among the working classes than middle classes. Among the middle classes, there is greater interaction with and reliance on people of similar class, educational background or occupation and less reliance on kin support. The middle classes would also have greater access to formal institutions such as banks and the capacity to purchase some forms of care, thus having less need to rely on kin support (see also Wenger 1984; Sinclair *et al.* 1990). Those who move up into middle-class occupations or incomes are also more likely to move out of areas of high ethnic minority concentrations – thus, symbolically and physically, they become more distant from where other kin are likely to be concentrated. However, in both these studies there are relatively few social networks across racial or religious boundaries – support networks remain largely confined to people's own ethnic groups.

Kin networks are often characterized by residential concentration: with differential class mobility among a kin group there is some distancing between kin occupying different class positions, which is usually, though not necessarily, reflected in residential segregation. Werbner notes that the three different types of Pakistani migrants (traders, students and workers) had different residence patterns reflecting their class position: the working-class Pakistanis living in inner-city areas and the middle classes living in the suburbs. However, class mobility in the working classes is followed by a movement to suburbs, which results in the older settled migrants in those suburbs moving further outwards. This also happens in terms of ethnic differences where ethnic differences are closely tied to class positions. For example, Ballard (1990) and Werbner (1990a) have noted that Muslims moving upwards in terms of the housing market often buy properties from Sikhs, who in turn move upwards and outwards into the more expensive and suburban housing stocks.

Material obligations

As already noted, social and material obligations played an important part in the immigration process. They continue to play an important, though changing, role in the survival and prosperity of minority ethnic communities. In earlier years remittances to families in the Indian subcontinent represented a major form of material obligation. This decreased with family unification in Britain but remains a significant source of financial support to a large number of families in the sub-continent. The strength of ties with the family in Britain is reflected in the visible wealth and consumption by those in the sending villages; and migrants and their second generation have kept strong relationships with families in the subcontinent (Carey and Shukur 1985; Ballard 1990). For example, remittances from the UK and the Middle East were significant sources of foreign exchange, at $600 million in the mid-1980s, for Bangladesh (Carey and Shukur 1985).

In the British context, family and *biraderi* networks remain crucial for economic success and employment for Asians. The vast majority of Bhachu's (1985) and Anwar's (1979) respondents found work through family networks and Bhachu notes that her respondents were afforded considerable choice in jobs through such networks.

Clearly, with changing economic circumstances, and in other sectors of employment, such networks may be less effective in securing employment but there is one area where success is largely dependent on family and *biraderi* support, networks and reciprocities. Asian business success owes much to family support through loans, information and family labour – the inadequately acknowledged contribution of women to this area is particularly important (Westwood 1988; Anthias 1992). In a study by Sally Westwood (1988), women had a strong commitment to family business and contributed by working in low-status occupations to support family business ventures. However, they regarded the commercial sphere as a male preserve. Family employment in small family businesses often makes the difference between success and failure, in that few such ventures would survive if they had to pay full wages for the labour of family members.

Many commentators have emphasized the importance of communal modes of accumulation to the economic survival and success of Asian communities (Banton 1979; Warrier 1988; Werbner 1988). Examples here are house purchases and the setting up of businesses paid for by interest-free loans from family members – reflecting both positive reciprocal relationships and enforced encapsulation through limited access to mainstream economic institutions. Werbner considers the importance of strategies that rest on personal knowledge, expectations and trust. She explains the relative economic success of the Pakistani community in Manchester in terms of credit distribution networks rather than the pooling of income. In terms of business success, she argues, alongside rational planning and business skills, the collective willingness to take risks on the part of the lenders and borrowers, wholesalers and their customers is vitally important.

Although such norms and behaviours have been important in the survival strategies of Asian communities, not all ethnic groups, or individuals within an ethnic group, are equally well equipped to benefit from, or have access to, such resources. At the level of the ethno-religious groups, Hindus and Sikhs are financially better off than Pakistanis and Bangladeshis, are less reliant on family support for business success and show greater signs of social change in terms of family size and adaptation. Ethnic businesses, relying heavily on their own communities for trade as well as labour, remain marginalized and do not enjoy the same support from financial institutions as the mainstream business sectors. What is true, however, is that at both intra- and inter-family levels, material obligations play a vital part in family obligations among Asian communities.

Family obligations and cultural traditions: continuity and change

Social change affects migrants and natives alike. In Britain, we have routine pronouncements by politicians, policy-makers, the media and academics about loss of family values and the breakdown of traditional responsibilities and reciprocities. This presumed breakdown is publicly linked to a diverse range of troubles, such as teenage pregnancies, truancy, vandalism, football hooliganism, homelessness, domestic violence and the 'crisis of care'. In the New Right analysis, the presumed over-protective and interfering state is argued to play a retrograde role in this breakdown of self-reliance and family responsibility (Minford 1987). However, social change is a natural phenomenon confronting all societies, although the pace of change may vary across societies and across time, for a variety of reasons (see, for example, Qureshi 1996).

In relation to India, for example, Rao (1977: 25) notes numerous influences on social change: 'Sanskritisation; secularisation; westernisation; nationalism and revivalism; democracy and election; socialism and egalitarianism; planning; industrialisation; urbanisation; education; politicisation; new outlook for submerged classes; change in family, caste and Hindu social institutions; science and technology; regionalism; and modernisation.'[1] The family as an institution is important in discussing social change. Although the relationship between the family and society is a dynamic one, rapid changes in family structure, values, customs and systems of obligations are argued to be a major catalyst for social change and alter the family's desire and ability to meet traditional obligations (Young and Wilmot 1957; Gore 1977). There is also a dynamic relationship between the family and economy, with changes in one having a potential effect on the other. For migrant communities both the structure and reciprocities within the family and the family's relationship with the economy are potential agents for social change and therefore important to consider. Below I consider several aspects of continuity and change in family formation and obligations.

Social change is not easy to explain, partly because it requires an understanding of the relationship between norms and behaviour when norms themselves may be contested, and may not bear a direct relationship to action (Finch and Mason 1993). Norms vary both across people (influenced by gender, age, class, religion and ethnicity, as well as other personal and structural factors) and across time; behaviour too is mediated by a complex range of factors. To complicate matters further, there is also considerable overlap in norms and behaviours across ethnic and social groups, across genders and across historical periods (Ahmad 1996). It seems that three types of considerations may be important in affecting social change.

First, as Anderson (1971) argues, one view on social change is that people will break out of prevailing patterns of behaviour if they perceive it to be in their interests to do so *and* if they can do so without suffering severe social sanctions for contravening existing normative beliefs (see also Qureshi 1996). He also argues that once new patterns of behaviour are established new normative beliefs will emerge to support them. In this respect, Ballard and Ballard (1977) discuss the changing role of the older generation and the extended family in the maintenance of marriages among the younger generation – marriages are essentially unions of families rather than individuals and therefore the family and kin have a considerable stake in the marriage. Within the new environment, parents and grandparents, because of education and 'cultural' differences with their children, may have fewer skills to make sound marriage choices. The Ballards also note that the relative fragmentation of the extended family and the trend towards nuclear households among many younger people may mean that couples' lives are open to greater strain than they would experience among other family members (although we need to acknowledge that living with the wider family can itself lead to friction and failure of marriage). Finally, traditional sanctions of public shame, threats of violence and material sanctions may be absent or less effective in the British context.

Second, however, as some have argued, normative beliefs may continue to exert symbolically significant influence on behaviour long after the conditions which supported them have changed. Thus, for example, some Pakistani and Bangladeshi women might stay out of the labour market even if the opportunities for paid work were present. Further, Thomas (1992) argues that despite the fact that few Indian Hindus follow the practices of the three Brahminic age-related lifestages of householder (*grhastha*), hermit (*vanaprastha*) and wandering ascetic (*sannyasi*), these stages remain normative for most Hindus. Similarly, Pillsbury (1978) reports the resilience of beliefs in 'doing the month' – characterized by prescriptions and proscriptions in relation to physical and spiritual care of women after childbirth – even among professional women of Chinese descent in America. Such normative beliefs, although no longer sufficiently strong to have a major influence on behaviour, can lead to guilt. Despite the reproduction of distinctive institutions to maintain the continuity and stability of religio-cultural values, migrants must, at least at a minimal level, adapt to function in a new environment. The rate of social change for immigrants may be faster than for the 'natives', and differences between generations may be greater at the level of both normative assumptions and behaviour (Modood *et al.* 1994). Equally importantly, the perceived difference in norms between generations may also lead to a change in expectations and thus affect behaviour.

Third, maintenance or change of cultural values and behaviour may depend on their consistency with personal identity and the ease with which certain traditions can be maintained. Among Sikh girls, for example, most adhere to the Sikh edicts of long hair (kesh) and wearing a bangle (kara) – both of which are consistent with the prevalent ideas about femininity, and are easily maintained (Drury 1991). The same may not be true of Sikh men. Personal identities are multiple, situational and complexly interactive: gender, 'race', sexuality etc.

Others reluctantly change their behaviour because of external social, economic and legal constraints. Examples here include the banning of headscarves for girls in French schools (a cause of considerable grievance for Muslims), some schools not allowing pupils to wear jewellery (hence problems of wearing the kara) or the informal pressure which led many Sikh men to cut their hair in the early years of migration. Interestingly, resistance to such hostility can itself give rise to new identities.

In the sections below, I discuss how migrants attempt to preserve cultural traditions and how various forces for change impact on the normative values and behaviour of minority ethnic populations. An important lesson of this discussion is that *continuity* and *change* are *not* diametrically opposed but complementary concepts, which at times are difficult to disentangle.

Reproducing culture

Ideological, structural and personal factors are important in reproducing ideas and norms of family responsibilities (Finch 1989). The reproduction of cultures is not a simple process of implanting the norms, behaviours and aspirations of one generation into the minds and hearts of the next. Reproduction takes place within a dynamic space involving negotiation and engagement, encompassing conflicting values within the family, influences of the wider society, personal agendas of various actors, the role of the economy, legal frameworks and the impact of and resistance to a racialized external world. If debates about agency and structure in social change are complex they are even more complex for minorities who live within their own as well as the wider society's structures and institutions. Below, I discuss three main forces for cultural retention: family and socialization, ethnic organizations and the part played by external factors.

First, and a recurrent theme in research, the role played by the family in reproducing values and behaviours is regarded as vital (Anwar 1979; Warrier 1988; Afshar 1994). Anthias (1992) notes that the reproduction of cultural values of honour and shame, identity and religion, obligations and expectations, relations with kin and ethnic group, and gender roles is regarded as the prime responsibility of parents, especially women. Family-based socialization serves two main functions: it imparts religious and cultural values regarding gender roles, mutual responsibilities of family members, obligations towards kin etc.; and it counters the presumed harmful and contradictory influences of the wider society, i.e. individualism, secular morality, presumed sexual permissiveness, presumed lack of respect for elders, and loss of family values (Anwar 1979; Afshar 1994). Parents and family are responsible for equipping children with culturally appropriate norms and behaviours and positive religious and ethnic identities (some of these debates are taken up below). Further, as Werbner (1988) has noted, women's (and less crucially men's) role in ceremonial exchange or *vartan bhanji*, a system of mutual help, is crucial in the maintenance of cultural traditions. Appropriate conduct in *vartan bhanji* is vital to family honour and, especially, to a woman's moral reputation.

Second, minority ethnic religious and cultural institutions play a crucial part in cultural retention. These include: religious organizations; ethnic media such as newspapers, radio and television both in English and other community languages; weekend and evening schools for religious education or mother tongue teaching; community centres and voluntary organizations; ethnic businesses; and art and cultural organizations (Rex *et al.* 1987; Rex 1991). Through these, minority communities seek 'to reproduce in the British context the social characteristics which used to shape their way of life' in the country of origin (Joly 1987).

Third, concerns about the values and institutions of the wider society, as well as external hostility, reinforce encapsulation and reduce the opportunities for excursions into other cultural traditions; though this is less true of the second generation, whose knowledge of the wider culture and the English language may potentially make such excursions easier (Werbner 1990a, b; Modood *et al.* 1994). External hostility also fosters newer forms of (often inclusive) identity formation and mobilization (Samad 1992). This encapsulation is sustained by minority ethnic institutions, as discussed above.

Some of the major forces for continuity and change in cultural traditions and family obligations are discussed below.

Immigration process and social change

The immigration process itself is a change agent in family life and affects people's roles, expectations and reciprocities. For most primary migrants, migration was as single men or women and few then could rely on direct family support in Britain. However, as noted, the immigration process itself rested heavily on kinship obligations. Ballard (1990) notes some tensions even in those early days. For example, those who sent money to their families often felt that those reaping the benefits had little appreciation of the hardships endured in generating these remittances. This remains an issue currently between migrant workers in the Middle East and their families in the Indian subcontinent. Second, new tensions were created after family reunions in Britain. There was now less chance of having savings which could be remitted to relatives, leading to feelings of migrants having reneged on financial obligations to the wider kin, who were, often, responsible for facilitating their migration in the first place (Saifullah Khan 1977).

The differences in patterns of migration among groups, and the enforced migration of various refugee populations, also have an impact on available family support. For example, whereas most Sikh and Hindu families joined in the 1960s and early 1970s, Pakistani and Bangladeshi families joined (and are joining) later, amid markedly stricter immigration policies. Restrictive and racialized immigration rules have often kept families apart for decades. Often, people are left in both places without important family support. Those in Britain, though deprived of family, retain social, moral and material obligations towards their younger family members in the Indian subcontinent (see Modood *et al.* 1994). Strongly felt, but difficult to meet, obligations towards family members divided by immigration rules were causes of significant distress for many older people in a study by Ahmad and Walker (1996).

For refugee populations (e.g. Vietnamese, East African Asians), official dispersal policies were a more formal element of the state's role in family and community breakdown, although secondary internal migration has led to considerable geographical concentration, facilitation of community networks and organizations (Lam and Green 1995).

Concerning women, Saifullah Khan (1977) notes some changes in rules of seclusion after migration. In most villages, kin make up the bulk of co-villagers and seclusion rules are relaxed, with women enjoying a variety of supportive networks and freedom of movement. Saifullah Khan argues that in the new situation with the greater necessity to deal with non-kin, and in a locality containing kin and non-kin, women may experience restrictions on movement and loss of social support. However, considering the tendency to residential concentration according to ethnic boundaries (Chinese people are a major exception), and the emergence of women's employment-related networks, this may be less of a problem now than when Saifullah Khan's work took place.

Finally, an unacknowledged but significant issue concerns men (*mangeters*) entering Britain to marry British women. The tendency to bring over marriage partners from the Indian subcontinent rests partly on kinship obligations and the desire to strengthen family relationships with kin, and partly, according to Ballard (1990) in relation to marriage of men, on concerns about the likelihood of young women, exposed to the presumed individualism and permissiveness of the Western culture, being suitable wives, daughters-in-law or mothers. Although the marriage of a woman from the Indian subcontinent to a British man and settlement in Britain can result in loss of support networks for the women, it none the less represents continuity with the expected norms of patrilocal forms of family formation. For men coming to Britain for marriage, in contrast, it represents change in expectations, traditional hierarchies of power and living arrangements. Within the Asian community, for men to be dependent on in-laws is regarded as, at least, suspect and often dishonourable; and this in itself causes problems. Male fiancés are initially dependent on the spouse and in-laws for accommodation and employment. Their residence status in Britain is subject to evidence of a 'successful marriage' as assessed after one year – this is often regarded as giving undue powers to the wife and in-laws, who can have an 'unsatisfactory' spouse repatriated with the consequent loss of honour. Anecdotal evidence suggests that such marriages experience additional tensions, with men bemoaning reduced ability to meet their obligations towards their kin and women concerned about their husbands' unreasonable expectations and behaviour.

Gender, employment and change

Imperial notions of oppressive family structures of various colonized people, especially the marginalized position of women, are well known. These concerns were often offered as the legitimation of colonial rule over India (Brah 1992) and the Middle East (Ahmed 1992), where imperialism was presented as a liberating force for women whose cultures and religions were thought to be socially, economically and morally oppressive. The remarkable consistency in these discourses and those which socially construct Asian women's experience in contemporary Britain is noted by Brah (1992). These fears were rehearsed at length recently in the media treatment of the marriage between Pakistan's Imran Khan and Jemima Goldsmith, daughter of a wealthy British businessman (see also Parmar 1982; Alibhai-Brown 1993).

This having been said, as in the white society, the various migrant communities confront problems of sexism and many in these communities vociferously marshal notions of cultural tradition and religious values in support of patriarchal ideology (Wilson 1979; Mumtaz and Shaheed 1987; see also a collection of feminist poetry edited by Rukhsana Ahmad 1991). Wilson (1979) notes how discourses of *sharm* and *izzet* (shame and honour) legitimate keeping women 'in their place', as mothers and homemakers, and as the site of and threat to male honour. Alongside selective interpretations of tradition and religion, relative economic marginalization and limited access to inherited property remain important factors in sustaining gender inequalities and ensuring the primacy of women's role as mother, wife and carer. Warrier (1988), recognizing the link between gender roles and the economy, notes that many social scientists have argued that women's entry into the labour market will be a major force in changing the 'traditional reciprocities' in the Asian family. The strength of Asian groups is, reportedly, in their communal mode of accumulation, which provides more effective economic competition and accumulation of wealth and property, and gives the older generation control over younger generations (including marriages). These established hierarchies are said to be greatly weakening in Britain, with women seizing employment opportunities, leading to the renegotiation of gender-based household responsibilities (see Westwood and Bhachu 1988). This is Parminder Bhachu's thesis (Bhachu 1985, 1988, 1991).

Bhachu notes the relatively high level of labour market participation of Sikh women and stresses the two-way relationship between gendered cultural norms and the economy. As resource producers, these women influence the household gender relations and restructure their social as well as moral identities. Although many are in low-status jobs, their income provides the necessary clout to renegotiate the gendered responsibilities and the patrilaterally oriented obligations of their husbands and in-laws, as well as women's own obligations towards in-laws. In many cases, Bhachu argues, the personal income enhances their capacity to meet (and create) obligations, through (say) personal contributions to own or daughters' dowries, and to develop female (kin and non-kin) centred 'non-compulsory' ceremonial activity (Bhachu 1988: 96). Bhachu argues that women's employment

> has resulted in more than just the increase in women's personal autonomy and decision making powers. It has resulted in changes in culturally defined notions of 'female' and 'male' roles and duties and also in the social fabric of Punjabi society itself, which is becoming more loosely organized and increasingly bilateral due to shifts in household patterns, a move away from the stronger patrilaterility prior to migration
>
> (Bhachu 1988: 96–7)

Following Bhachu, women's personal income through child and other benefits is also likely to have some impact on patterns of personal expenditure, with income being used for personal consumption, to help kin or to contribute to *vartan bhanji*. Bhachu impresses the importance of the economy to self-determinative aspects of identity and the renegotiation of household relationships. Significantly, she moves the argument away from an emphasis on identities being determined by cultures of 'the homeland' or the exclusionary forces of racism. Her analysis, therefore, is important, if perhaps over-optimistic. Her argument that women's employment radically alters household responsibilities and gender roles is not shared by other researchers.

In contrast to Bhachu, Warrier (1988) found that few of her factory worker respondents regarded paid work as a 'liberating experience'. Most were in paid jobs to supplement family income, employment being an extension of their perceived primary role as wife and mother. In the case of conflict between the roles as homemakers and workers, the former was privileged. Husbands played a strong role in decisions about female employment. Westwood's (1988) study confirms these findings. However, in both studies, although paid work was not 'emancipatory', it made an important contribution to the household budget and was important for social life and personal development: 'While factory work added immeasurably to the amount of work in their lives most of the younger women guarded their right to work outside the home, for the sense of independence it gave them, the good friends they made and the fun they had' (Westwood 1988: 125).

Leaving aside the vexed question of whether paid work affects gender-based reciprocities, it is clear that it offers some advantages in terms of personal consumption, female-centred networks and making a significant financial contribution to meeting personal and family obligations. However, as Qureshi and Walker (1989) show, women's paid employment also has consequences for family-based care of disabled or older family members. Women in full-time jobs are less likely to be providing care for a family member than those who stay at home. However, not surprisingly, most of the women in Warrier's and Westwood's studies were enabled to work because close kin, usually mothers-in-law, provided childcare. Childcare arrangements with distant relatives or non-kin were rare. I have concentrated on possible changes in women's roles, but there are a range of issues affecting young men (education, unemployment etc.) which are relevant to this discussion.

'Independence and other rude things': the second generation

Images of cultural conflict between the first and second generations are common in academic, professional and lay discourses. For example, in the aftermath of the troubles between Asian youth and the police in Bradford, the Chief Constable of the West Yorkshire Police Force stated: 'Cultural and religious leaders have been worried for the past 10 years or so that the younger generations don't follow their teachings and feel that they have great difficulty in controlling them' (quoted in the *Independent*, 12 June 1995: 2). This was a major focus of the news coverage and a convenient form of analysis for policy-makers, who could thus abdicate responsibility for the events. As I will discuss, generational conflict is neither inevitable nor universal; nor is it confined to minorities. However, there are a number of elements of social change which need to be acknowledged.

Migration can upset traditional hierarchies of authority, with the younger family members often possessing greater socially valued skills, such as knowledge of customs, values and institutions of the wider society, literacy and fluency in English and perhaps a greater earning potential. Among the Asian communities, children routinely act as cultural and literal interpreters in their families' dealings with the welfare state and other agencies (Ahmad and Walker 1996). The absence of such skills in older people may affect both the perception of authority as well as actual hierarchies of familial reciprocities, competencies and control. Equally, it shows the vital role of younger family members in facilitating access to services.

Perceptions that new freedoms are threatening traditional cultural values of migrants, such as parental authority and family obligations, a perceived trend towards marriages based on ideals of individual choice and romantic love, and concerns about sexual permissiveness, are strongly held by the older generation (Anwar 1979; Modood *et al.* 1994; Shaw 1988; Afshar 1994). Modood *et al.* (1994) note that although social norms of inter-generational obligations are recognized by the first as well as second generation, their fulfilment is tempered by the social realities of present-day Britain. The first generation mentioned the greater independence of their children, a relative equalization of power relations between generations and a more ambitious second generation, with women especially being seen as partly responsible for the change. The following quotation from one of Anwar's respondents sums up these concerns, and shows the efforts of this parent to provide appropriate support to his children:

> I do this because if we teach them from the very beginning with good reasons, they will respect us and follow the cultural values without questioning. However, if we leave it too late, they learn independence and other rude things at school and it becomes difficult to counter these influences at a later age.
>
> (Anwar 1979: 59)

These perceptions of change affected the older generation's expectations of the younger generation in relation to family obligations. However, as shown by Drury (1991) and Afshar (1994), the second generation is not homogeneous in its views and behaviour and the fears of the first generation are not always borne out in experience.

Afshar, for example, studied the preservation and change of values in three generations of Pakistani women. Her hypothesis that the 'youngest generation in these households would show the greatest resistance to old norms and values and would be most likely to rebel against traditional notions of Islam and the kinds of identities that it would have imposed on the family' was not supported. Instead, many chose an Islamic identity for struggles both within families and outside. Some utilized symbols of Islamic identity as markers of political independence. Afshar found a variety of views about family roles and responsibilities, from hierarchical to egalitarian, in relation to genders and generations – these were characterized as much by educational, class and denominational factors as by age.

Drury's (1991) study of cultural change in Sikh girls is instructive and emphasizes modification of cultural norms and behaviour and negotiation between generations, with little evidence of wholesale rejection of cultural values or intergenerational conflict. She found that for these girls identity was situational and varied, in that some girls confined some Sikh traditions to specific contexts while others maintained them in all situations. Gender played an important part in adherence to certain traditions and the girls resented the relative freedoms enjoyed by Sikh young men; for example, to 'go out, even with girlfriends, and have a good time' (Drury 1991: 396). The vast majority expected to have arranged marriages. Even those who did not support the idea of an arranged marriage, considered the costs of rebelling and possibly losing family support too great (see also Shaw 1988; Modood *et al.* 1994). Drury divides *conformity* to parental norms into *willing* or consensual and *unwilling* conformity (see also Anderson 1971). In willing conformity, the views of the first and the second generations were consistent and the second generation, with parental approval, conformed at a general level (across the board) or selectively. Unwilling conformity refers to traditions being maintained in deference to parental requirements and could lead to some tension in relationship between generations. In *non-conformity*, *established* non-conformity refers to the abandoning of traditions with parental consent. Finally, *breakaway* non-conformity reflects either covert or overt rejection of tradition in defiance of parental views. Only in the last case was there open conflict between generations.

Other factors which influence conformity and change in the second generation include education, religiosity and the social class of both generations. In a study of cultural retention among Indian-origin Hindus in Canada, Dhruvarajan (1993) shows that whereas greater religiosity and lower social class are related to greater traditionality (for example, in relation to sons' marriage or daughters' dating), the better off and the better educated showed a tendency towards individualistic values. What is unclear, however, is whether this is characteristic of change influenced by migration or simply a reflection of class differences. Modood *et al.*'s (1994) work provides some support for these findings. They note important similarities and differences in terms of notions of family obligations between generations, as well as between the Indian (more prosperous) and Bangladeshi and Pakistani (generally less prosperous) groups. They note that the first generation placed greater emphasis on extended family, both in Britain and in countries of origin, as the major focus of social contact and support and obligation. Although the second generation recognized the importance of family relations for 'reassurance, stability and support' (Modood *et al.* 1994: 26), their views differed markedly from those of the first generation. Of the three groups – Bangladeshi, Pakistani and Indian – the first two had greater involvement in family affairs, including financial support. The second generation were less involved with the extended family and compared to the first generation had more involvement in extra-familial relationships and leisure pursuits, with friendship-based networks often across ethnic and racial boundaries. Modood *et al.* (1994: 31) note that 'Much of the value, the emotional, moral and material support that the first generation placed on the extended family, the second generation placed on the immediate family, meaning parents, siblings and probably grandparents.'

However, as is clear from this discussion, the 'second generation' is heterogeneous in its views and behaviour. Fears about rejection of the cultural and religious values are not borne out in research studies. On the whole, the second generation shows much continuity with parental traditions, alongside areas of modification. And even where values conflict, as in approaches to marriage, personal values are carefully balanced against the loss of family support. Despite its popularity, there is little, if any, evidence of the second generation being caught in a cultural 'no-man's land' between parental values and those of the wider society. And far from change being the sole prerogative of the second generation, Drury shows that first generation people adapt their expectations of appropriate behaviour for their children. But equally, the evidence points to a process of change which sustains an uneven continuity with traditional values. The significance attached to specific instances of change can vary dramatically depending upon the intra-ethnic relationship of the observer to the actor, or particularly when the observation is made from outside the ethnic community (Burghart 1987).

Concluding comments

Neither social norms nor behaviours are unified within ethnic groups. Behaviour is negotiated within a complex space where cultural norms are important influences on but not the sole determinants of action. Economic situation, gender and moral identity, age, personal relationships and competing obligations all impinge on the construction of and ability to meet obligations. This is not surprising. Scholars of religion, for example, differentiate between 'scriptural' and 'lived' religion (Burghart 1987; Ahmed 1988). Whereas there are differences within a broadly defined religion (say Islam or Hinduism) in terms of scriptural allegiance, the lived experience of people within a tradition shows both greater diversity and remarkable similarities with other religions. That minority ethnic communities are given official unitary identities, or construct such identities in their dealings with the state or the media (as Hindus or as Bangladeshis), gives the impression of homogeneous needs, norms and behaviour (see Chapter 3, this volume; Ahmad, 1996). Realities of social norms and behaviour remain complex and contested. Burghart's work in relation to the construction of the public image of Hinduism in Britain is instructive in this respect (Burghart 1987). He argues that the Western attempts at achieving an intellectual understanding of Hinduism, and the desire of many Hindus to 're-package' it in a discourse which would be understood by outsiders, have imposed upon it an artificial unity where there is actual diversity, and artificial diversity where there is unity. He notes this in relation to the National Council of Hindu Temples' publications, which, in the British context, package Hinduism as an 'ethnic religion', emphasizing the unity of the tradition rather than the diversity of beliefs. Such fictive unities are of concern to practitioners, who may only have access to these 'authenticated' versions of ethnic minorities' traditions and values, including those of family obligations. However, as this chapter shows, realities remain somewhat more complex, ambiguous and contested.

In their work on family obligations in contemporary Britain, Finch and Mason (1993) are struck by the similarities of perspectives and experiences between their Asian and white respondents. As this chapter shows, there is diversity of experiences and expectations within the Asian communities as well as similarities between the Asian and other communities. This chapter has drawn together literature from disparate sources, few of which have family obligations as a central focus. Literature on other, especially smaller, minority ethnic communities is even more sparse. Policy and practice in community care will benefit considerably from a fuller understanding of obligations in minority ethnic communities. There is a strong need for further research in this area, to provide a sophisticated understanding of family-based obligations and their negotiation, as well as processes of social change.

Acknowledgements

My thanks go to Hazel Qureshi for helpful comments.

Note

1 Sanskritization is the process by which low caste Hindus adopt values, beliefs and practices of the high caste Hindus.

Annotated bibliography

Anwar, M. (1979) *The Myth of Return*. London: Heinemann.
Anwar provides a detailed study of kinship and obligations among a Pakistani community. He explores the importance of the hierarchy of relationships within the family, the relevance of age and gender to expectations and obligations, and attempts to ensure cultural continuity against perceived internal and external forces of change.

Finch, J. (1989) *Family Obligations and Social Change*. Cambridge: Polity.
Janet Finch has synthesized considerable literature on family obligations and social change with some discussion of minority ethnic groups. She explores the continuity and change in family obligations and considers the economic, legal and demographic context of family-based support.

Westwood, S. and Bhachu, P. (1988) *Enterprising Women: Ethnicity, Economy and Gender Relations*. London: Routledge.
This collection explores the impact of women's labour market participation on household gender relations. Essays by Bhachu, Werbner, Westwood and Warrier provide useful accounts of Asian women's employment and its implications for gender roles and female-led and female-oriented relationships.

5

Looking after their own? Family care-giving among Asian and Afro-Caribbean communities

Karl Atkin and Janet Rollings

Introduction

Care in the community increasingly means care by the family (Finch 1989), regardless of ethnic background (Atkin and Rollings 1993a, b). More older and disabled people are supported at home by their relatives than by statutory provision (Twigg 1992). The increasing reference to carers in guidance associated with the NHS and Community Care Act further reflects their importance to the success of community care (Department of Health 1990). More specifically, the growth in research on informal care that has taken place over the past decade means there is a relatively good understanding of the nature of caring – its origins, incidence, patterns and experiences (see Parker 1992; Twigg 1992). The General Household Survey (GHS),[1] for example, provides extensive quantitative material on the incidence and pattern of care (Green 1988), and subsequent secondary data analysis is beginning to build up a sophisticated account of how care-giving is organized (Arber and Ginn 1990; Parker and Lawton 1994). We are also beginning to understand how health and social services respond to family carers (Twigg and Atkin 1994).

This accumulated knowledge has led some commentators to question the need for more research, particularly small-scale local enquiries that repeat previous work (Twigg 1992). This view certainly has its merits. None the less, much of the mainstream research on care-giving neglects the experience of black and ethnic minority carers. These studies, by default, focus on the experience of white people, and provide little or no information about the circumstances and experiences of family carers from black and ethnic minority groups. Nor is there any other large-scale information source; the GHS, for example, does not have a sufficient sample of black and ethnic minority carers to enable useful analysis.

The aim of this chapter – by reviewing a mix of empirical studies and policy debates – is to provide an insight into the experience of family care-giving in Asian and Afro-Caribbean communities.[2] First, the chapter will explore the sparse literature on care-giving in black and ethnic minority communities. Much of the empirical material in this area is speculative and descriptive. None the less it is possible to provide an introduction to family care-giving in Asian and Afro-Caribbean communities by exploring demographic changes as well as potential similarities and differences between the experiences of white and minority ethnic carers. Second, the chapter will relate this material to more general discussions about policy and practice in informal care, the delivery of services to black and ethnic minorities and the theoretical development of the mainstream carer research.

The demography of care

Next to economic factors, demographic changes are powerful influences on policy formulation and successful implementation, and provide the context within which community care policy operates. Relevant demographic changes include those that affect or appear to affect those who need care and those who might take on the responsibility of care. Within this context three general factors assume particular significance: age, gender and disability. These will be examined now. Other more specific demographic influences, such as family structure and female labour market participation, are considered later in the chapter, within the wider context of myths and assumptions about the availability of informal care in Asian and Afro-Caribbean communities.

First, the potential relationship between age and disability indicates the importance of the age distribution of black minority communities for the discussion on informal care. Not all old people are disabled. However the incidence and severity of disability increases with age, thus creating a potential demand for family care (Parker 1990). Minority groups are, on average, younger than the white population (Owen 1993). Fewer than 20 per cent are aged over 45 and 3 per cent are over 65. The comparative figures for the white population are 22 per cent and 17 per cent respectively. There are also differences in the age structure of the various ethnic minority groups, resulting from the patterns of migration from the respective countries of origin. Bangladeshi and Pakistani communities, for instance, are generally younger than Indian and Afro-Caribbean people. Fourteen per cent of Pakistani and Bangladeshi people are over 45. By comparison 30 per cent of the Afro-Caribbeans are aged 45 or over. More generally, demographic trends indicate an imminent steep growth in the numbers of older people of Afro-Caribbean and Asian (especially of Indian origin) descent over the next ten years. Potentially this could put increasing pressure on the caring responsibilities of Asian and Afro-Caribbean families.

Second, gender affects those who need care, as well as those who take

on the responsibility of care (Parker 1990). At present there are significant gender differences both between the white and minority ethnic groups
and within the various minority ethnic groups (Owen 1993). Fifty-one per
cent of the white population is female compared with 49 per cent within
minority ethnic groups. Within the minority ethnic groups, the lowest
ratio of males to females is displayed among Afro-Caribbeans (949 males
per 1000 females). This figure is similar to the white population. Among
South Asians there is an excess of males over females (1013 males per
1000 females). This is most striking among the Bangladeshi group where
the male to female ratio is 1090: 1000. For both Afro-Caribbean and
South Asian groups, the excess of males over females is greatest among
those over 65. It is difficult to know the full implications of these gender
imbalances because so little is known about the organization of care among
Asian and Afro-Caribbean families. For the white population it is assumed
that females provide the bulk of care for older or disabled relatives (Parker
and Lawton 1994). A smaller number of females, therefore, would reduce
the potential population of carers. On the other side of the equation, older
women are more likely to be disabled than older men (Parker 1990). Again
it is difficult to assess the impact of this proposition for older people from
black and ethnic minorities because so little is known about disability
among these people.

Third, the incidence of disability among black communities obviously
affects those who are likely to need care. Of course, the relationship between 'disability' and the need for family care is complex. 'Disability' and
'care' are both socially constructed: 'all the factors that transform an
impairment into disability also tend to transform family members and
friends into informal carers' (Parker 1992: 17). Further, people with disabilities can choose to live independently of relatives. Nor do statistics
on the incidence of impairment provide any insight into the experience of
disability. These are issues to which we return later in the chapter. None
the less, publications of findings from a national survey of impairment
have produced a supposedly comprehensive picture of the incidence and
nature of disability in Great Britain (OPCS 1988). There are, however,
few studies describing the extent, nature or experience of disability among
people from black and ethnic minorities (see McAvoy and Donaldson
1990). The number of surveys assessing the incidence of disability in black
people, however, is slowly growing (RADAR 1984; Farrah 1986; GLAD
1987). There is also a growing body of work on specific conditions, such
as cardiovascular disease, stroke, diabetes, haemoglobinopathies and
mental health problems among black and ethnic minorities (CRD/SPRU
1996). Despite this interest, significant areas of neglect remain. There is still
little material, for example, on the prevalence, nature and experience of learning disability and mental infirmity among older people. Another dimension
to this debate is whether the incidence of disability is greater among black
and ethnic minorities in comparison to the general population. Although

some studies support this view (Bhalla and Blakemore 1981; Donaldson and Odell 1986; Farrah 1986; Moledina 1988), data from the OPCS survey of physical disability (OPCS 1988) showed that when standardized for age the prevalence of disability among Afro-Caribbean and Asian people, compared with that of the white population, was roughly the same. Preliminary data from the 1991 census suggest that people identifying themselves as Black Caribbean, Pakistani, Indian and Bangladeshi have a higher incidence of long-standing illness than white groups (Owen 1993). The relationship between ethnicity and illness becomes more pronounced with age. This incidence of disability across ethnic groups remains an area of interesting debate where more information is required.

The visibility of Asian and Afro-Caribbean carers

Whereas care-giving among white families has gained considerable visibility over the past decade, informal care in minority ethnic communities remains largely invisible (Atkin and Rollings 1993a, b). Parker (1990) argues that one of the most persistent misconceptions about 'modern society' is that the family no longer cares for disabled and older people. This, however, is not an argument usually applied to black, and particularly Asian, families. Indeed, their commitment to care for older and disabled relatives is assumed to be greater than that of white people, to the extent that service providers think they need not concern themselves with the support of people from these groups (Walker and Ahmad 1994). Asian and Afro-Caribbean people are assumed virtuously to 'look after their own' (Baxter 1989b; Atkin and Rollings 1993). Consequently, for carers from minority ethnic communities, their general invisibility is often exacerbated by service professionals' racist stereotypes (Walker and Ahmad 1994), and these carers remain one of the most 'neglected and invisible groups in the country' (Hicks 1988).

The assumption that Asian people live in self-supporting families is simplistic for a number of reasons (Ahmad and Atkin 1996). The extended family, although common among Asians, is by no means universal (Chapter 4, this volume; Bhalla and Blakemore 1981; Barker 1984; Fenton 1987) and there are still a significant proportion of Asian people who live alone, with few relatives in this country (Cameron et al. 1989). Further, socio-economic and demographic factors may influence both the willingness and ability of families from Asian communities to provide care. Asian households, for example, are slowly changing in response to internal and external pressures (Owen 1993). The availability of appropriate housing and occupational mobility may have an impact on the extended family, and thereby, on the ability to provide family-based care (Lalljie 1983). Cameron et al. (1989), for example, concluded that changes in family structure, household structure and geographical dispersal of close and extended kin made it difficult for the extended family network to offer support for older and disabled relatives. Although feelings of obligation may still be strong, changing family structure made it difficult to fulfil these obligations (London Borough of Camden 1990). This in turn can have psychological consequences for the role of family care-giving among Asian families. Chauhan (1989), for instance, described the situation of older black people who have looked after their parents and expect to be looked after in turn by their offspring. If these expectations are not fully realized the older person may experience shock, disappointment, shame or loss (Coombe 1981; Moledina 1988). The changing role relationship in Asian families is often a source of stress for older people. Fenton (1987) described 'inescapable tensions' as older Asian people found it difficult to comprehend changes which have occurred in the attitudes and lifestyles of their sons and daughters. Cameron *et al.* (1989) observed the 'conflicting expectations' of different generations.

Overall family size is shrinking within Asian communities generally and particularly among Hindus and Sikhs (Owen 1993). This is accompanied by challenges to marriage patterns both internally and those forced by immigration rules. Brah (1978) notes that as early as the late 1970s, Asian adolescents were expressing some unease with traditional marriage customs and many looked forward to forming a 'nuclear' household, while keeping in close contact with the 'joint family'. These findings are supported by Bhachu (1988). Further, restrictive immigration policies often leave families divided across continents (Ahmad and Walker 1996), and this perhaps begins to explain the gender difference among South Asian and Afro-Caribbean groups (Fenton 1987). At the same time, Asian – predominantly Hindu and Sikh – women's increasing participation in the paid labour market is argued to be leading to a renegotiation of household responsibilities (Bhachu 1988), although not all would agree with this interpretation (Wilson 1979). Although the effect of these changes on family-based care is not clear, it is reported that daughters and daughters-in-law who are in full-time employment are less likely to be involved in caring (Qureshi and Walker 1989).

The large extended family is uncommon among Afro-Caribbean communities (Lalljie 1983; Barker 1984), over a third of whom may be living on their own (Berry *et al.* 1981; Bhalla and Blakemore 1981). Among Afro-Caribbean populations, there is higher prevalence of single parenthood than the norm, as well as greater involvement of women in the labour market. Furthermore, a survey in Leicester suggests that a substantial minority (over 40 per cent) do not have frequent family contact (Farrah 1986).

The nature of care

Who cares within the family?

Regardless of the size or structure of the family network, research shows that when caring responsibilities are taken on, the locus of care is usually the immediate family (Cameron *et al.* 1989; McCalman 1990), and the main responsibility of day-to-day care falls to one family member, usually a woman (Bould 1990; Cocking and Athwal 1990; McCalman 1990). In this respect Asian and Afro-Caribbean families are no different from white families (Qureshi and Walker 1989). Walker (1987), who identified fifteen Asian families caring for a child with a severe learning difficulty, concluded that all aspects of care were the responsibility of the mother. McCalman (1990) observed, in her study of Asian and Afro-Caribbean families, that help received from other family members was incidental or occasional, or at best called on for any lack of alternative. There is no doubt that caring is gendered. None the less, recent research has begun to focus on the role of men, particularly as fathers looking after a disabled child (Beresford 1994) or as spouse carers (Arber and Ginn 1990; Parker 1992). There is however, little research on Asian and Afro-Caribbean men's experiences of caregiving.

The physical aspects of care-giving

Generally carers experience a level of physical exertion in their daily living, far above that experienced by other people (Parker 1990). Common tasks include offering help with bathing, dressing, getting in and out of bed, lifting, toileting and household activities (Nissel and Bonnerjea 1982; Lewis and Meredith 1988). The limited literature available suggests that the experience of Asian and Afro-Caribbean carers is not different from that of white carers. Many carers find the physical burden of care too great and express a need for assistance with tasks such as lifting or bathing, particularly when they suffer from ill health (Farrah 1986; McCalman 1990).

The emotional aspect of care-giving

Research on white carers suggests that caring brings about increased levels of stress or emotional strain (Parker 1990). Although there is a lack of systematic exploration of these issues in relation to Asian and Afro-Caribbean people, the limited evidence available suggests that their experience of caring is similar (Walker 1987). Mothers who look after a child with sickle cell disorders, for example, express feelings of hopelessness and frustration (Midence and Elander 1994). The literature also documents the general isolation and loneliness of caring (Barker 1984; Guilliford 1984; Powell and Perkins 1984; Watson 1984; Holland and Lewando-Hundt 1987; Uppal 1988; McCalman 1990; Eribo 1991). Bould (1990), for example, described how many black carers felt trapped within four walls, with no alternative but to care. Over half of the carers spoke of experiencing depression. The emotional consequences may be exacerbated by the organization of services. Lack of provision of bilingual workers or

even adequate interpreting facilities, often coupled with the lack of culturally appropriate support services (such as appropriate food, respite or
foster care facilities) or barriers to services imposed by non-recognition of
need, exacerbate the emotional consequences of care-giving (Donaldson
and Odell 1986; London Borough of Camden 1990).

Generally, female carers appear to experience a greater sense of isolation and loneliness than male carers, exacerbated by the tendency for male
carers to be more likely to receive formal support than female carers (Twigg
and Atkin 1994). This seems true irrespective of ethnic origin (Bhalla and
Blakemore 1981; Donovan 1986; McAvoy 1990; McCalman 1990). In
many ways, however, this feeling of isolation is heightened for female
Asian carers by external factors (Bhalla and Blakemore 1981; McCalman
1990). They may be restricted in their houses through a fear of an alien
outside world, where their own norms, values and social skills are often
regarded as inappropriate, where their behaviour is in danger of being
misinterpreted and where overt racial hostility or violence, for many, is a
daily experience (Currer 1986; Cameron et al. 1989).

The mainstream literature on informal care suggests that caring can
cause potential tensions within the family, with non-disabled siblings and
partners feeling neglected (Quine and Pahl 1985; Beresford 1994). Female
carers particularly worry about neglecting their spouses and other family
members by concentrating on the needs of the disabled or older people
(Glendinning 1983). Afro-Caribbean and Asian families describe similar
experiences to those reported in the general literature (Powell and Perkins
1984; McCalman 1990). Bould (1990), for example, described how Asian
women looking after a disabled child often experienced tensions in their
marriage, as well as finding it difficult to give attention to the non-disabled
children in the family. Similarly, Pai and Kapur (1981), studying the burden placed on the families of psychiatric patients, reported that carers find
their role most difficult in terms of the disruption of normal family activities caused by looking after their relative.

Caring for a disabled or older person can also disrupt a carer's social life
(Lewis and Meredith 1988). Carers may be afraid to leave the disabled
person; exhaustion from caring may also preclude the maintenance of
friendships and contribute to feelings of isolation (Twigg and Atkin 1994).
Afro-Caribbean and Asian carers express similar feelings (McCalman 1990;
Eribo 1991). Afro-Caribbean mothers caring for children with sickle cell
disease, for example, reported disruption of their social life because of
need to be available at all times (see Ahmad and Atkin 1996). Other forms
of emotional stress among Afro-Caribbean and Asian carers include a lack
of knowledge about the disabled person's condition (Cocking and Athwal
1990; Walker 1987; Baxter et al. 1990). McCalman (1990) reported that
a lack of knowledge made black carers feel insecure and undermined their
confidence in providing appropriate care. Zamora (1988) described a similar feeling expressed by black carers looking after people diagnosed as
having mental health problems.

The material consequences of care

Caring has material consequences. Financially, carers tend to be worse off than the general population (Glendinning 1983). Around 90 per cent of families are reported to have extra costs – including laundry, heating and transport – associated with the disability (Baldwin 1985). Afro-Caribbean and Asian carers experience similar additional financial costs to those described by white carers (Guilliford 1984; Bould 1990; McCalman 1990; Eribo 1991).

Other costs facing carers arise principally from restricted employment, which leads to reduced income (Parker 1990). There is considerable evidence, for example, that caring for a disabled or older person impacts on the carer's employment opportunities (Glendinning 1983; Baldwin 1985; Hirst 1992; Smyth and Robus 1989) and this is equally true for black carers (Bould 1990; McCalman 1990; Eribo 1991). McCalman (1990), for example, found that none of the eight Asian carers she interviewed was in employment, yet all these women had the responsibility of financially supporting their families owing to the severity of their husband's disability. They felt that the 'burden of care' would make it difficult for them to keep a job. In contrast, eight of the thirteen Afro-Caribbean carers interviewed were engaged in full-time work, with a further two in part-time employment. All stated that they had to work in order to maintain themselves and the person they looked after. Social security benefits, they felt, were inadequate.

Although all families face financial costs in caring for a disabled child, the impact on black and Asian families may be even greater. Guilliford (1984) notes, for example, that Bangladeshi families looking after a child with a severe learning disability experienced greater financial difficulties than white families because of an unequal structuring of opportunities. Evidence on racial inequalities in income, employment and housing is overwhelming (Skellington 1992). Though far from homogeneous, in general income levels of Asians (particularly Pakistanis and Bangladeshis) and Afro-Caribbeans are lower than the norm and their unemployment rates are about twice those in the white population. Within the Pakistani and Bangladeshi communities, there is relatively little participation of women in the labour market, affecting family income and access to contributory benefits. For a variety of reasons, Asian and black families are also less likely to receive their full social security entitlements, and may not qualify for some benefits that are related to contributions or residence requirements (Gordon and Newnham 1985). Perceptions of state benefits are also strongly influenced by religious and cultural factors: in a study of eligible non-claimants, people from Bangladeshi, Pakistani and Chinese communities were most likely to attach stigma or 'shame' to claiming welfare benefits (Law et al. 1994). Housing is also an important factor in the overall environment of providing care (Oldman 1990). There has been no systematic examination of housing issues in relation to Asian and Afro-

Caribbean carers, although housing inequalities have been documented by various researchers – with minority ethnic communities more likely to be in older, unmodernized, inner-city housing which is lacking in central heating and other household amenities, such as gardens and washing machines (see Skellington 1992). Housing inequalities, in owner-occupied as well as council sectors, are particularly marked for Pakistani, Bangladeshi and Afro-Caribbean communities, who also carry a disproportionate burden of homelessness (CRE 1988). Housing problems for carers from minority ethnic communities have been reported (Farrah 1986; Gunaratnum 1990; McCalman 1990). Damp and draughty housing, lack of appropriate heating and the financial inability to keep the house warm are significant problems in looking after a disabled or older person. Further, Bhalla and Blakemore (1981) reported that 25 per cent of disabled Asian people and 33 per cent of disabled Afro-Caribbean people experienced housing problems and wanted to move. Farrah (1986) found similar dissatisfaction among older Afro-Caribbean people. Thirty per cent expressed a desire to move and of these 7 per cent needed single-level accommodation and 12 per cent wanted improved toilet access.

Service provision for Asian and Afro-Caribbean carers

There has been no systematic exploration of the delivery of services to Asian and Afro-Caribbean people and few large-scale empirical studies exist. None the less, by referring to the general literature it is possible to gain an insight into service delivery to Asian and Afro-Caribbean carers. Two themes emerge as significant: the general relationship between carers and service provision; and the difficulties faced by services in meeting the health and social care needs of ethnic minorities (Atkin and Rollings 1992).

The NHS and Community Care Act and the subsequent policy guidance associated with it placed carers centre stage. Carers' contribution to community care was recognized as was the need to support them to continue their contribution (DH 1990). Despite the greater visibility of carers in the policy debate, policy itself has remained undeveloped and rarely goes beyond bland statements about the importance of supporting carers (Twigg and Atkin 1994). There has been little in the way of strategic thinking on the subject among policy-makers, planners and practitioners. Consequently, there is limited understanding of how carers' needs are, and are not, incorporated into policy-making and the delivery of mainstream services (Twigg and Atkin 1994). The problems this causes affect all carers, irrespective of ethnic origin. For example, service support to carers is often thought of in terms of a specialist carer-oriented service. This, however, misses the degree to which services in general can help the carer. Day care not only provides an activity for the cared-for person, but also a valuable break for the carer (Parker 1992). Other services, such as community nursing, although aimed at 'the patient', can also offer considerable support to carers, by referring on to other services as well as giving the carer someone to talk to (Twigg and Atkin 1994). None the less, the traditional focus on the patient or client can cause problems for the carer. Carers are rarely the focus of intervention and can exist on the periphery of service provision. Their position is uncertain and ill-defined, making it easy for them to be marginalized in the process of service delivery (Twigg and Atkin 1994).

The policy and practice guidance associated with the NHS and Community Care Act has also begun to recognize the 'particular care needs' of Britain's ethnic minority populations (see Cmnd 849; Audit Commission 1992a, b). Recognition of the 'particular care needs' of minority groups at the 'highest level of policy-making' has been described 'as something of a breakthrough' (Walker and Ahmad 1994). There is no doubt that government policy on health and social care creates important opportunities for black and ethnic minorities by presenting the opportunity of need-led care planning, the opening of consultation and planning processes to direct local influence, a new awareness of carers' needs and a recognition of the particular circumstances of black and ethnic minorities (Walker and Ahmad 1994). These opportunities, however, arise in the context of existing demands, and in particular the long-standing challenges of providing appropriate community care services to black and Asian communities (Butt 1994). Empirical evidence suggests that community care provision experiences considerable differences in recognizing and responding to the needs of people from black and ethnic minorities (Dominelli 1989; Atkin and Rollings 1993a, b; Butt 1994; Walker and Ahmad 1994). Service organizations frequently ignore the needs of ethnic minorities by assuming that their policies, procedures and practices are equally appropriate for everyone (Atkin and Rollings 1993a, b; Blakemore and Boneham 1994). Consequently services become, by default, organized according to a 'white norm'. Straightforward examples include the inability of health and social services to provide support for people who do not speak English, or more specifically the unavailability of vegetarian food or halal meat in day care and domiciliary services. Such practices legitimate non-recognition of the community care needs of minority ethnic communities. Other common problems faced in services include the use of cultural stereotypes in explaining the experiences of their black and ethnic minority users (Durrant 1989) and the racist attitudes held by frontline practitioners (Cameron *et al.* 1989; Ahmad *et al.* 1991; Bowler 1993).

Conceptualizing care-giving in Asian and Afro-Caribbean families

As this chapter has demonstrated, there is little material describing the experience of Asian and Afro-Caribbean carers. This is in contrast to the vast literature on family obligations and care-giving among white families (see Twigg 1992). The sparse research evidence that does exist is descriptive and often based on small-scale locally based surveys that are difficult to generalize (see Bradford Social Services Department 1989; McCalman 1990). Further, there has been no attempt to link the findings to those of the mainstream literature. Engagement with this mainstream carer literature, and the theoretical conceptualizations it offers, will prove useful in our developing understanding of care-giving in Asian and Afro-Caribbean communities. Specifically, this mainstream literature reminds us of the conceptual importance of issues such as family obligation, the feminist critiques of community care, social class, the shift from 'burden' to 'coping' in describing the experience of care and the disabled peoples' critiques of informal care in the understanding of care-giving.

The general literature emphasizes the importance of discussing caregiving within the wider context of family relationships and obligations. Qureshi and Walker's (1989) analysis of the family care of older people established the normative priorities governing who gives care in the family; and Finch and Mason (1993) provide a detailed sociological exploration of the ways in which kinship responsibilities are negotiated in specific concrete situations. This understanding of how family obligations operate has been influential in the way the debate on informal care has developed. For example, Ahmad (Chapter 4, this volume), points to the importance of issues such as gender, financial resources, legitimate excuses, prior or competing obligations and expectations of reciprocality in the negotiation of family obligation. However, as Ahmad also demonstrates, there is little empirical material available on how family obligations operate in ethnic minority families. Consequently, an important 'building block' in our conceptual understanding of care-giving among Asian and Afro-Caribbean families is missing.

Feminism is another important strand informing the current debates about family care-giving. However, its impact on writings about caregiving in Asian and Afro-Caribbean communities is minimal. None the less, the feminist critiques of community care exposed the ways in which social policy contained an implicit family policy, in which the position of women was assumed and unchallenged (Finch and Groves 1980; Land and Rose 1985; Graham 1991). Women were seen as a new service army of labour that could be exploited by community care. Asian and Afro-Caribbean women do not seem immune from these policy assumptions. Indeed, as we have seen, they may be regarded as particularly virtuous when it comes to family-based carers.

More recently, the discovery of unexpected numbers of male carers seemed to undermine the assumption that caring was exclusively a women's issue. Further analysis of the GHS, however, revealed that the majority of male carers were spouses or were involved in the lighter end of care-giving (Parker and Lawton 1994). Interpersonal care involving long hours and intimate personal tending were still heavily gendered. The GHS figures, however, made visible the extent to which caring was carried out by men as part of spouse relationships. This redressed the early imbalance in feminist critiques, which regarded carers solely as wives, daughters or daughters-in-law. Recent feminist analysis has also begun to take account of 'differences' among women. For example, it has begun to expose the degree to which previous carer research was based on the experience of white middle-class women, while excluding those of black and working class women (Graham 1991). The emerging analysis of care-giving has attempted to show the ways in which women can be subject to different forms of oppression, of which gender is only one (Williams 1989). More generally, several commentators have argued that the debates around care-giving have failed to incorporate the dimension of social class (see Atkin 1992).

Other aspects of how caregiving is conceptualized have been subject to debate. Much of the empirical work describes the impact of caring in terms of 'stresses' and 'burdens' – physical, emotional and financial (see Beresford 1994). Within this tradition carers are not seen as women or families but as people whose lives have been severely disrupted by care-giving. This approach has been criticized (Zarit 1989). Not only are carers unlikely to see their role wholly in terms of burden, such an approach can also pathologize the experience of disabled people (Twigg and Atkin 1994). Consequently, recent research has begun to focus on exploring the ways families cope, using varying strategies and with varying degrees of success, with the care of a disabled or chronically ill child, rather than simply describing the 'burdens' of care (Beresford 1994). However, despite the merits of such a focus, over-emphasizing the coping aspects of care-giving could remove carers from the discourse of justice and individual 'need', thus undermining the importance of public intervention and support. The tensions generated by this debate have important implications for our perception of care-giving among Asian and Afro-Caribbean people.

The most recent influence in the debate on caring has been the increasingly powerful critique of the disability movement, which, first, emphasizes the repression inherent in medical constructions of disability and, second, challenges the lay emphasis on disability as personal tragedy (Oliver 1990; Morris 1991; see also Chapter 6, this volume). Out of these perceptions has developed a critique of the debate on informal care, which argues that policy should not endorse dependence through an emphasis on supporting carers, but underwrite the independence of the disabled people they care for (Oliver 1995). The recent emphasis on the needs of carers, according to Oliver, diverts attention from the support of disabled people (Oliver 1995). Such assertions have, however, been challenged (Parker 1993). For instance, the provision of health and social services to supersede carers may run counter to what the disabled people in their relationships want. Further, displacing the need for carers is more likely to meet the needs of younger disabled people than those of, say, frail older people who have mental impairments, or those who have a chronic illness (Parker 1993). None the less the disability lobby's critique reminds us that care-giving takes place within a relationship. The cared for person is as important as the carer. The disability critique has rightly argued that caring cannot be examined separately from the needs and wishes of disabled people. On the other hand, it is not possible to focus exclusively on the disabled person (this, of course, only applies when there is such a carer). Caring is embedded in relationships arising out of marriage, parenthood, kinship and occasionally friendship, in which people feel a sense of responsibility and obligation to provide care (Twigg and Atkin 1994).

Conclusion

Little is known about the nature and experience of informal care among black communities. Much of the available material is speculative and descriptive. It is, however, possible to provide an introduction to informal care among Asian and Afro-Caribbean people by discussing the limited understanding of informal care within these communities with reference to wider issues such as service delivery and racism as well as the general problems faced in conceptualizing caring relationships. Asian and Afro-Caribbean carers have not shared the general recognition given to carers over the past five years. Their general invisibility is made worse by assumptions about extended family networks being able to provide full support for older and disabled people.

None the less, the experience of care-giving among Asian and Afro-Caribbean carers is broadly similar to that of white people. The physical, emotional and financial consequences of care-giving affect all carers, irrespective of ethnic origin. However, for Asian and Afro-Caribbean carers these consequences are often exacerbated by structural disadvantage, non-recognition of need and racism. As we have seen, evidence on racial inequalities in income, employment and housing are overwhelming. Not surprisingly, Asian and Afro-Caribbean carers often experience greater material hardship than white carers. More generally, the inaccessibility and inappropriateness of community health and social services to minority ethnic groups has been well established. Asian and Afro-Caribbean carers, therefore, often find it more difficult to obtain formal service support than white carers.

Future research, besides taking account of racism, would also benefit from engaging with the mainstream carer literature and the theoretical conceptualizations it offers. For example, the problems faced by incorporating carers into the practice of mainstream services are relevant to all carers, irrespective of ethnic origin. Further, the importance of discussing care-giving within the wider context of family relationships and obligation is well established. Yet our understanding of family obligation among Asian and Afro-Caribbean communities is limited (see Chapter 4, this volume).

Within this wider context this chapter has attempted to provide an introduction to family care-giving in Asian and Afro-Caribbean communities.

Given the importance of carers to the success of community care and their increasing recognition in the policy literature, care-giving in Asian and Afro-Caribbean communities is likely to become central to future debates about care in the community. For the same reasons, understanding care-giving in other minority groups, such as Somali or Chinese communities, is equally important. If anything these communities are even more neglected than Asian and Afro-Caribbean communities. Considerable work is necessary before our understanding of care-giving in all these communities can compare to that of the white families.

Notes

This chapter develops ideas first presented in two other papers (see Atkin and Rollings 1992; Ahmad and Atkin 1996).

1 The General Household Survey, organized by the Office of Population Censuses and Surveys, is a continuous survey of adults in private households in Great Britain. Since 1985, the GHS has included a section on carers.
2 The chapter confines itself to the two largest ethnic minority communities in Great Britain because most of the material in this area describes the experience of Asian and Afro-Caribbean carers.

Annotated bibliography

Atkin, K. and Rollings, J. (1992) Informal care in Asian and Afro-Caribbean communities: a literature review, *British Journal of Social Work*, 22, 405–18.
The authors, by reviewing a mix of empirical studies and policy debates, examine the experience of care in Asian and Afro-Caribbean communities. By discussing topics such as the demography of care, the nature of care-giving and service provision to carers, the paper gives coherence to a fragmented literature and illustrates gaps in present understanding.

McCalman, J. A. (1990) *The Forgotten People*. London: Kings Fund Centre.
This is one of the few books that presents empirical material on the experience of care-giving among black and ethnic minorities. The author contacted thirty-four carers looking after a close relative, living in Southwark. The book describes their experience.

Twigg, J. and Atkin, K. (1994) *Carers Perceived: Policy and Practice in Informal Care*. Buckingham: Open University Press.
This book explores how service practitioners, such as doctors, social workers and community nurses, respond to the needs of family care-givers. The book also examines the broader policy issues raised by trying to incorporate carers' interests into service provision. Although not dealing explicitly with carers from black and ethnic minorities, the book raises many issues about their experience.

Part III

CASE STUDIES IN COMMUNITY CARE

6

'Yes, we mean black disabled people too': thoughts on community care and disabled people from black and minority ethnic communities

Ossie Stuart

Introduction

A discussion of the pertinent issues concerning black disabled people[1] cannot take place without recognition that disabled people and their organizations continue to provide an important critique of social policy and, specifically, the way in which community care services are delivered. The growing importance of disabled people's organizations in the formulation of social policy has meant that the disabled person's voice is fast becoming indispensable in the planning of community care services for disabled users. That the voice of black disabled people still remains largely unheard and the effectiveness or otherwise of services for this group continues to be poorly understood has exposed white disabled people and their organizations to the charge of not being appropriately sensitive to difference (Stuart 1992). Yet black disabled writers themselves have failed to move beyond the rhetoric of racist practice and continue to emphasize the victim status endured by many black disabled people. At a time when the community care reforms provide some opportunities for the creation of innovative services for disabled people, the theoretical conceptualization of disabled people from minority ethnic communities as merely the victims of racism suggests that they will continue to receive inadequate services.

This chapter is a polemic. Its purpose is to look again at the theoretical conceptualization of disabled people from black and minority ethnic communities. At the heart of this discussion will be the exploration of difference, in the form of social class, gender, disabilities other than physical, age and, of course, ethnicity, and its impact upon an individual's experience. Is it appropriate or even possible to describe the experience of disabled people from minority ethnic communities solely in terms of their perceived ethnicity, without including other factors which help to shape their identities? Indeed, 'black disabled person' might not always be the most appropriate identity around which to build service provision for this group of people. So the purpose of this polemic is to question the idea that black disabled people as a homogeneous group have similar experiences, with the intention of moving on the debate. This chapter considers the definitions of disability, the problems of assigning a single identity as 'disabled' to black disabled people, their popular but unhelpful 'double disadvantage' thesis, issues around autonomy and independence for black disabled people, as well as the prospects for a user-oriented service in the new community care.

Definitions of disability

The starting point for any discussion about disabled people must be the definition of disability. In a world constructed by non-disabled people and dominated by their assumptions, how disability is defined has a profound impact upon how disabled people, both black and white, are perceived. And it has implications both for the provision of services and the ability to control one's life (Morris 1993; Oliver 1993).

The definition of disability is also related to the politics of control between disabled people and professionals who design and deliver services to disabled people. Who should be in charge of the rehabilitation process, disabled people or professionals? Should disabled people receive the services professionals think they need or those that they choose for themselves? How these questions are answered depends upon where the problem of disability is thought to be located. Disability is commonly thought to describe the limitations of impaired people. In contrast, disabled people reason that the problem of disability is located in the physical and social environment, which does not take account of the needs of disabled people. The former represents the individual model of disability; the latter, the social model (Oliver 1990).

Emphasis upon the individual informs the medical model of disability. In this model disproportionate emphasis is placed by the medical profession upon clinical diagnosis, the very nature of which is destined to lead to a partial and inhibiting view of the disabled individual (Brisenden 1986). This is perceived as biological determinism, in which disability is defined solely in terms of physical (and psychological) malfunctioning which requires medical intervention.

The medical profession presents a powerful image of disabled people as a unified and dependent population. The growth of specialist professions and their publicly visible role as gate-keepers to medical, social and welfare services provides an effective reinforcement of the view that disability is a personal problem requiring medical solutions (Finkelstein 1993). The medical approach towards disability still dominates current social policy legislation and provides the main criteria for defining categories of people who will have access to services and benefits. For disabled writers, the overriding political feature of interventions administered by medical practitioners is that they bring all disability groups together under a single medical interpretation of the cause behind their marginalized position in society: the medical model of disability (Oliver 1990; Finkelstein 1993).

Vociferous criticism of the medical model, largely by disabled people, has challenged the dominance of the medical discourse. There are increasing signs that services are moving away from medical control to those provided by community services. However, this shift to social and welfare interventions does not necessarily result in disabled people having greater control over their lives. Indeed, it is pointed out that community-based service purchasers have a wider perspective than their medical colleagues in identifying areas of disabled people's lives for their professional assessment and evaluation. From the architecture of the home to advice and counselling for intimate personal and sexual problems, this new breed of worker is there to provide 'expert' assessment and advice (Finkelstein 1993).

Service purchasers and providers still perceive the lives of disabled people in terms of problems to be solved. The large and extremely expensive specialist services organized nationally provide ample evidence that a characteristic of a disabled group is that they are confronted with a series of problems which they cannot solve on their own. Instead, the state has to administer through the provision of specialist services the means to alleviate these problems. From this perspective, disabled people are socially dysfunctional or described as being 'socially dead' (Miller and Gwynne 1972). Called the 'administrative model' of service intervention, this role was given, in the first instance, to the medical profession when it was unable to 'cure' individual impairments. The move towards community-based services is merely the transfer of this duty to other professions.

It is suggested by disabled writers that the common feature underlying these differing models of disability is that each is concerned with the disabled individual. Each assumes that intervention is necessary to assist an individual deemed to be unable to function 'normally' either physically or psychologically. As a consequence, the focus is upon the body as the 'cause' of disability. It is from this starting point that disabled people can be understood as a collective within the context of a single medical interpretation, in need of service intervention (Finkelstein 1993).

In contrast to these oppressive models, disabled people posit an alternative. The social model, or the 'social oppression theory', views disability as a social oppression which locates disability in people and ignores the social and structural aspect of disability. This model must be located within the experience of disabled people themselves and their attempts to redefine disability (Oliver 1990). In this second interpretation disadvantages experienced by disabled people are perceived as the collective consequence of an uncaring and unknowing society rather than as a consequence of individual impairment. The focus is shifted away from the individual to the ways disability is produced. It is within the context of society and social organization that disability ought to be understood – in other words 'on the way the experience of disability is structured' (Oliver 1990).

The dispute around the definition of disability has meant that the threefold definition of disability, which is predominant both nationally and internationally, underwrites the medical model of disability according to disabled writers (Oliver 1990, 1993). This interpretation arose from work carried out in Britain during the late 1960s in a national survey on the behalf of the Office of Populations Censuses and Surveys (OPCS) (Harris 1971). It has been subsequently refined and a version was adopted by the World Health Organization (WHO) as the basis for its definition of disability (Wood 1981). The international debate concerning which definition of disability the WHO should adopt brought into sharper relief differences in interpretation between disabled people and their organizations and international bodies, as well as other non-disabled organizations. The WHO definition is divided into three parts, 'impairment', 'disability' and 'handicap'. In this scheme 'impairment' is concerned with the abnormality of function. 'Disability' is understood as not being able to perform an activity considered normal for a human being of a given age, gender etc. 'Handicap' is interpreted as being the inability to perform a normal social role (Oliver 1990). Taken together, these definitions eschew the medical model and include a recognition of a social dimension to disability. However, the WHO scheme has failed to win the support of disabled people and their organizations.

Disabled people and their organizations oppose this scheme because they perceive it to be based upon able-bodied assumptions of disability and, as a consequence, to fail to accord with the personal realities of disabled people (Oliver 1990). Disabled writers point out that the WHO scheme reifies the idea of 'normality' without acknowledging that the question of 'normality' remains purely subjective. While it is acknowledged that the WHO scheme does include social dimensions, these same writers suggest that it ultimately fails because it does not interpret disability as arising from social causes. Instead, its fundamental rationale rests upon the impaired individual, with disability and handicap arising as a direct consequence of individual impairments (e.g. Oliver 1993).

In response to the international debate, disabled people and their organizations proffered a twofold definition of disability first proposed by Disabled People's International (DPI) in 1981 (Driedger 1989). The DPI avoided the complexity of the definitions described above and instead proposed the following twofold classification of 'handicap' and 'disability'. Most British disabled people substitute 'impairment' for 'handicap', although the latter has a wider currency and acceptance internationally (Barnes 1991). Nevertheless, 'impairment' is described as lacking part of or all of a limb, or having a defective limb, organism or mechanism of the body. 'Disability' is the disadvantage or restriction of activity caused by contemporary social organization, which takes little account of people who have physical impairments and thus excludes them from the mainstream of social activities (Oliver 1990). As Oliver reminds us, at stake here is the issue of causation. Previous definitions are reducible to the individual and attributable to biological pathology. The definition of disability proffered by disabled people and their organizations locates the causes of disability squarely within society and social organization (Oliver 1990). It is this difference which allows disabled writers to insist that both the OPCS and WHO definitions have oppressive implications for disabled people (Oliver 1990).

The corollary to this dispute about definitions is the question of a common identity for disabled people. The growth of organizations of disabled people has been equated with the development of the black and feminist movements for civil rights (Abberley 1987; Driedger 1989; Oliver 1990; Morris 1991). Yet in recent years the common features of gender, race and disability discrimination have been superseded by the reminder that each has its unique characteristics (Finkelstein 1993). Emphasis upon these differences coincide with an appeal for a common identity among disabled people. How disabled people identify themselves will assist the development of interventionist strategies for services and help with personal development. So disabled people and their organizations strive to forge a common identity as a united front to confront medical and administrative dominance (Finkelstein 1993).

Disabled writers argue that the very nature of disability entitles them to claim that disabled people are a distinct social group to be placed alongside black and ethnic minorities and women. They remind us that disability, as it is constructed in modern society, means that all disabled people endure both a common and unique experience of oppression. It is reasoned that, as a consequence, the image of a disabled person is and will remain utterly negative. This is not the case within other oppressed social groups, such as ethnic minorities or women. Rather, it is around the issue of the medical model that an understanding of the unitary nature of the oppression of disabled people has been built. Implicit in this is the assumption that this oppression is a central analytical concept which facilitates the privileging of disability over other social divisions (Finkelstein 1993).

Current methods of service delivery ensure that the image of disabled people is one of a unified and dependent population. The administrative approach to disability draws different groups of disabled people together in the assessment process for problem-solving and service provision. It is within this context that modern organizations of disabled people seek to bring disabled people together and foster a common identity both to reflect the growth of a united front against medical and administrative dominance and to redefine disability in positive terms (Finkelstein 1993). As a consequence, the cultural identity of disability is closely associated with the politics of disability. The experience of individual oppression informs a disabled person's cultural identity, part of which includes the aspiration for individual autonomy and empowerment.

Black disabled people and the singular disability identity

The assumptions implicit in the social model of disability place black disabled people in a very exposed position, because the language and philosophy of disabled writers and their organizations do not take into account
the complex concerns of black disabled people (Stuart 1992). Nevertheless,
the response of disabled people to their subordination is equally attractive
to black disabled people. As a consequence, black disabled writers have
begun to ask which should take precedence, their identity as disabled people or their ethnic identity. How these writers have sought to answer this
question will occupy the next section of this chapter. However, it is appropriate at this point for me to explore what is meant by 'cultural identity'
in this context.

It is no accident that the term 'culture' has expanded to displace
any overt references to 'race' in the biological sense of the word. As far
as national identity is concerned, culture is reductively conceived and is
always primarily and 'naturally' reproduced in families or communities.
The nation is, in turn, conceived as a neat, symmetrical accumulation of
family units, and the supposedly homogeneous culture culminates in the
experience of unified and continuous national identity. The teaching of
history, for example, is part of the transmission of this 'authentic' national
culture, which reveals the confluence of 'race', nationality and culture in
the contemporary politics of racial exclusion (Gilroy 1993b). The relationship between racism and nationalism has also emerged as the mainspring
of a populist politics, bolstered by debates around immigration, crime,
religion, education and social services.

This new cultural racism is one example of what Gilroy (1993b) describes as ethnic absolutism. This is the reductive, essentialist understanding of ethnic and national difference, which operates through an absolute
sense of culture so powerful that it is capable of separating people off from
each other and diverting them into social and historical locations that are
understood to be mutually impermeable and incommensurate. Ethnic absolutism may not trade in the vocabularies of 'race'. It may be remote from
the symbolism of colour and, most important of all, it can afflict anyone.
That those who experience racism themselves may be particularly prone to
the lure of ethnic absolutism is important for this discussion. They often
seize on simple, self-evident truths as a way of rationalizing their subordination and comprehending their own particularity.

The lure of ethnic absolutism has indeed beguiled black disabled writers.
Macro-structural and economic conditions in the West shape the locations
in which black and minority ethnic communities reside. Indeed, it is not
possible to talk about these structural factors and black expressive cultures
autonomously. The identity expressed by disabled people from minority
ethnic communities also makes reference to this context. As a consequence,
unlike for their white peers, the main concern identified by black disabled
writers is not the kind of community services they receive, but that they

receive a service at all (Begum 1992). In response to this perception of subordination, black people tended to prize highly the ideals of ethnic absolutism and the comfort of cultural sameness. Indeed, over the past eight years, we have seen black disabled writers make demands for sameness to distinguish black disabled people from others, including other disabled people and black non-disabled people, (Confederation of Indian Organisations 1987; Begum 1992, 1994; Stuart 1992, 1993; Hill 1994).

The rhetorical language of double discrimination has changed a great deal since it was first introduced in the mid-1980s. Nevertheless, whether it is described as a 'double disadvantage' or, more recently, 'simultaneous oppression', black disabled writers hanker after the assurance of a pure, simple and essential black disabled identity (Stuart 1992). The pursuit of these comfortable certainties ignores or represses intra-racial differences based on class, ideology, gender etc. (Gilroy 1993b). That this essential black disabled identity has been inadequate to capture the experience of disabled people from minority ethnic communities will be explored below. The pursuit of homogeneity in itself cannot answer the problems faced by this group. Homogeneity can signify unity but unity need not require homogeneity (Gilroy 1993b). These assumptions have profound implications for service delivery to this group of disabled people.

Black and disabled, a double disadvantage?

The appeal to a crude homogencity did not initially come from black disabled writers, but their white peers. However, the pursuit of a simple race essence by black disabled writers should be understood in the context of an evocation of a disability narcissism which underplays difference. The response of black disabled writers to this homogeneous disability identity has not been a rejection of this claustrophobic, victim-oriented emphasis upon disabled people's subordination, but the opposite. Black disabled writers have, instead, sought to manufacture identities which reflect their particular subordination. Initially they described the experience of disabled people from minority ethnic communities as of being 'doubly disadvantaged' or of a 'double oppression'. These descriptions of the black disabled persons' experience was first proffered in the late 1980s and ought to be understood within the context of 'institutional racism'. Perhaps the most complete description of 'double disadvantage' is provided by Confederation of Indian Organisations, which defined it as follows:

All attitudes, procedures and patterns – social and economic – whose effect, though not necessarily whose conscious intention, is to create and maintain the power and influence and well-being of white people at the expense of black people.

Or, in other words . . . the able-bodied have now become white and the disabled people black. It therefore follows that the black or Asian

disabled person faces a double disadvantage: that of being both black
and disabled.

(Confederation of Indian Organisations 1987: 2)

'Institutional racism' is a term which originated in the Black Power
Movement's struggles in the United States of America (Williams 1989;
Rattansi 1992). It is a term which signifies the myriad taken-for-granted
ways in which routine institutional procedures end up discriminating against
and disadvantaging black and ethnic minorities. Unfortunately, this concept has frequently been used in a reductive manner to imply that racist
processes are the only primary cause of all the unequal outcomes and
exclusions which black people experience. In the education system, for
example, some writers have tended to characterize the poor experience
of black students solely within this context (Troyna and Williams 1986).
The significance of difference, especially class or gender inequalities, being
intertwined with the racism that black people encounter is underplayed.
This flaw seriously undermines the analysis and suggests inappropriate and
possibly divisive polices, which ignore discriminations and disadvantages
common to black and white people (Rattansi 1992) as well as the fact that
racisms are differently experienced by different black people.

It is for this reason that black disabled writers have demurred from
'double disadvantage' as an interpretation of the experience of black disabled people and propose an alternative (Stuart 1992). Instead of double
disadvantage, black disabled writers describe their experience as being a
form of 'simultaneous oppression'. This term was first coined by black
women, whose experience has informed that of black disabled people. At
the beginning of the 1980s black feminist writers began to assert strongly
that their experience of oppression differs in substance and intensity from
that understood by their white peers. Carby makes this point clearly:

> The experience of black women does not enter the parameters of
> parallelism (the attempts to parallel race and gender divisions). The
> fact that black women are subject to *simultaneous* oppression of
> patriarchy, class and 'race' is the prime reason for not employing
> parallels that render their position and experience not only marginal
> but invisible.
>
> (Carby 1982: 73, her emphasis)

The idea of simultaneous oppression, as described by Carby, appeals to
black disabled writers because it meets some of the criticisms levelled at
'double disadvantage'. Simultaneous oppression incorporates a notion of
difference in the form of class, gender and even ethnicity. However, it does
retain the oppressor – oppressed dichotomy so attractive to black disabled
writers (Stuart 1992, 1993; Begum 1994). Indeed, 'simultaneous oppression' serves to emphasize the subordination and singularity of black disabled persons' experience. This disability oppression separates black disabled

people from all other groups and justifies the construction of a distinct and separate black disabled identity (Stuart 1992).

However, black disabled writers' adherence to simultaneous oppression leaves other complex considerations untouched. Indeed, the claims made by Carby (1982), Parmar (1982) and Bhavnani and Coulson (1986) for the specificity of black women creates a paradox. 'Black women' is a term used by some black feminists to incorporate a diversity of lifestyles, but it is also retained as an undifferentiated category for analysis on the grounds that black women are united by racist oppression (Knowles and Mercer 1992). Black disabled writers too often represent black disabled people as a homogeneous group. Rather than explore diversity, they fail to recognize it as a central aspect of the experience of black and minority ethnic communities. Instead racist processes remain the primary cause of inequality and discrimination, in which we see just an eternal struggle between binary opposites, the victims and perpetrators (Gilroy 1987). Inevitably, this perspective fails to focus upon black people, disabled or otherwise, except as victims.

The idea of a common, invariant racial identity capable of linking divergent black experiences across different spaces and times has been fatally flawed. The dogmatic assertions of homogeneity upon which black disabled writers have latched can neither conceal nor answer the charge that this sense of sameness did not exist prior to their attempts to manufacture it. Curiously, the popularity of such an appeal comes at a time when the effects of race discrimination, inequitable service provision and, even, the painful history of ethnic inferiority marked by slavery and colonialism can no longer be relied upon to establish the feelings of connectedness assumed to be a precondition for racial survival (Gilroy 1993b). Nevertheless, the therapeutic importance of an adherence to a black essential identity in the reproduction of a political movement cannot be denied. However, there is a high price to be paid for insisting upon the representation of black disabled peoples' experience in this way. This price is simplistic, inappropriate and divisive social policy initiatives which ignore difference and fail to help those for whom they are designed. Such policies are hostages to fortune to the New Right ideologues, as in the case of education, who would interpret their inevitable failure as proof of the inappropriateness of intervention (Flew 1984).

This begs the question: what is the alternative? There are limits to what ethnic minority populations can blame on the inequities of white supremacy. Indeed, continually to present black people as the victims of subordination denies them the opportunity to demonstrate that there is far more to the content of black social and cultural life than the effects of racism alone (Gilroy 1993b). Closely associated with this particular insight is the fact that there are two sides to the black experience of subordination, that which is afflicted from without and the response to this from within. It is the latter which is of considerable importance: the acknowledgement that, as well as being the victims of subordination, these communities have to share responsibility for some of its consequences, such as urban fratricide, the highly topical and controversial issue of youth criminality and even the disabilism within black and minority ethnic communities towards black disabled people.

An alternative to this victim fixation is the reflexive position, which is becoming more evident within black and minority ethnic communities. The encouragement of black business interests and economic strategies towards self-reliance are just two examples. If these Victorian ideals of individualism and racial uplift resound too closely with the Thatcherite brand of nationalistic, populist and racially coded conservatism, their similarity is superficial rather than fundamental and inevitably limited. However, at their heart is the well-being of the black and minority ethnic communities and an indication of the growing sophistication of black political responses. Conservatism is not an inevitable consequence of a more reflexive, self-critical spirit. As Gilroy suggests, it can usher in a different perspective on self and sociality, detached from conservative individualism, in which black communities are able and willing to take a measure of responsibility for changing their situation; to participate as full actors rather than just as the victims (Gilroy 1993b).

There is substantial evidence to suggest that this more reflexive and positive approach has been adopted by many black and minority ethnic organizations in both the health and social 'care' field. Indeed, the Sickle Cell Society, the Asian People with Disabilities Alliance and numerous small black voluntary organizations demonstrate that black and minority ethnic people are active agents in their struggle for equity. However, the problem still remains that black disabled people do not benefit from those social policies designed to empower disabled people. At this point it is appropriate to look at some key community care services designed for disabled people and contrast them with the experience of disabled people from black and minority ethnic communities. What will quickly become apparent is that poor service design, coupled with the extreme subordination experienced by black disabled people, account for the failure of services to assist this group. What should be apparent by now is that new thinking is required to overcome these obstacles.

Autonomy and independence, and black and minority ethnic communities

Nasa Begum, in a discussion about appropriate community care services for black disabled people, appeals for a strategy to 'promote independent living and autonomy for black disabled people'. This can be achieved through 'a strategy for tackling institutional and individual racism' (Begum 1994). An appeal such as this is familiar to all disabled writers because they are committed to the social theory of disability. For disabled writers, both black and white, the key to this philosophy is the achievement of autonomy, independence and empowerment in the face of oppression within an able-bodied society. However, in the context of community care policy, black disabled people have not been the main beneficiaries of services, such as those characteristic of the independent living movement, which are designed to empower them.

One of the main controversies over community care policy is the association of physical impairment with dependence (Ellis 1993; Morris 1993). That the assumed inability to do things for oneself means that a person is dependent is rejected by disabled people. Those deemed dependent are assumed to be unable to take control of their lives. As a consequence, the need for personal assistance is translated into a need for 'care' in the sense of being looked after. The 'carer', whether a professional or a relative, becomes the person in charge of the person in need of care. Disabled people are denied any personal responsibility or choice (Morris 1993). It is acknowledged that 'caring' within the family is not as clear cut as this, and disabled writers do point to the reciprocity between the 'carer' and the 'cared for' (Morris 1993). Nevertheless, most disabled writers would also reason that informal care as the principal way of delivering personal assistance is likely to result in the oppression of disabled people (Morris 1993).

Disabled people and their organizations see 'independent living' as the embodiment of the aspiration to achieve autonomy and independence in relation to social policy. At its most basic, this interpretation is the ability to have control over personal assistance in order to go about daily tasks. In accordance with the social model, disabled people and their organizations consider the ability to participate fully in society through 'independent living' as both a civil and a human right (Morris 1993). It is this control which enables the expression of individuality and from this flows the assertion of disabled people's human rights and their status as citizens (Morris 1993).

Service provision and poverty

In policy terms the 1990 NHS and Community Care Act has attempted to meet user demands for greater choice and control over the services they receive. By giving users and carers greater control over the assessment process and choice in any resulting services, these reforms are intended to enhance user independence and choice (Department of Health 1989). However, despite its being replete with the language of autonomy and independence, it is not clear whether or how the Act ensures that the views of the disabled person will no longer remain subordinate to those of the service purchaser and the 'carer' (Ellis 1993). Nevertheless, the Act does mean that individual 'care' solutions can be better tailored to the needs of both users and carers.

Today, a variety of initiatives exist to allow disabled people, with the support of their social services department, to establish their own independent living schemes. Disabled people in Greenwich, Hampshire and

Derbyshire have been able, with the help of a local service provider, to run their own service through centres for independent living (CILs). These allow them to recruit their own personal assistance and tailor assistance to suit their needs exactly. In other places, social services departments have attempted to provide similar, if inferior, services for local disabled people. However, despite all this activity, black disabled people continue to be under-represented as recipients or, in the case of CILs, as providers of these services.

The absence of disabled people from black and minority ethnic communities from community care schemes and as provider organizations has not gone unnoticed by black disabled writers. They reason that this is the result of both institutional and individual racism. The services available take little account of the culturally specific needs of disabled people from black and minority ethnic communities (Begum 1992; Francis 1993). Instead, they point out that service providers frequently make culturalist assumptions about black and minority ethnic communities. The myth held by service purchasers, that South Asian families prefer to look after their own impaired family members rather than endure the intervention of Western style social services, is a well known example (see Chapters 4 and 5, this volume).

The failure of the independent living initiatives to reach black disabled people is partially the result of the subordinate economic position black people occupy in British society. Black and minority ethnic communities are primarily located in the poorest regions of Britain. Recent research on disabled people in one of the poorer inner London regions demonstrates how this in-built disadvantage is translated into deprivation for black disabled people in particular (Doyle *et al.* 1994). The local authority which served the majority of the informants of this research suffered from severe under-funding. Its departments were poorly managed or under-staffed or both, with a consequent impact upon efficiency. For example, the local social services department failed to implement a systematic method for finding people in need of support (Doyle *et al.* 1994). The absence of people with disabilities from lists compiled by local authority care managers created a vicious circle for the informants, especially those from black and minority ethnic communities. Those most likely to have the least contact with their social services department were either supporting themselves in local authority flats or living in similar accommodation with informal carers, usually their mothers. In this climate, black disabled people are in danger of being and often are completely forgotten (Doyle *et al.* 1994; see also Chapter 5, this volume).

The oppression of disabled people within minority ethnic communities

A view frequently expressed by the African Caribbean informants in the London project, described by Doyle and colleagues, was that they were more disadvantaged than their neighbours with disabilities from the white population. However, the researchers were unable to confirm that the white disabled people in the study, who lived in circumstances very similar to those of their black peers, were much better off. Nevertheless, these sentiments ought to be taken seriously. The project's researchers interpreted them as an expression of hopelessness, lack of opportunity and powerlessness felt by their black informants (Doyle et al. 1994). However, these views can also be explained in a different way. They might be an example of people seizing on simple, self-evident truths as a way of rationalizing their subordination and comprehending their own particularity. That the white informants in the project experienced similar deprivation provides a caution against explaining the subordinate position disabled people from minority ethnic communities endure in solely a racist context. Policy initiatives designed to alleviate racism alone would certainly fail and compound the isolation felt by all the disabled people living in regions similar to the one studied.

Despite the inclusion of the structural context into its perspective, the research by Doyle et al. ignored the issue of widespread and frequently expressed disablist attitudes held by many within the black and minority ethnic communities. This is an extremely sensitive topic and few black disabled writers have chosen even to acknowledge it. Those who do only make a brief reference to it (Stuart 1992). Partially, the reason for this reticence is the fear that service purchasers might lay an emphasis on this oppression out of all proportion to its significance and use it as an excuse for their own culpability. That the oppression of disabled people occurs in black and minority ethnic populations, as it does in the rest of society, should come as no surprise. In the absence of research on this issue, the extent of the problem and its impact upon black disabled people is unknown. Nevertheless, disablist attitudes to disabled people do appear to vary between ethnic communities. Within African and African Caribbean communities, for example, sexuality and the ability to procreate appear to govern some of the attitudes to disability. In contrast, family honour and social status appear to influence some of the attitudes to impairment within South Asian populations. It is important to acknowledge that alongside the many strengths of black and minority ethnic community identity, weaknesses also reside. If black and minority ethnic communities are to be seen as being more than just the victims of their oppression then appropriate research to obtain a better understanding of the isolation disabled people experience within black and minority ethnic communities would be of considerable importance.

Nasa Begum is correct to suggest that services to disabled people from minority ethnic communities need to be improved (Begum 1994). However, the assumption that this can be achieved by simply eradicating racism from service provision is too simplistic. It is clear that the communities to whom Begum refers are both complex and multifaceted. Services designed for the regions in which black and minority ethnic communities are found predominantly must both alleviate the ills common to that region and involve the communities in both the design and provision of local services. However, beyond social class, gender and locality, the impairment a black disabled person has will have a considerable impact upon his or her experience. This is because disability within black and minority ethnic communities is as stigmatized as any other aspect of black peoples' experience in the United Kingdom. The racialization of the impairments found within black and minority ethnic communities serves to add to the subordination of disabled people. Likewise, it is another way in which these people perceive their experience to be a homogeneous one. Yet this form of subordination provides further evidence that black disabled people cannot evoke a simple sameness or a homogeneous identity (for a discussion see Sheldon and Parker 1992; Ahmad 1993, Chapter 3).

Appropriate community care policy

Most of the discussion of community care legislation in relation to disabled people has been inclined to concentrate on its known weaknesses (Ellis 1993; Morris 1993). Writers who have looked specifically at black disabled people's experience of the new policy have also followed this trend (Begum 1994; Doyle et al. 1994). That there is a great deal to criticize about this new initiative is not at dispute. However, sole emphasis upon the policy's weaknesses can quickly become rhetorical and a distraction from what is positive about this initiative. The context of the new community care policy initiative was a number of earlier studies which highlighted the failure of care in community as it existed at that time. Disabled people, especially, bore the brunt of this failure, receiving a notoriously poor service from the demarcated agencies operating within artificial barriers which represented health, social services and other sectors. It has been acknowledged that services for people with disabilities nationally were patchy and inadequate. The number of health staff with the necessary skills for this group was extremely variable. The most vulnerable were disabled people living in the most disadvantaged regions, where the majority of disabled people from minority ethnic communities are still to be found. For this group, in particular, care in the community was usually being left to informal carers, usually members of family with little service support.

The new legislation is a distinct improvement on what preceded it. The twin objectives of community care reforms are the promotion of greater independence and choice (Department of Health 1989). One example specifically relevant to black disabled people is the guidelines given to care managers, which for the first time include specific recommendations concerning black and minority ethnic communities. These include: consultation with representatives from these disadvantaged groups; information to be published in appropriate languages and in accessible forms; staff recruitment from backgrounds similar to those who use the services; and monitoring systems to measure the achievement of organizational change in this area (SSI 1991). In addition, the legislation enshrines greater user and carer choice and full participation in the needs assessment process. Despite what appear to be very positive guidelines it should be remembered that they only partially compensate for the deprived environment in which the majority of minority ethnic communities are to be found. The community care legislation's purchaser–provider split and encouragement of competition to deliver services might even harm this vulnerable group. For example, the cheapest provider of block contracts might not be best placed to meet the needs of all the people within the local community.

Unfortunately, the literature on disabled people from black and minority ethnic communities continues to characterize them as passive victims of racism and disabilism. To ensure that the community care legislation works best for these disabled people it is important to remember that they are actors too. As actors their views and opinions may or may not coincide with the 'problems' characterized in the literature. Disabled people, whether black or white, are the product of neither racism nor disabilism alone. They have wider concerns and interests, which cannot always be accounted for within these twin prisms of oppression. This simple fact represents a tremendous challenge to both those who write about disability and those who are responsible for designing services for people living in the poorest regions in Britain. That one of the central characteristics of black disabled people is their heterogeneous nature should not frighten those charged with the responsibility to provide services for people from different ethnic backgrounds. What might appear to be a daunting prospect can only be mitigated by careful listening to the views of both users and carers from minority ethnic communities. Furthermore, it is vital to remember that as well as discrimination, social class, gender, the family and the environment are equally important factors which influence the outlook of all disabled people. Only then can the opportunities which the community care legislation has to offer be fully exploited.

Conclusion

The community care reforms provide an opportunity to improve and create innovative services for disabled people within black and minority ethnic communities. In order to gain from these reforms families of disabled people within minority ethnic communities will also be required to play a full part. The context within which most of these people live is one of deprivation and disadvantage and this begs a question: will poverty undermine any benefits the reforms might bring? This question cannot be fully answered until the theoretical problems in conceptualizing the experience of disabled people within black and minority ethnic communities have been resolved. The continued characterization of disabled people and their families as victims of circumstance and not as actors in their own right, rather than assisting them, adds to their continued neglect. Perceived ethnicity is only one aspect of an individual's experience, as is a person's disability or gender. To break this cycle future services must be sensitive to the social, economic and cultural context which structures an individual's life. Certain services might be both applicable nationwide and relevant locally. Furthermore, the provision of 'ethnic sensitivity' will have different implications for different services and for different disabled people. The very nature of sensitive service delivery rests on an acknowledgement and respect for diversity. This requires service purchasers to listen very closely to those on whose behalf they are charged to purchase services for.

Note

1 The term 'black', used in this context, is merely a social construct. Throughout this chapter I use the term 'black' to describe people of New Commonwealth origin in the UK and including people of Arabic, Vietnamese or Chinese origin.

Annotated bibliography

Swain, J., Finkelstein, V., French, S. and Oliver, M. (eds) (1993) *Disabling Barriers – Enabling Environments*. London: Sage and The Open University.
This major theme of this key text is that disabled people are presented with numerous social, structural and economic barriers that deny them full citizenship rights. In particular the book explores how definitions of disability disempower disabled people and discusses how the politics of disablement can challenge these definitions.

Stuart, O. (1992) Race and disability: just a double oppression?, *Disability, Handicap and Society*, 7(2), 177–88.
This article explores the experiences and identities of black disabled people. It provides an account of oppression by describing the experiences of disability within the context of inequitable services, poverty and racism. It demonstrates that a disabled person's identity is informed by factors other than his or her impairment.

Donald, J. and Rattansi, A. (eds) (1992) *'Race', Culture and Difference*. London: Sage and Open University.
The book focuses on the mainstream debates on race, culture and identity in Britain. It includes a comprehensive treatment of: multiculturalism, anti-racism and ethnicity; New Right approaches to difference; and race and feminism.

7

Representations and realities: black people, community care and mental illness

Charles Watters

Introduction

Studies undertaken in Britain over the past two decades have indicated clearly that black people's experience of mental health services differs in important ways from that of the white population. Studies have tended to focus on three key areas: the pattern of psychiatric hospital admissions among defined 'ethnic minority' groups, specifically Afro-Caribbeans and Asians; the prevalence of specific psychiatric diagnosis among these groups, particularly schizophrenia and depression; and cultural factors in the treatment of black people in primary health care settings. By contrast, little attention has been given to the ways in which community-based mental health services are delivered to black people and the influence specific forms of service provision may have on black people's access to mental health care. Furthermore, studies have tended to focus almost exclusively on the role of doctors, particularly psychiatrists, and have paid scant attention to the complex institutional, professional and policy contexts in which black people receive services in Britain.

In considering the relationship between black people and mental health and social services in this chapter I shift attention to the complex, pluralist contexts in which black people may receive mental health services, and consider the role that specific representations of black people's mental health problems may have in determining the types of treatment offered.

Black people and mental health services in Britain

An oft-cited and consistent finding is that Afro-Caribbeans are significantly more likely to enter mental health services through compulsory admission involving the use of Section 2 or Section 3 of the Mental Health Act 1983 (Cope 1989). Cope has reported that, during the 1980s, while fewer than

10 per cent of all admissions were compulsory, for Afro-Caribbeans the figure was between 20 and 30 per cent. Particular attention has been directed at the use of Section 136 of the Act, under which the police have specific powers to detain persons for up to 72 hours in a 'place of safety', if they are regarded as being a danger either to themselves or to others. Numerous studies have indicated that Afro-Caribbean people are particularly likely to be detained under this section (Ineichen *et al.* 1984; Littlewood and Lipsedge 1989). Research findings suggest further that the use of compulsory admissions relates particularly to young Afro-Caribbean males, with those between the ages of 16 and 30 being up to seventeen times more likely than white males to be admitted in this way (Cope 1989).

A more recent study conducted by Bebbington *et al.* (1994: 747) in two London boroughs confirmed the tendency for 'Black Caribbeans' to be more likely than the white population to be admitted compulsorily, although the rate was not as high as Cope suggests. They note that for both Afro-Caribbean men and women, 'nearly half of all admissions were compulsory, compared with only one-fifth for whites.' The authors argue that there is a strong link between ethnicity and diagnosis, but argue against the view that ethnicity is in itself related to decision-making regarding use of the Mental Health Act in admissions. In other words, the authors appear to support the view that there is an 'ethnic vulnerability' to mental illness, particularly schizophrenia, and go so far as to suggest the possibility that this could be due to a 'hazard arising during pregnancy or postnatally' (Bebbington *et al.* 1994: 748).

Researchers have consistently distinguished between the experience of Afro-Caribbeans and that of Asians. Cope (1989: 345), for example, eliminated consideration of the experience of Asians with respect to compulsory admissions on the basis of preliminary findings to the effect that the 'results were similar to those of whites'. By contrast, research has focused less on custodial dimensions of the service and more frequently on a consideration of the links between psychiatric hospitalization and migration or on 'culturally specific' ways in which Asians may present their mental health problems. In this context, particular attention has been given to the extent to which Asians may have difficulty in communicating mental health problems within primary health care settings. Studies have tended to focus on producing broad generalizations of Asian 'culture', treating the latter as though it was a homogeneous entity and proposing that difficulties in communication are produced through deficiencies in Asians language and culture. Julian Leff, for example, suggested that this may be due to the fact that people from some non-Western cultures may lack a language for describing emotional states (Leff 1973). Philip Rack has argued that Asians perceive mental health problems in terms of social dysfunction. For example, once Asian patients are functioning normally they and their family consider them 'cured', and there is perceived to be no need to explore the emotional or psychological condition (Rack 1982: 110).

Discussion of diagnosis is generally orientated around the representation of Afro-Caribbean males as susceptible to schizophrenia or other forms of psychosis, while Asians, particularly women, are frequently characterized as being likely to suffer from depression and possibly suicidal (a newspaper article went so far as to speak in terms of a 'suicide epidemic among young Asian women: *Observer* 29 August 1993). The characterization of Afro-Caribbeans as being susceptible to schizophrenia has been strongly challenged in a number of studies. Fernando (1988: 138), for example, has argued that the instruments which are used as diagnostic tools, such as the 'present state examination', involve the making of judgements regarding the patient's culture and background, which are 'likely to be influenced by the stereotypes in society'. According to Fernando (1988: 140), a diagnosis of schizophrenia is arrived at in a context in which

> The psychiatrist has to decide whether the (prospective) patient's beliefs are true or imaginary, whether the patient is thinking in an organised way, and whether emotions are blunted or in keeping with what is expected. All this is largely dependent on judging interactions between persons, usually the doctor and the patient, but influenced by society's norms which are institutionalised in education, training and so-called common sense.

Thus assessment and diagnosis are dependent on perceptions of what constitutes 'normal' behaviour. This perception is, according to Fernando, imbued with white, middle-class values on the basis of which black people may be labelled as suffering from mental health problems. A further important consideration is the way in which representations of the mental health problems of black people (for example, of Asian women as suffering from high rates of depression and Afro-Caribbean males as suffering high rates of schizophrenia) may themselves influence diagnosis. Cecil Hellman has cited a study undertaken by Temerlin, which indicated that groups of psychiatrists were highly influenced by advice on the problems of patients given prior to formal assessment and diagnosis (Hellman 1990: 225). According to him there is a high degree of subjectivity in the assessment of patients: 'Most psychiatric diagnosis is based on the doctor's subjective evaluation of the patient's appearance, speech and behaviour, as well as the performance in certain standardised psychometric tests' (Hellman 1990: 225). While there is no conclusive evidence that psychiatrists may be influenced by general representations of the 'problems' associated with Afro-Caribbean or Asian people this is an area in which research would be timely.

The issues raised here are of crucial importance when we are considering the development of community care for black people with mental health problems. The existence of high rates of compulsory admissions points to the fact that a high proportion of black people are not accessing mental health services through the route of 'voluntary' admission, usually involving a process of referral from a GP to a psychiatrist or mental health team. Evidence that Asian people may have difficulty in accessing appropriate services at a primary health care level and 'communication difficulties' with GPs indicates that community-based services may be both inappropriate and inaccessible. Before we consider this further it is appropriate to place the relationship between black people and mental health services within a broader context of developments in community care.

Developments in community care

The development of community care for people with mental health problems has been a key policy objective for successive governments since the late 1950s. Despite this long-standing commitment, however, there has been little consistency of view regarding what is meant by community care for the mentally ill. A number of commentators detected a crucial shift which took place in the 1970s, from viewing community care as the provision of statutory health and social services in the community to a view in which the community itself was seen as a key source of care for individuals (e.g. Allsop 1984; Evandrou 1990). The latter interpretation was apparent in key policy documents, such as the Barclay Report on the role of social workers. According to the report,

> Community social work implies a focus on individuals and families set in the context of all the networks of which they do, or might, form a part. Community social work requires of social workers changes in attitudes; increased understanding of the interactions of people in groups and communities; and an increased capacity to negotiate and to bring people together to enable networks to grow.
>
> (Barclay Report 1982: 217–18)

It was also supported by a number of initiatives, both national and local, aimed at harnessing and developing the caring capacities of communities (e.g. Hadley *et al.* 1984). Such approaches were informed by active discussion in both the USA and Britain on the potential role of social networks as repositories of care, and the role of the mental health and social work professional in harnessing the caring capacity of communities (Gottlieb 1981). In this context black people are frequently represented as living within relatively homogeneous communities with well established networks of care, which the health or social services worker can 'tap into' to generate support for individuals or families. This perspective is particularly apparent with respect to Asians. In addressing the interweaving of formal and informal care Martin Bulmer observes that

> A degree of social distance characterises relations between different ethnic groups and informal ties tend to be within each group. This is particularly marked among those coming from the Indian subcontinent.
>
> (Bulmer 1987: 186)

Later in this chapter we will consider the impact that the idea of homogeneous black or ethnic minority communities may have on the development of mental health services.

Two central policy developments affecting community based services for the mentally ill introduced in the late 1980s and early 1990s are care management (which of course is more generally applicable to recipients of social services) and the care programme approach.

Care management

The development of care management was a consequence of proposals contained within the Griffiths Report, which recommended that social services' key role should be as 'enablers' rather than as direct providers of community care. In the words of the report, local social services should act, 'as the designers, organisers and purchasers of non-health care services, and not primarily as direct providers, making the maximum possible use of voluntary and private sector bodies to widen consumer choice, stimulate innovation and encourage efficiency' (Griffiths 1988: 1). The role of the 'care manager' is to assess the needs of individuals and develop a 'package of care' to address these needs through making significant use of services offered by local independent including voluntary sectors.

The Griffiths Report only makes reference to the specific needs of a multiracial society in one brief paragraph. Here it is stated that 'The emphasis on the responsibility of the social services authority to assess need, and arrange appropriate packages of services *for individuals within their own situations*, should help to ensure that the different needs of people with different cultural backgrounds are properly considered' (Griffiths 1988: 26). The implication here appears to be that these new arrangements will, in themselves, lead to services being more responsive to the needs of black communities. However, unless the care manager has appropriate training in assessing and addressing the needs of black people and has a commitment to confronting issues of racial inequality, it is difficult to see how the introduction of care management in itself will improve social services for black people. Arguably the distance that is created between the commissioner and the provider of care makes it more difficult for the care manager to ensure that services are responding to individuals' needs (see also Chapter 9, this volume).

Care Programme Approach

The Care Programme Approach (CPA) is a parallel development and shares strong similarities to care management. The principles are the same; a worker is responsible for assessing individuals' needs, drawing up a care plan in accordance with these and ensuring its implementation. The CPA differs from care management in that it is exclusively directed towards those with mental health problems and its implementation is primarily the responsibility of health services. The introduction of the CPA was a response to mounting concern regarding the extent to which individuals were leaving psychiatric hospitals without appropriate care plans being put in place. While the development of hospital discharge arrangements was a feature of the approach, the CPA is currently viewed as being applicable to all those receiving specialist mental health services (Department of Health 1993). The focus on the pivotal role of the key worker is designed to ensure that care in the community is closely coordinated.

However, this development highlights the importance of key workers receiving training to meet the needs of black people and to identify the forms of racial discrimination black people may face in both mental health services and other relevant agencies, such as those concerned with housing and employment.

Furthermore, the development of both care management and the CPA is focused on developing and coordinating the activities of staff in relation to individuals who have, as it were, already entered the system. As such these measures are not primarily focused on ways of improving access. Indeed, in the light of well publicized incidents in which mental health patients in the community have harmed themselves or others, recent policy on the mentally ill has stressed the importance above all of addressing the needs of those with 'serious and/or long term mental health problems', with emphasis being placed on the development of a 'supervision register' of all those deemed to be of serious risk to themselves or others. The emphasis has thus been placed strongly on the coordination of services for those already in the system and suffering from serious problems, rather than on the improvement of access and development of preventative approaches for those in the community.

Service priorities and organizational change

The process through which mental health services are prioritized must be seen in the light of the organizational changes introduced through the NHS and Community Care Act 1990. As a result of this legislation, health services were divided into separate purchasing and providing organizations, with health authorities assuming responsibility for assessing the health care needs of their local population and placing contracts with provider organizations to meet these needs. Within this context, it is the purchasing health authorities' responsibility to determine the amount of money to be spent on mental health services and to agree with the providers quality standards for the service and the ways in which the service is to be monitored. In negotiating contracts, both parties seek to reach agreement on the priorities for the service. In the light of recent policy it is likely that the contract will ensure that resources are focused on meeting the needs of those regarded as having serious mental health problems, with less emphasis being placed on preventative work and on those with 'minor' problems. A consequence of these developments is that less emphasis is being placed on reaching communities perceived to be 'under-utilizing' services, while increasing the surveillance and control of those perceived to be 'dangerous'.

This development in community care policy towards the mentally ill is of particular significance to black people. Fernando (1988) has noted the tendency within psychiatry to associate black people with dangerousness. Citing a study by Harrison, Fernando (1991: 122) notes that black people are 'being seen as dangerous without adequate objective reasons for doing so'. Littlewood and Lipsedge (1989: 275) reiterate the point, citing American evidence which demonstrates that 'black psychiatric patients are less violent than white patients'. Despite a lack of evidence to show that black patients may be more dangerous, the stereotype of black people as dangerous persists and suggests that they are likely to receive services involving higher degrees of supervision and surveillance.

Despite the significant differences between black and white people in patterns of access to mental health services and in diagnosis, policy developments in mental health continue to pay scant attention to identifying and addressing the needs of black people. Where guidance is offered, the emphasis tends to be on stressing factors relating to perceived ethnic and cultural differences between black and white people. A small section of the *Health of the Nation Key Area Handbook – Mental Health* (Department of Health 1993) addresses the differences in service provision 'for people of different cultures and religions'. Emphasis is here placed on three areas: 'professionals from similar cultural backgrounds, interpreting services, and special dietary arrangements and other culturally specific requirements' (Department of Health 1993: 35). Here the emphasis is on cultural particularity, which highlights the 'otherness' of black people. The continuous reference to the difference and specificity of the needs of black and 'other ethnic minorities' carries an implicit assumption that there is a homogeneous white British culture of which black people are not a part. A further serious implication of this approach is that those responsible for the provision of mental health services in a multiracial society may assume that by appointing some 'black or other ethnic minority' workers and providing some interpreting and particular food they are addressing black people's needs without consideration being given to the broader issues of the inequalities and discriminatory practices that may underpin the distinctive experiences of black people in relation to mental health services.

Filters to care

It is unfortunate that in much of the writing on the relationship between black people and mental health services in Britain, little attention has been paid to the role of the general practitioner, the key gate-keeper to mental health services. According to the highly influential model of mental health care in the community, proposed by Goldberg and Huxley (1980), people with mental health problems pass through a series of 'filters' before gaining access to different levels of mental health services. Initially the mental health problem is identified within the community and in a high proportion of cases the matter is taken to a GP, whose ability to detect the disorder crucially influences the extent to which the individual is able to gain access to specialist mental health services. Depending upon the GP's ability to detect disorder and the nature of the diagnosis, the patient may then be referred to a psychiatrist, and then, based on her assessment, be referred to a psychiatric hospital. The model gives central place to the role of GPs and consultants in mental health care, presenting the former as the crucial 'gate-keepers' whom patients must normally pass. As such, the model fails to address the complexity of pathways to mental care in an environment in which there is now a plurality of purchasers and providers.

While Goldberg and Huxley do give some attention to the differences in access to services experienced by women and men, they give little attention to the particular difficulties which may be experienced by members of black and ethnic minority groups. As we have noted, a wide range of studies have indicated that the pathways to mental health care experienced by black minorities may be profoundly different from those experienced by other sections of the population. Studies demonstrate that, for example, Afro-Caribbeans are significantly more likely to enter psychiatric hospitals compulsorily under Section 136 of the Mental Health Act, thus, to follow Goldberg's famous model, circumventing the two intermediate filters between community and hospitalization.

Further studies have indicated that members of black minorities may face significant difficulties in gaining access to a range of health and social services. In some instances there is a lack of basic knowledge relating to services, in others difficulties may be due to the fact that black populations may see existing community services as being inappropriate (Atkin and Rollings 1993a, b). Given that GPs do have a significant role in detecting mental ill health, offering treatment and referring to specialist services, the extent to which GPs can detect and respond effectively to the mental health needs of their black patients may be a crucial determinant in black people gaining access to specialist services.

Studies of the relationship between GPs and their black patients, however, suggest that GPs may perceive the health needs of their black patients on the basis of negative stereotypes. For example, in the context of a study of GPs' attitudes to Asian and non-Asian patients, Ahmad et al. (1991: 54) reported that GPs regarded Asians as 'requiring longer consultations, to be less compliant, and perceived to make excessive use of health care'. GPs viewed proportionately high numbers of Asian patients as presenting with trivial complaints and thus wasting valuable time, despite there being no empirical evidence to support this view. This perception is supported in a

GP handbook designed to inform them of appropriate ways of treating Asian patients presenting with mental health problems. The author here describes

> Asian women whose days are spent in loneliness and social isolation, cut off from family and social networks. Many older Asian women speak little or no English. Some are confined to their home, by their husbands or by their own timidity, and are seldom seen; others may become surgery-haunters – perhaps because a visit to the doctor is one of the few opportunities for a culturally sanctioned outing.
>
> (Rack 1990: 290)

Assumptions to the effect that Asians are particularly predisposed towards somatizing their psychological problems (for example, presenting in GP surgeries with chest or back pains when they 'really' are depressed) are not generally supported by research findings and may be underpinned by ethnocentric dualistic views of the relationship between mind and body (Krause 1990; Watters 1994). I have argued elsewhere that in instances where Asian people may present with a somatic disorder and have a psychological problem the physiological symptoms should not be assumed to constitute a 'masking' or 'denial' of the mental health problem. When questioned about views on the cause of the physical problem, Asian people may freely and explicitly relate it to social or psychological factors (Watters 1995).

Given the GP's central role in diagnosing and referring people with mental health problems the issue of communication is of central importance. Where GPs may be influenced by stereotypes regarding the ways in which black people present or are susceptible to mental health problems, inappropriate treatment or referrals may follow. It is essential that, in this context, broad generalizations are avoided and attention is given to what Fernando (1988: 184) describes as the 'overall culture of each individual and the social pressures that influence the person's life'.

The role of short-term projects

In an examination of the relationship between black people and mental health services it is appropriate that the complex institutional context in which black people receive community-based mental health care is considered. Evidence from around the country suggests that where services are developed which seek to meet the needs of black people they are frequently in the form of short-term centrally funded projects (Watters 1994; see also Chapter 9, this volume). The ubiquity of such projects is indicated by the report of the government's Mental Health Task Force into mental health services for black people (Department of Health 1994). While the report brings attention to the work of many of these projects and presents them as examples of good practice which should be encouraged elsewhere, it pays scant attention to the marginal status of such projects in relation to mainstream mental health services. Such projects demonstrate a variant of what Dominelli (1992: 116) has characterized as the 'inclusive' and the 'exclusive' tendencies within institutional responses to the social and health care of black people. While here black people may be the focus for the work of such projects, and they are therefore 'included', the projects themselves are 'excluded' as a consequence of their marginal status in relation to mainstream services. While projects themselves frequently offer excellent services to black people, they are at best a piecemeal response (see also Chapter 3, this volume). In the context of a study of a local authority's response to black people, Ben-Tovim et al. (1986: 138) drew the conclusion that 'There is a tendency on the part of local authorities to restrict race relations initiatives to one-off, high profile measures rather than develop a sustained, mainstream orientated programme of action.'

Such projects serve an important role for purchasers and providers in that they give the latter the opportunity to say that they are doing something for black populations and thus to deflect criticism, while at the same time creating a forum in which black people's needs are addressed that is separate from mainstream services. The sources of funding for such projects are varied and include direct funding from the Department of Health under specific initiatives relating, for example, to developing services for those with serious mental illness, funding through the Mental Illness Specific Grant, joint finance initiatives involving health and social services, and the use of Urban Programme moneys by local authorities. A few projects may also be funded through collaborative arrangements with the private sector.

A characteristic of such projects is their short-term nature, with funding normally secured for a two- or three-year period. This has serious implications for the recruitment and retention of staff. Given the length of time recruitment may take, it is common for staff to be in post for only one year or so after the outset of the project. This offers very little time for staff to become familiar with the mental health services within the area and to establish mechanisms for referral and liaison with key professionals, such as community psychiatric nurses, social workers, GPs and psychiatrists. It also offers little time for them to become familiar with a local black population and to consult with it in order to help to identify what mental health needs there are and to plan services accordingly.

A further difficulty arises from the fact that these are often seen by statutory services as 'pilots', which are expected to monitor and evaluate their activity to assist the funding body to determine whether and to what extent the service will be funded at the end of the two- or three-year period. While managers from health and social services often emphasize the need for monitoring and evaluation in this context, there appears often to be little guidance as to the criteria by which this will take place and determine whether the service has been 'successful' or not. This can create a high degree of anxiety for those working in projects, who may be uncertain as to what response their report will elicit from potential funders. Given the fact that high numbers of referrals to a project are unlikely until it has been well established in a community, the two- to three-year time span suggests that an evaluation based primarily on quantitative data may fail to impress funders.

Placing emphasis on the need to evaluate the outcomes of short-term projects before taking action to address the mental health needs of black people may serve to delay action being taken within mainstream services. When pressed regarding what services are being offered to meet black populations' needs, managers are able to respond that they are running a project which is being monitored and evaluated. However, in practice it appears that often when monitoring and evaluation data are provided by project teams they receive scant attention from service providers and purchasers. One leader of a project initiated through Urban Programme moneys and subsequently inadequately funded by the health authority described her position as follows:

> I have done all this evaluation work for them but they [the health authority] don't seem to be interested in it. I want to develop the service but I don't know who to go to to discuss this. I'd like to talk about new developments but I don't know who to talk to. There is no dialogue, no coordination. I don't mind doing more evaluation work but I don't know what is the point.

A further feature of special projects directed to meeting the mental health needs of black people is that whereas mainstream services are now divided between the functions of purchaser and provider, with the former responsible for assessing health or social care needs, black workers involved in special projects may be required to assume a dual responsibility for assessing the mental health needs of local black people and developing and providing innovative services to meet these needs. As a consequence of these dual functions, mainstream purchasers and providers may delay action on the grounds that 'we need to find out more about the needs of these populations' or on the grounds that 'we need to find out what services are effective before we introduce these more widely.'

This dual responsibility may result in projects occupying a rather nebulous position with respect to purchasers and providers. One project I studied had originally been funded through a central government initiative. After a period of three years the funding for the project was 'picked up' by the local health authority, which contracted for the service and required monitoring and evaluation data on an annual basis. With a splitting of responsibilities between purchasers and providers in 1991, the service was contracted for by the NHS provider trust, which reduced funding to the organization. Part of the organization's brief was to identify the health needs of the local black populations and needs which were unmet. With the trust focusing more exclusively on the provision of services, this information was viewed as a 'purchaser concern'. The project found itself operating in an increasingly complex institutional context, in which there was some confusion as to the statutory agencies with which it should relate. Information that indicated, for example, the need for an increase in services and funding for the organization was regarded as a 'purchaser concern'. However, the formal contract was with the trust, and the purchasing health authority was reluctant to address the detailed issues relating to the organization expanding its services beyond pointing to general components in the trust's contract relating to providing 'appropriate services for black and ethnic minority groups'.

A second project was set up with a specific brief to establish innovative services for black and ethnic minority groups living in an inner-city area. It was funded initially by a three-year grant from the Department of Health under an initiative aimed at improving mental health services for those with serious and/or long-term mental health problems. The health authority agreed in principle to pick up this funding subject to a satisfactory evaluation being conducted. During the three years health service managers maintained a distance from the project and allowed highly innovative approaches to service delivery to be adopted. Project 'teams' were established to address the mental health needs of the Asian and Afro-Caribbean populations of the inner city. To make the team more 'accessible' traditional professional titles such as community psychiatric nurse and social worker were dispensed with, in favour of titles such as Asian development worker or Afro-Caribbean support worker. The team experimented with innovative approaches to management and developed consultative and steering groups which included representation from the local Race Equality Council, service users and the voluntary sector.

A wide range of initiatives were developed, involving innovative therapeutic approaches, close links to primary health care, drop-in services and relatives' support groups. Systems were developed for monitoring the teams' activities, including the collection of data on the location and source of referral and the types of therapeutic interventions. These initiatives bore fruit in terms of a rapid increase in the number of referrals to mental health services for Asian and Afro-Caribbean people. For example, in the year prior to the introduction of the project there were about six referrals of Asian people to mental health services, while in the two years following the establishment of a specialized service for Asian people there were in excess of a hundred referrals. The source of referral diversified to include significant numbers of self-referrals and referrals from a range of primary health workers, such as health visitors and district nurses.

At the end of a three-year period of central government funding the project was 'integrated' into mainstream local services. As the integration drew closer, health managers developed an interest in studying data deriving from this ongoing monitoring, particularly as it related to the levels of activity of individual workers. The process of integration involved health managers taking the following steps:

1 Stringent rules were applied to ensure that referrals were not accepted from outside the authority's catchment area (previously these rules had not been imposed in a rigid way). Those existing clients who lived outside the area were discharged to their local health authority regardless of whether there were any comparable services available to them.
2 Workers were required to adopt a 'generic' caseload. In other words, they were no longer able to specialize exclusively in addressing the needs of Afro-Caribbean or Asian populations and were required to develop a caseload which included significant numbers of white people.
3 The innovative management structures were abolished in favour of direct management and accountability to the mental health services manager.
4 Workers were required to develop closer links with local GPs and psychiatrists.

It is notable that following integration there was a marked decrease in referrals of black people to the team and in the innovative approaches to service provision.

The above examples illustrate that even in instances where the funding of projects has been 'picked up' by mainstream services it may be at a cost of reducing innovation and specialization. What is also of concern is the impact this may have on local black communities. The process of building trust between a service and local black communities is often slow and difficult as black people's experience of mental health services has often been in the context of compulsory admissions or of services which are tailored to the needs of white communities. After years of building communication and trust with local communities the experience of black users was of a service aimed at meeting their needs being cut or at best altered substantially without consultation with them.

The above comments are not intended to detract in any way from the work done by the numerous people involved in such projects. My experience indicates that workers involved in them have achieved a great deal in often very difficult circumstances. In setting various projects up as examples of good practice, the NHS Management Executive has acknowledged the value of the work being done. What I do wish to argue is that this work is often done in a specific institutional context which keeps community mental health services for black people in a marginal position in relation to mainstream mental health services.

Representations of black communities

Underpinning the articulation of community care policy is a view of community as a repository of caring networks which the skilled professional can 'tap into' in order to mobilize support for clients. Community care policy documents notoriously lack specificity with respect to what is meant by 'the community' (see also Chapter 3, this volume, for a discussion). In seeking to work within communities, health and social services have developed 'quasi-communities' deriving their boundaries from electoral wards or GP practice areas. For the purposes of developing community-based working these are defined as 'patches', 'localities' or, in the case of community psychiatry, 'sectors'. The parameters of community are thus often defined more as a result of administrative expediency than through consideration of residents' own perceptions of 'belonging'.

In the case of black minorities, communities are represented as transcending these localized boundaries. Asian and Afro-Caribbean communities are frequently construed as though they were relatively homogeneous entities about whom generalized statements can be made regarding their mental health needs. Such a view has been supported by anthropological and sociological writing on ethnic minorities, which presents communities not only as homogeneous but as having certain essential characteristics. The Durkheimian notion of 'altruistic solidarity' explicitly underpins a view of Asian communities presented by John Rex (1982).

Such a view has also been supported in the writings of anthropologists who have studied ethnic minority communities in Britain. In this context both Asians and Afro-Caribbeans have been characterized as maintaining strict boundaries between their communities and those of the white British. Robinson (1986: 84), for example, has observed that

> It seems that Indian and Pakistani migrants to Britain not only avoid contact with the indigenous population, but also minimise the need for interaction with other Asians whom they feel to be members of out-groups (on whatever criteria appear appropriate at the time). They employ similar strategies for both purposes and these strategies produce similar spatial, social, and institutional outcomes.

The idea of the 'boundary', deriving from Barth's work on ethnic groups, has been highly influential in anthropological writing on ethnic groups in Britain (Barth 1969). The anthropologist Roger Ballard has argued that within these boundaries ethnic groups cultures may be seen as 'coherent systems' or 'systematic totalities' (Ballard 1979). In writing about the role of social workers in relation to these groups Ballard compares the social work experience of otherness in this context to that of Alice as she passes through the looking glass: 'once across the ethnic [boundary] . . . they can never be quite sure whether things really mean what they seem to, or rather what they would have done had the rules of the more normal and familiar world continued to apply' (Ballard 1979: 149). Here black people's cultures and communities are, to use Hall's (1992: 255) expression, 'fixed and naturalized' in a context in which the difference between 'belongingness and otherness' is stressed. Communities are represented as fixed and immutable entities within which the more exotic aspects of cultures are stressed.

Within the context of health and social service responses to the perceived mental health needs of black people, the terms 'Afro-Caribbean' and 'Asian' are used as though they denote relatively homogeneous communities about whom generalized statements can be made. As such they constitute what Werbner (1991: 115) has characterized as a 'fictive unity, analogous in many respects to a territorial community'. Werbner has argued that the construction of such communities by policy-makers derives from notions of administrative equity according to which 'there can only be one community centre, one service for the aged, or one battered wives refuge for each specified ethnic group' (Werbner 1991: 115). In other words, in a context in which resources are limited, local government or health authorities cannot subdivide resources among smaller groupings, such as Gujarati-speaking Hindus or Rastafarians. The implication here is that those developing policy or delivering services may be aware of the multiplicity of communities which exist under the broad categories 'Afro-Caribbean' or 'Asian', but owing to limited resources being available have to treat these as corporate unities.

However, this argument ignores the fact that in the minds of policy-makers and those delivering services in the mental health sphere and in other areas of health and social service activity, the categories Asian or Afro-Caribbean are frequently regarded as representing homogeneous communities with particular characteristics. In the context of the provision of mental health services, representations are constitutive and may be regarded as functioning at three levels. The first of these may be referred to as the 'institutional level', at which decisions are taken regarding the funding and development of services for black people. Second, there is the 'service level', by which I refer to the organization of services within a particular locality. Third, there is the 'treatment level', that is the level at which there is interaction between black people and mental health professionals.

Institutional level

Decisions regarding the funding and development of mental health services for black people may be taken in a wide variety of contexts and using a range of funding mechanisms. Local government initiatives may be derived through joint finance, the Urban Programme or other sources. The health service may derive money through special one-off initiatives, from joint finance or the mental illness specific grant. Typically, funds will be allocated to specific initiatives by a group of representatives of different agencies involved in the provision of services to people with mental health problems. Such groups may not include black community representatives and the representatives of the various agencies may have no particular knowledge of, or interest in, services for black people. In this context generalized 'common sense assumptions' regarding the mental health needs of black people may be made, and the extent to which proposed projects accord with these will influence decision-making. For example, initiatives relating to community provision for Asian women suffering from depression or for Afro-Caribbean men with severe mental health problems may accord with 'common sense assumptions' and be considered a 'good idea' without specific consideration being given to the local needs of black people and their expression of these needs.

Service level

At the level at which local services are organized and delivered, what I refer to as the 'service level', special projects and specific initiatives relating to black people are established in a broader context of statutory service provision. In order for such services to function effectively they have to interact constantly with key professionals in the locality, such as GPs, social workers and community psychiatric nurses. Given the crucial role GPs play as gate-keepers to mental health services, the extent to which referrals will be received depends on the GPs' capacity to diagnose mental health problems accurately. As indicated above, there is some evidence to suggest that GPs may carry negative stereotypes with respect to their black patients. Such stereotypes are apparent in literature advising GPs on the psychiatric problems faced by Asians, who are described as presenting with trivial complaints and as somatizing psychological problems.

If black workers exist only at the margins of mental health services they will be unable to influence mainstream service and challenge misleading stereotypes. While GPs and other professionals may welcome the prospect of having a local specialist service to which they can refer black patients, the majority of black people will continue to be dependent upon mainstream community mental health services and it is within this context that the main challenge for change exists.

Treatment level

In what I have termed the 'treatment level' within which black people come face to face with service providers, the idea that black people live in relatively homogeneous and supportive communities may have direct bearing on the services they receive. In this context black people may be characterized as being able to 'look after their own', while the negative effects of racism are not addressed. The perception that Asians, for example, live in supportive communities may undermine the potential for professionals to treat black people on an individual basis and to take into account the reality of their particular circumstances (see Chapters 4 and 5, this volume). As noted above, Fernando (1988: 184) has argued for a more individualistic approach to treatment, which moves away from generalized and stereotypical views to a view that stresses the 'importance of the overall culture of each individual and the social pressures which influence the person's life'. The potential dangers of adopting generalized and stereotypical views in treatment are illustrated by the following excerpt from a case study.

HK was a 56-year-old Gujarati Hindu man. In 1972 he and his family were expelled from Uganda, where he had had a steady job. Following his migration, his marital situation deteriorated and he began to feel depressed. He attributed his depression to the fact that he could not find a job in England. He increasingly spent more and more time away from his wife and children, and after a violent domestic incident was admitted into a psychiatric hospital. Following this he was admitted to hospital on several other occasions and was diagnosed as suffering from schizophrenia. In his time outside hospital he lived in a bedsit in a part of the city where there was a large Afro-Caribbean population. He had very little to do with local Asians, as he felt many of them knew about his past and held him in low esteem. As the community care policy developed HK was assigned a social worker and attempts were made to reduce his hospital admissions by improving the level of social support. The social worker felt that it would be helpful for HK to be more closely integrated with his 'own' community, and to this end encouraged him to attend an Asian day centre. He was not keen on the day centre (which was attended primarily by Punjabi-speaking women) and asked to join an Afro-Caribbean mental health group. This group was attended by people he knew, some of whom had on occasions been helpful to him. His request was granted and he became a regular member and felt that he benefited from the group a great deal.

The above case study illustrates some of the key issues with respect to the development of community care for black people. The idea that an ascribed identity as 'Asian' or 'Afro-Caribbean' is a sufficient basis for assuming the existence of a network, based on principles of a form of 'altruistic solidarity', follows a range of fallacious and misleading stereotypes which fail to take account of the complexities of black cultures and black identity. As Brah has observed, understanding of black people in Britain must move beyond the crude essentialism implicit in multicultural approaches. Identity is not a 'fixed core', but shifts in a context in which 'cultural identities are simultaneously cultures in process' (Brah 1992: 143). Within this context, taken-for-granted 'common sense assumptions' regarding black people's allegiances and networks must be scrutinized and challenged if effective and responsive community care is to be developed.

I have suggested that constitutive representations operate at all three levels identified above. They are not confined simply to contexts in which black people receive treatment but may be instrumental in determining the very contexts in which mental health care is received. A description of the approaches to treatment adopted within projects, such as that undertaken by the Mental Health Task Force (Department of Health 1994), is an inadequate reflection of the response of mental health services to black people. I suggest that two ingredients are missing. First, the shifting of attention to 'special' projects deflects from consideration of attitudes within mainstream services, the context in which most black people continue to receive mental health care. As Fernando (1988) has observed, for issues of institutional racism to be addressed requires a concerted commitment within key professions to addressing structural inequalities. Second, the broader contexts in which projects operate should be examined, specifically their marginal and persistently insecure position in relation to mainstream services.

Conclusion

In the development of community care for black people with mental health problems, there have been a number of initiatives, often in the form of short-term projects. While the work of these projects is often exemplary, they exist in institutional contexts in which black people's needs are marginalized. Projects may act as a 'buffer', deflecting demands for change in mainstream mental health services. While projects may introduce mechanisms for consultation with black people, this consultation may only take place on the periphery.

Within services crude stereotypes and generalizations regarding the mental health needs of black people and black communities persist; for example, that black people can 'look after their own' and live within supportive networks.

There is an urgent need for service providers to address the complexities of the so-called communities they serve and to respond to black service users' individual experiences. While the development of quasi-markets in health and social care ostensibly provides opportunities, attention must be given to the training and experience of care managers and key workers involved in the care programme approach if we are to avoid familiar racist stereotypes and practices simply being reproduced, albeit in a new institutional context.

Annotated bibliography

Littlewood, R. and Lipsedge, M. (1989) *Aliens and Alienists: Ethnic Minorities and Psychiatry*. London: Unwin Hyman.
This book offers a scholarly and comprehensive examination of the relationship between psychiatry and ethnic minority groups in Britain. The authors, who are both psychiatrists, use material from case histories to illustrate issues which may arise at the interface between psychiatrists and service users from black and ethnic minority groups. A historical perspective is provided on the development of racist thinking within psychiatry, and the authors draw on a wide range of cross-cultural research in developing their arguments. The book contains an extensive bibliography.

Fernando, S. (1988) *Race and Culture in Psychiatry*. London: Croom Helm.
Fernando's book is more tightly focused and polemical than the above and concentrates on developing a sustained critique of racism in psychiatry. He traces the

development of racist thinking from the 19th century to its manifestation in the theory and practice of psychiatry in the present day. Fernando's emphasis is on developing an agenda for action and he offers practical ideas on the ways in which psychiatry could address racism.

Werbner, P. and Anwar, M. (eds) (1991) *Black and Ethnic Leadership – the Cultural Dimensions of Political Action.* London: Routledge.

This book contains a number of highly informative essays on race and ethnicity in present-day Britain. It has the merit of addressing directly complex issues relating to culture and community and exploring the political contexts in which cultures and identities are formed. While specific consideration of mental health policy and practice falls outside the scope of the book, it contains a number of valuable insights into the way in which agencies within the public sector construct and respond to the perceived needs of black and ethnic minority 'communities', which are of considerable relevance to the mental health field.

8

Social security, community care – and 'race': the marginal dimension

Gary Craig and Dhanwant K. Rai

Introduction

This chapter reviews the contribution of social security benefits to the alleviation of poverty among ethnic minority communities, both as cash benefits in their own right (i.e. to replace or supplement income) and as a substitute for or supplement to care services. We focus in particular on the role of research in shaping policy. The structure of the chapter is as follows. First, we review, briefly, existing evidence about the growth of poverty among ethnic minority communities. We then discuss the place of cash benefits within the development of community care programmes. Next we examine the (limited) evidence about ethnic minority communities' experience of the social security system in general, and of 'cash-for-care' benefits in particular. We conclude that we know very little about the experience of black and ethnic minority communities, in relation either to social security provision or, more specifically, to their use of 'cash-for-care' benefits.

Social policy as an academic discipline, as opposed to sociology, has not always engaged with issues of 'race' and racism. In sociology, as Saggar (1993: 35) notes, 'even the most casual observer of the sociology of contemporary Britain cannot have failed to notice the extent to which challenging questions regarding British multi-racial society have been taken on in many of the leading textbooks.' The central concerns of social policy – social security and personal social services particularly in this context, but also housing, health and education – absorb enormous sums of public expenditure. Social security alone accounts for an annual outturn of £100 billion (or about one-eighth of annual GDP). They are, correspondingly, the subjects of extensive research activity.

While there is relevant research literature on housing, health and education, social security research fails to recognize the existence of Britain's minority ethnic communities (Dutt and Ahmad 1990). To take just two examples from different contributions to social policy debate: first, a recent wide-ranging reader on ethnicity, inequalities, opportunities and policies contained only one reference to social security benefits and that to an article then six years old (Braham *et al.* 1992); second, an otherwise comprehensive account of models of benefit take-up had effectively nothing to say on the subject of 'race' in relation either to past or future research (Craig, P. 1991).

In relation to the policy process, it is clear that institutional and individual racism affect the ways in which cash benefits are structured and delivered. However, we also believe that part of the problem lies in current research practice on social security, which effectively continues to marginalize 'race' as a fundamental organizing concept in the commissioning, design, fieldwork and analysis and interpretation of data. In the final section of this chapter, therefore, we consider the limitations of current approaches to locating a 'race' dimension within social policy research. We do so, with Farrar (1992: 54–5) on the assumption that 'race issues cannot be discussed neutrally . . . [or] . . . neatly packaged within the academic text . . . [and that] . . . these issues should be analysed not simply for their intrinsic interest but in order to influence events.'

Poverty: the black experience[1]

Between 1977 and 1991, the number of people living in poverty, defined as less than half average income, rose from three to eleven million (DSS 1993a), with the poorest tenth of the population no better off than in 1967, while the richest 5 per cent had increases of almost 60 per cent in income since 1979 alone (Jenkins 1994). At the same time, measures which have led to increasingly restricted eligibility for many benefits and the 'restructuring' of benefit provision have been introduced. These have included: the replacement of certain benefits by others of more limited scope and generosity; further emphases on means-tested and discretionary benefits within the state sector and on private income-replacement provision outside it; and a reduction in the real value of certain key benefits. These developments have all been accompanied by highly publicized allegations of fraud and inappropriate claiming. Taken together, these processes reduce the role of social security to a creaking 'last-resort safety net' through which increasing numbers of claimants are wholly or partially slipping. Within this dismal general context, the ability of the social security system to maintain ethnic minority households at reasonable income levels must be seriously questioned. This is all the more unacceptable in the light of widespread and long-standing allegations against the system of, at best, indifference to the needs of ethnic minority communities and, at worst, racism (see below).

Remarkably, neither the DSS nor any of the agencies (of the DSS) created under the Next Steps 'revolution' (Ditch 1993) have in place a credible ethnic monitoring system. The agencies continue to operate, as the DSS did before them, a system of benefits delivery unshaped by a coherent strategy of racial equality, whose 'colour-blindness' is mitigated only by certain provisions at the margins. As a result, targeted and large-scale research (whatever its other limitations) funded by the DSS, which aims to explore the specific experience of ethnic minority communities, is virtually impossible to execute. It is still not unusual for relatively well funded and otherwise experienced research teams to go into the field, for example, not knowing the ethnic origin of respondents, not being able to draw a sample based on ethnic origin and having little idea as to whether translation or interpretation facilities are necessary or whether the design of research instruments incorporates an appropriate understanding of the cultural and social contexts of all respondents. Similarly, the official DSS annual review of data (DSS 1993b) provides no analysis based on ethnic origin. Thus we may find within it a gender-based analysis of the length of spells on sickness benefit, for example, or the age distribution of households in receipt of community charge benefit, but not the ethnic origin of claimants or other household members in either case.

The continuing opposition of successive Secretaries of State to ethnic monitoring precludes much useful 'race'-related social security research from being undertaken. Given the difficulties to date in introducing a single, widely accepted 'ethnic' question within the Census, the prognosis is not encouraging for those wishing to explore and act on issues to do with the impact of 'race' on the delivery and receipt of social security benefits. Nor is the position in relation to the delivery of care services much better: a fairly recent NISW (1991) report observes that very few local authority social services departments have effective systems in place for ethnic monitoring and record-keeping.

This is alarming because, as a review of ethnic minority communities' experience of poverty demonstrates, there are numerous structural factors which increase the likelihood of their experiencing poverty compared with the population as a whole (Amin and Oppenheim 1992). These include the higher than average, and increasing, unemployment levels of ethnic minorities, largely as a result of: the decline of the older industrial sectors and the international restructuring of capital; the racist way in which people are selected for jobs or made redundant (TUC 1994), despite, as the 1991 Census shows, ethnic minorities now having a higher rate of attainment of advanced educational qualifications than their white counterparts (Ouseley 1995); the greater likelihood of working in low-paid jobs; and a more limited access to good health care and adequate housing conditions.

In this situation, it should fall to the social security system to provide a more general compensatory mechanism, at least in terms of the maintenance of adequate income levels, but also to pay specific attention to the needs of those at greatest risk. However, Amin and Oppenheim

(1992) identify a further set of factors which, far from allowing the social security system to achieve this compensatory function, effectively undermine its ability so to do. The most significant of these are the following. First, the emphasis within contributory schemes (such as still exist) on non-interruptions of contributions militates against those who cannot maintain steady contributions because of irregular earnings, short working lives in the UK and absences abroad (Patel 1990). Second, the consequent enforced reliance of such groups on means-tested benefits, which are notorious for low take-up levels resulting from limited knowledge of benefits and individual or structural racism, creates significant blockages to accessing benefits. For example, take-up of free dental care for ethnic minority claimants was recently estimated at 44 per cent, whereas for white claimants it was 62 per cent (still very low). Third, they experience direct and indirect discrimination through conditions placed on 'people from abroad', such as sponsorship, residence and 'public funds' tests. For example, eligibility for severe disablement allowance requires residence in the UK for ten of the twenty years prior to a claim, and claiming of benefits such as income support and family credit is defined as 'having recourse to public funds'. Finally, many experience discrimination and racism in the delivery of social security benefits, including the failure to provide adequate translation and interpretation services. For example, Youth Training Schemes, membership of which is a condition for receipt of Income Support (IS) between the ages of 16 and 18, frequently fail adequately to cater for the cultural and religious needs of young Asian women (Craig, G. 1991). The position of women from ethnic minority communities is particularly precarious in relation to eligibility and access to social security benefits (Cook and Watt 1992).

Why are cash benefits important in a discussion of community care?[2]

Debates about community care have focused, in relation to questions of finance, largely on questions of overall resources and only more recently on the extent to which carers and users of care services might be willing or able to contribute to the costs of care. There has been little discussion of the role of social security (and other sources of cash help) in meeting individual care needs. However, with pressures on local government finances and central government controls over targeted resources for community care through the annual 'settlement' with local government, local authority social services departments are, through the imposition of charging systems and other means, increasingly becoming concerned with 'cash for care' issues. As a result, the traditional boundary between the central government 'cash' (social security) role and the local government 'care' (provision of services) role is becoming blurred.

A number of contradictions are now beginning to emerge out of the rhetoric of community care legislation and policy statements. Choice, for care users, appears to be at the heart of official community care policy (Department of Health 1991). In reality, however, current policy lays stress upon the provision of services rather than cash, as has recently been evidenced by government reluctance to legislate for the widespread provision of direct cash payments to disabled care users and by the effective demise of the Independent Living Fund (Kestenbaum 1992). As a result, the 'choice' which, as the independent living movement has so powerfully argued, would offer care users individual (and cultural) sensitivity in developing personal care plans, is severely constrained (Barnes 1995).

Similarly, the Griffiths Report, the Community Care White Paper, the 1990 NHS and Community Care Act and subsequent government policy guidance have all apparently attached importance to promoting the involvement of care users in the planning and delivery of services. Despite a national 'User Task Force' being set up (criticized by some user groups for its under-resourcing and exclusiveness) and sporadic indications of good practice at a local level, the general picture remains bleak. A combination of constraints on resources and the maintenance of traditional 'top-down' modes of service delivery effectively excludes all but the most determined user groups from participation in the planning and delivery of care services (Craig 1993). These constraints create even greater barriers to those from ethnic minority communities.

At an individual level, the same factors, together with the development of private care markets, but only for those with substantial personal resources, confront most care users with the likelihood of an increasingly residualized care service that offers little effective choice. As Knapp (1989: 245) points out, '"residualisation" of the poor may be the price of freedom of choice for the rich.' Without state direction or intervention, there is little evidence that market mechanisms alone are likely to meet the needs of small, unpopular or poor groups of service users, or of those whose needs may be more difficult to identify or meet.

In this context, the needs of poor ethnic minority care users are likely to be marginal to most care provision (Craig 1992a, b). The Community Care White Paper did acknowledge that 'people from different cultural backgrounds have particular care needs and problems' (Department of Health 1989). However, the NHS and Community Care Act itself made no explicit reference to ethnic minority communities. Chapters elsewhere in this book reflect on the uneven but generally low level of activity which has been directed to date at the needs of ethnic minorities (Craig 1993). It may be theoretically accurate to say that because 'community care policy focuses on vulnerable groups, its implications for the black populations require close scrutiny' (Walker and Ahmad 1994: 52). The reality, however, is that there is little understanding of their needs or appropriate provision, even by the generally under-developed standards of community care provision nation-wide (IRR 1993). This is even more the case when we consider 'cash for care' issues.

Black and minority ethnic experience of social security

Five and a half per cent of the British population (or roughly three million people) are members of minority ethnic communities, including 1.6 per cent black (including Afro-Caribbean, black African and black 'other'), 2.7 per cent South Asian (mainly Indian, Bangladeshi and Pakistani) and 1.2 per cent Chinese and 'others'. This population lives mainly in or near the large English cities (Owen 1993). For example, 14 per cent of the ethnic minority population lives in the West Midlands (compared with 9 per cent of the Great Britain white population), with other major concentrations in the West Yorkshire, London and Greater Manchester areas (see also Chapter 4, this volume). Almost two-thirds of all ethnic minority communities live in areas characterized by traditional manufacturing industry and in parts of central and inner London (Owen 1993: 8), areas where, as noted earlier, there has been a significant restructuring of local employment opportunities leading to unemployment, under-employment or low-waged employment. Data from Labour Force surveys show that compared with a 'white' unemployment rate of 7 per cent in 1989–90, the corresponding rate for African-Caribbeans was 14 per cent, for Pakistanis 22 per cent and for Bangladeshis 25 per cent. By 1993, the position had deteriorated: compared with an unemployment rate of 5 per cent among the white population, the rates were 25 per cent for black populations and 30 per cent for Pakistanis and Bangladeshis (Sly 1994).

There are also significant variations by age and gender: for example, the peak unemployment rate for Pakistanis is in the age range 16–24, whereas for Bangladeshis it is in the 45–64 range (Jones 1993). An analysis of ethnicity and gender in the West Midlands labour force (Andersen 1993), based on the 1991 Census, suggests that the unemployment rate for economically active Pakistani females was 42.5 per cent compared with 7.5 per cent for white females.

The household and age structures of different ethnic minority groups are diverse and this also has implications for the structure and use of different social security benefits. Thus, for example, about 60 per cent of South Asian families comprised couples with children, twice the rate for white and black families (Owen 1993). On the other hand, proportionately about four times as many black families comprise lone parents as white or South Asian families, and this may have implications for the assumptions underpinning the Child Support Act.

At the other end of the age spectrum, although one-sixth of the white UK population was aged 65 and over in 1988, the ethnic minority groups with the highest proportion over the age of 65 years were the Indian and African-Caribbean groups, at only 3 per cent (FPSC 1991). While there is some evidence that access to informal carers is markedly greater among some ethnic minority groups than in the UK population as a whole (Wilmott 1986), there are grounds for concern regarding access to income for ethnic minority elders. Given their shorter employment careers, while in the UK, and greater likelihood of unemployment and low pay, it is likely that ethnic minority pensioners will both have reduced access to and levels of occupational and state pensions, and other contributory benefits. As a result, their income is likely to be lower in general than that of their white counterparts (Jolley 1988).

Similarly, gender has an important impact on an individual's relationship to the social security system and the interrelationship of gender and 'race' needs to be explored far more fully than has hitherto been the case. Female economic activity rates are higher for Afro-Caribbean women than for women in general and almost four times as high as those for South Asian women. However, Afro-Caribbean economically active women are only slightly more likely to be working full-time than women of South Asian origin, and both groups are far more likely to be working full-time than white women. Afro-Caribbean households are overall far more likely to be dependent on just a woman's wage than white households, but because of what Lister (1992) describes as the 'gender-blind' nature of the poverty statistics, it is not easy to establish the extent to which the social security system responds adequately to the differing economic and social situations of ethnic minority families. Lister's review of the literature indicates that ethnic minority women are over-represented among the low paid and the unemployed and that women in general are more vulnerable to poverty than men. Although social security statistics do not provide consistent gender-based analyses, it is clear that women's access to contributory benefits is much lower than men's. Yet again, however, although take-up of some pre-pension age benefits (particularly family credit, severe disablement allowance and invalid care allowance) is dominated by women, we know virtually nothing beyond the anecdotal about the extent to which the dimension of 'race' affects patterns of take-up of such benefits, or the impact of failure to take up such benefits on the quality of life of ethnic minority families.

In general, for those ethnic minority groups whose overall demographic profile is 'younger' than that of the British population as a whole, dependence on income-replacement social security benefits will be higher than that of the general population. The key point, however, for all ethnic minority groups is that dependence on certain kinds of social security benefits (and on means-tested benefits in particular) is likely to be higher than in the population as a whole. Issues of access to, knowledge of, and delivery of benefits are therefore more significant. What, then, do we know about ethnic minority communities' experience of the social security system? The most startling observation to be made is that, prior to a recent small-scale research project funded by the DSS (Bloch 1993), there is little evidence that the Department of Social Security has taken this issue at all seriously. Indeed, in one early evaluation of social security administration and delivery, the (then) DHSS impeded the publication of findings which revealed a significant level of overt and indirect racism among DHSS officials (Cooper 1984). Although the DSS appears rather more open now to discussion about the needs of ethnic minorities, the level of official disinterest, during the 1980s and early 1990s, is in marked contrast to the attention paid to the needs of ethnic minority communities in some other areas of social policy, such as what Harrison (1993: 2) refers to as the 'startling development towards ethnic pluralism . . . in the social housing field.' Prior to Bloch's (1993) study, it was left almost entirely to individual academics and to the voluntary sector to raise even limited questions about the ethnic minority communities' access to social security and the appropriateness of the DSS's responses.

Before the mid-1980s, there was little to suggest that issues to do with ethnic minority access to social security were regarded as a suitable focus for social research at all. The third Policy Studies Institute survey into 'the circumstances of the British black population' (Brown 1985), covering the question of household income within a brief section on 'support and care', noted the relatively very small proportion of pensioner-only households and the varying – but generally higher – levels of dependence on different key social security benefits (especially unemployment benefit, child benefit and supplementary benefit) compared with the white population.

Respondents to this study were asked in a subsidiary question if they believed people of 'Asian/West Indian' origin were treated the same, better or worse than white people by social security offices. This revealed a clear divide between the beliefs of white respondents (where males responded 65 per cent 'the same', 20 per cent 'better' and 5 per cent 'worse') and those of ethnic minority male respondents (for Afro-Caribbeans, the corresponding figures were 46 per cent, 2 per cent and 24 per cent). The generally low level of interest in and knowledge of 'race' issues in relation to social security was also reflected in a bibliography published at the time (Gordon and Klug 1984). Compared with sixty-six entries under 'Citizenship and Nationality' (itself part of a very extensive section on immigration and nationality), there were only fourteen entries under 'welfare rights' and no separate 'social security' section at all, although there were forty-seven entries under 'social services'.

Recent research findings

From the mid-1980s, research into the experience of ethnic minority claimants appears to fall into three broad categories in terms of the auspices of the study: small-scale, sometimes anecdotal, research based on the work of local community organizations (e.g. Tarpey 1984; Mahtani 1992); reports analysing wider ranging sources of information on specific 'race'-related issues to do with social security benefits, delivery and administration (e.g. Gordon and Newnham 1985; NACAB 1991; Amin and Oppenheim 1992); and more general research accounts (based on either small-scale qualitative or large-scale survey research) of social security issues, which include some specific focus. We briefly review the findings of some of these key reports below.

An innovatory report published by the Child Poverty Action Group reviewed evidence relating to racism in the social security system (Gordon and Newnham 1985). As the report observed, 'little has been done to highlight the plight of one particular group of welfare claimants – black people – who . . . are second-class claimants'; the report commented that the absence of research was 'surprising'. Where the position of black people as claimants was examined, the 'problem' was defined as 'one of language and culture – for example, the absence of information translated into minority languages' (Gordon and Newnham 1985). This was, the authors concluded, certainly one problem but only a part of the 'racism which permeates the whole social security system'.

Much of this report focuses on the connections between social security benefit entitlement and issues of nationality and the control of immigration, which, as Walker and Ahmad (1994) observe, led to black people being fearful of making claims to which they are fully entitled (see also Skellington 1992). The report also reviewed the extent of institutional and individual racism within the social security system. By the time of its publication, the DHSS was in the process of translating key leaflets into the major Asian languages, although it had been less than assiduous in ensuring their effective distribution. It had also, at that time, only two offices where interpreters were officially employed 'in cases of special difficulty', relying instead in the remainder of its over 400 offices on claimants' 'younger family members and friends' to undertake interpretation.

The 1986 Social Security Act, and after

A major impetus for re-examining the ethnic minority experience of social security came from the 1986 Social Security Act, with its increased emphasis on discretionary and means-tested benefits (notably the Social Fund); although, as we have seen, the Act itself did not directly address this question of ethnic minority experience. One early, largely descriptive, commentary on the Social Fund in practice (Craig 1989) reflected the concern that discretion based on notions of deserts would lead to discrimination against ethnic minority claimants. Such evidence as was available was anecdotal and ambiguous on this question (Becker and Silburn 1990).

Discretion has historically had an important place within the social security system. Although the scope of discretion may deliberately give the appearance of generosity, the practice of discretion at a local level may deny this (Adler and Asquith 1981). Discretion allows for political adjustments in the face of uncertain situations and thus provides a mechanism both for the rationing of benefits and for the classification of claimants in a way which is obscure but which works to the disadvantage of those groups regarded by the state as the 'undeserving' poor (Craig 1992b). Given the minority ethnic people's often contested status as citizens and nationals it has not been difficult for politicians concerned to seek to limit expenditure by tacitly characterizing ethnic minority claimants as 'undeserving' and 'scroungers' (Gordon and Newnham 1985; see also Chapter 2, this volume). The impact of general ideological attacks on so-called 'undeserving' claimants is particularly significant for members of ethnic minorities, given their high physical visibility because of skin colour.

Despite widespread concern about the impact of this increased reliance on discretion, researchers conducting the DSS-funded official evaluation of the social fund, based on an otherwise creative mix of qualitative and quantitative methodologies, were not required to place any special emphasis on the needs of ethnic minority claimants; nor consequently were they able to offer, in the final report, any separate 'race'-based assessment of the fund's impact (Huby and Dix 1992). The only indication of a 'race' dimension in the study is a technical note stating that nine potential respondents out of 3553 sample addresses were discarded because of 'language problems.' Cohen et al. (1992) evaluated the more general impact of the 1986 Act, using semi-structured questionnaires and including within the two studies brought together in their report a significant sub-sample of Pakistani claimants, interviewed in their preferred language by Pakistani interviewers. Both studies reported institutional racism – for example, as a result of inappropriate assumptions about family and community life, which were reflected in the day-to-day operation of the social fund – and incidences of individual racism within local DSS offices.

Additionally, the study carried out in Bradford (where the restructuring of the textile industry had led to a rapid increase in unemployment among the local Bangladeshi and Pakistani communities) suggested that the DSS had made little progress even in the provision of translation and interpretation facilities. The Westfield House office, serving the Pakistani community in particular (one of the two offices referred to in Gordon and Newnham's report), had a full-time interpretation service (for Urdu and Punjabi) but 'the interpreter only wrote in English and translation into other written languages had to be carried out at another office' (Gordon and Newnham 1985: 52). In 1989, the Secretary of State had noted, in response to a written question on 'measures undertaken by the DSS to assist ethnic minorities in claiming benefits', that there were only five measures then in place: (a) publication in seven languages other than English of the key leaflet 'Which benefit?'; (b) a free Urdu and Punjabi telephone helpline; (c) training courses for local office staff servicing multiracial communities; (d) an interpreter and liaison service in Bradford; and (e) signs and posters in local offices and public areas (Hansard 21 February 1989: col. 593). This DSS response, however, was not only limited in terms of the remit of the department itself; it also failed to address the impact of wider structural processes of discrimination.

Mahtani's (1992) Sheffield-based study is typical of a number of small-scale investigations into wider policy issues facing local ethnic minority communities. This examined problems of credit and debt within a local Pakistani community, again through semi-structured interviews. The study revealed a familiar contradiction: that respondents were in greater poverty and generally greater need, facing increased levels of debt compared with the population at large, yet made relatively low use of debt advice services. Here, the findings, though also familiar, were not largely directed at the DSS but at the local advice networks: 'reasons advanced for not using advice services included the difficulty of language, a lack of awareness of where to seek advice, and the feeling that an adviser from a different background would not understand the Pakistani culture nor the implications of their advice' (Mahtani 1992: 37). Key recommendations were for specialist debt advice workers, better translation and publicity provision, and better training and information for all parties involved in local debt and credit work.

The report that perhaps provoked the most extensive response from the DSS to date is *Barriers to Benefit* (NACAB 1991). The Citizens Advice Bureau (CAB) service had increasingly dealt with queries from ethnic minority users during the 1980s, recruiting black and Asian advisers in response to this trend, and social security was one of its two major ongoing areas of advice work (accounting for about 1.8 million or 24 per cent of all enquiries in 1992–3). NACAB had occasionally reported on issues related to the needs of ethnic minorities (NACAB 1984; Cowell and Owen 1985; GLCAB 1986), but this report represented its first major national public statement. It was based on an analysis of a substantial number of cases focused on defined topics and culled from the information returns from almost 100 local bureaux.

The report's most substantial conclusions were that racism was common in the social security system and that 'black clients and clients who speak or write no or little English are not receiving full entitlement to benefit and their encounters with the social security system are often distressing and humiliating'. (NACAB 1991: 2). This arises, the NACAB report concluded, because the DSS 'refuses to accept responsibility for people who do not understand DSS communications in English'. As a result, NACAB recommended that the DSS should give a clear commitment to racial equality, and to improving its performance in terms of different language forms, translation and interpretation facilities, the images used in publicity material and training and support for those working with ethnic minority claimants: a distressingly familiar checklist.

One significant outcome of the NACAB report was the agreement of the DSS to establish liaison arrangements with NACAB in order to monitor developments. By March 1993, NACAB's informal soundings with local bureaux suggested that 'there had been good local initiatives in some areas but that overall there was still a long way to go.' By that time, however, the Benefits Agency had been established to administer benefit delivery and had committed itself, in writing, to 'providing services fairly and impartially, never discriminating on any grounds including those of race,

sex, religion or disability.' A further indirect outcome of the pressure generated by NACAB's work was that the DSS commissioned a small study,
completed in 1993, on the information needs of ethnic minority communities (Bloch 1993).

Bloch's study mainly comprises 101 'semi-structured interviews with
customers and potential customers from six linguistic groups in six urban
locations in England' (Bloch 1993: 4). The groups chosen were representative of different lengths of residence, religious affiliations and first languages.
Respondents were recruited in areas of high residential concentration of
the case study groups by systematic door-knocking in selected streets, supplemented by recruitment through community contacts. Significantly, when
asked what their most useful source of information had been about social
security provision, respondents most often mentioned local advice workers
and friends or relatives. The recommendations arising from the study
included suggestions that local offices of the Benefits Agency 'develop a
deeper understanding of the communities they serve', consult with local
community groups, hold benefits surgeries, improve translation and interpretation facilities and recruit more staff from ethnic minorities. It also
recommended that further research be undertaken, particularly through a
large-scale survey 'to obtain more detailed and statistically representative
data' (Bloch 1993: xiii) about claiming patterns.

Cash for care: the missing 'race' perspective

The major social security benefits relevant to this discussion are Income
Support, the key means-tested income maintenance benefit, and its associated premiums, together with the Social Fund; non-means-tested/extra
costs benefits such as Attendance Allowance (AA), Disability Living Allowance (DLA), Invalid Care Allowance (ICA), Invalidity Benefit (now replaced by a new, more restricted benefit, Incapacity Benefit) and Severe
Disablement Allowance; and contributory benefits such as retirement pensions and sickness and unemployment benefits. Other significant sources of
cash-for-care help include the Family Fund and the (now largely defunct)
Independent Living Fund. Here we limit the discussion to those benefits
which are more explicitly care-related.

As noted earlier, the literature on the 'race' dimension of 'cash for care'
issues is sparse. An extensive literature review of 'community care in a
multi-racial Britain' (Atkin and Rollings 1993a: 17) contains only one
reference to social security benefits within its index, and a short section
on the financial burdens of care, which notes that 'black people ... are
further disadvantaged because their incomes are likely to be lower than
those of white people' (p. 17), refers to only six published sources. One
database does exist as a result of the large-scale surveys of disablement
by the Office of Population Censuses and Statistics, commissioned by the
DHSS to inform its review of disability benefits. These surveys (OPCS 1988)
found that the rates of disability for 'Asians' and 'West Indians' were 12.6

and 15.1 per cent respectively, compared with 13.7 per cent for 'whites'. This database does not, however, appear to have been further utilized to explore benefit issues for ethnic minority communities; nor have the DSS's better funded explorations of 'cash for care' issues (McLaughlin 1991) had an explicit 'race' dimension.

One small-scale survey (MacFarland *et al.* 1989) indicates how even issues of access to care benefits become 'overlooked' within ethnic minority communities. This qualitative study in Glasgow asked Asian respondents about problems experienced in relation to a range of services, activities and issues. Although none of the sixty respondents identified welfare rights as a problem area, only 28 per cent of the sample mentioned the DHSS as a useful source of help and considerably fewer knew of other potential places to seek advice (such as the social services department and the Race Equality Council). The need for a 'major welfare rights and benefit campaign, utilising material in the main community languages, thus emerged very strongly' (MacFarland *et al.* 1989: 411). The issue, the researchers noted, was not low levels of need but 'barriers of awareness and communication'.

The difficulties of surmounting these 'barriers' are exemplified in another small-scale survey (Figgess *et al.* 1993) This was aimed at encouraging the development of effective services for people with disabilities in Oldham. The postal survey, sent to a sample of those in receipt of selected disability benefits (found through the council's Housing Benefit recipient list), achieved a good overall response rate but a very low representation (4 per cent of all respondents) from ethnic minority communities. The survey, which reviewed use of services, availability of carers and take-up of benefits, was not able to offer suggestions about how to improve provision for ethnic minority communities, although a number of respondents suggested the need for leaflets in languages other than English (see also Barker 1984; Confederation of Indian Organisations 1987; ADAPT 1993).

The response of the two major national 'cash for care' quangos to the needs of ethnic minority communities has also been limited. In the case of the Family Fund, which has provided modest cash help for over twenty years to families caring for severely disabled children under the age of 16, no ethnic monitoring was undertaken at all until early in 1994, when a decision was taken to include a question for applicants as to whether English was a first language. Given the connection between 'race' and ill-health (Ahmad 1993), this appears to be an area where more aggressive data collection might compensate for some of the deficiencies of DSS record-keeping. Similarly, the Independent Living Fund (Kestenbaum 1992), which paid weekly income to certain severely disabled adults (emphasizing the issues of choice and control) until its effective demise in 1993, only maintained a limited database on its users and its final reports were able to shed little light on whether the fund reached severely disabled ethnic minority adults.

The role of local authorities in promoting benefits take-up is a major issue to be faced by local authorities, which are, as noted earlier, now being drawn, often reluctantly, into the development of community care charging regimes. Charging arrangements are open to the accusations that they particularly penalize poorer clients and care-users or, where they attempt to 'claw back' disability benefits such as AA or DLA, that they effectively make disabled care users pay twice for services, once through council tax and once through a charge. The Association of Metropolitan Authorities (AMA) has attempted to develop a coherent charging policy for local authorities, which tries to reconcile the difference between the principle that the 'user pays' is fairer than spreading the cost of services across all local authority residents, and the recognition that most social services provision is used predominantly by those in receipt of social security benefits. Here again members of ethnic minority groups may be vulnerable, since the adoption of means-tested charging schemes, favoured by many local authorities, is likely to impact negatively on users' attitudes to services. The AMA acknowledges (AMA/LGIU 1991, 1992) that ethnic minority claimants may, because of under-claiming, not be entitled to concessionary 'passporting' schemes for free service use, but, to date, suggests only that effective benefit checking systems should be put in place as part of the care assessment process. Clearly, local authorities could, with adequate ethnic recording, plan focused take-up campaigns for specific benefits. Small-scale studies (Jadeja and Singh 1993) also reflect on both the impoverishment of black elders and ways in which charging policies that take no account of 'race' will disproportionately affect them.

'Race': the marginal dimension

Given these ten years of generally critical research about ethnic minorities' experience of social security cash benefits, why is it that the dimension of 'race' remains marginal to most policy discussion? We will argue that the answer derives not only from institutional and individual racism but also from the methodological limitations of many studies. However, given that the DSS is the largest funder of research into the social security system, it is particularly pertinent to again ask why there have been so few 'race'-related studies of the structure, administration and delivery of social security, and to examine the way in which implicitly racist assumptions still shape each stage of the research process, from the formulation of research questions and commissioning of research through to the analysis of data.

If we examine the limited number of studies that have addressed ethnic minority communities, it is perhaps not surprising to note that many have focused on identifying problems of access to information; this trend was noted by Gordon and Newnham (1985), who also highlighted how institutional and individual racism limited ethnic minority access to benefits. An assumption that the low level of take-up of benefit among ethnic minority communities is owing to a lack of appropriate or insufficient

information or advice about benefits (in written or oral form) for ethnic minority communities appears to underpin many of these studies (e.g.
Ritchie and England 1985). These key findings are sometimes supplemented
with suggestions that information dissemination among ethnic minority
communities takes specific cultural forms, such as through the informal
networks of friends and relatives (Bloch 1993).

There is no doubt that these studies highlight important problems. Access
to information is crucial to social security claims. However, a concentration on communication issues provides only a limited understanding of
structural problems when we consider the English-speaking ethnic minority communities: 'it is not clear why African-Caribbean black Britons appear
to be so disadvantaged in relation to social security. We may guess at the
answers and we know that the State cannot hide behind the same linguistic
and cultural reasons as have been proposed for Asian non-claimants' (*Benefits* Editorial 1994: 2).

We are thus faced with two questions. Why is it that 'race' remains
excluded from much social security research? And why is it that within the
limited 'race'-related social security research, the focus is on linguistic and
cultural differences? We start with the first question, drawing our arguments from a recent study (Rai 1995). One of the aims of this qualitative
study, based on consultations with a wide range of research organizations,
was to identify the range of approaches to conducting qualitative social
rescarch among Asian communities. One of its central findings was that
unless a research organization has a specialist role in addressing the 'race'
dimension, the inclusion of 'race' is dependent on the interest of individual
researchers. On rare occasions the funders or commissioners of research
may specify consideration of 'race'-related issues in research studies. Overall, in a culture where research agendas are set by funding bodies in consultation with the research community, 'race' tends to occupy a marginal
space.

Given that it is largely left to individual researchers to consider ethnic
minority communities in social research, it is worth looking at the conditions in which this practice prevails. Rai found, first, that in most research
organizations there is an absence of an organizational policy, strategy or
practice ethos to address the 'race' dimension. This inevitably results in
ad hoc and inconsistent practice patterns. The second reason relates to the
low proportional representation of ethnic minority communities in the
population as a whole, which, it is often argued, does not justify their
inclusion in samples of general population. Presumed extra costs, related
to requirements to meet the language needs of non-speakers of English,
and concerns about complex sampling designs are among the reasons
for this exclusion. Further, in quantitative research, it is argued that the
low numbers of potential respondents from ethnic minority communities
lead to results which are difficult to generalize. There are reservations
about using current sampling techniques for ethnic minority communities.
Researchers argue that samples drawn only from densely populated ethnic

minority areas are not representative and are biased against members of these communities who live elsewhere. In qualitative research, it is believed that low numbers of members from ethnic minority communities in small sample sizes lead to meaningless data and results. The third reason given was a lack of knowledge on how to address 'race' in research. Reasons cited included uncertainty about which ethnic minority communities to include in particular research studies and a lack of awareness of their cultural norms and social circumstances. A 'play safe' option is adopted, which results in ethnic minority communities being ignored in research.

Against these arguments, which reflect the dominant practice, Rai found that the few specialist organizations and interested individual researchers engaged in 'race'-related research observe the position of ethnic minority communities from a perspective based on the real circumstances and experiences of the UK's ethnic minority communities. These researchers recognize that ethnic minority communities often face the severest social problems, such as higher levels of unemployment and a higher level of dependency on state benefits, as demonstrated earlier. They also note the methodological limitations of, for example, the sampling techniques available for ethnic minority communities, as discussed above.

However, instead of these limitations resulting in a dismissive response on 'pure' methodological grounds, it can be argued that the social context of ethnic minority communities living in concentrated urban areas gives rise to specific problems – such as high unemployment, poverty, lack of adequate housing – which need to be addressed accordingly. Some official approaches in fact calculate the densities of ethnic minority populations as indicators in the assessment of levels of deprivation (Department of Health 1992).

Current practices in 'race'-related research

Rai's (1995) study explored current practices for addressing Asian communities in social research, noting the existence of three methodological approaches. These were categorized as 'invisible', 'partially visible' and 'visible'. In the traditionally dominant, 'invisible' approach, Asian communities are not treated as separate categories for analysis in research designs. However, attention is paid to ensuring that an adequate sample size is constituted to allow meaningful analysis. In quantitative methods, it is believed that if any differences exist between Asian people and others (i.e. white people), then these will emerge in the analysis, whereas in qualitative research, purposive sampling allows the possibility of including enough members of the Asian communities to produce adequate data for analysis. In the 'invisible' approach, no special regard is paid to the specific circumstances of Asian communities, except in ensuring that members of these communities are numerically represented. In quantitative research, if an Asian respondent does not communicate in English, she or he may be dropped from the sample or an interpreter might be arranged. In qualitative research, non-English-speaking respondents are generally excluded.

In the increasingly represented 'partially visible' approach, there is a recognition that Asian communities need to be considered differently. However, the extent of this recognition is limited to language or communication issues in data collection. The focus tends to be on ethnic and linguistic matching of interviewers with the research respondents. In quantitative research, this may involve translating questionnaires, and using 'specialist' language interviewers or interpreters. In qualitative research, where the prevalent practice is that project researchers are themselves involved in data collection, Asian researchers tend to be employed to assist with projects addressing Asian communities.

In the still rare 'visible' approach, the specific and different cultural norms and social circumstances of Asian communities are given prominence. All stages of the research process – design, data collection, analysis and interpretation of data – are considered within an appropriate 'race'-related context, which focuses on the Asian experience as the pivotal concern.

Rai's study found that the most common current practice is the 'partially visible' approach. While it may be argued that this position reflects an increased understanding of the different needs of ethnic minority communities, on the whole it remains inadequate. Attention is not paid to conceptualizing the research problem within the context of the experiences of ethnic minority communities. Analysis and interpretation of data tend to be carried out within the 'standard' analytic frameworks; in other words, relevant to the experiences of white communities.

As a result, the focus on cultural and linguistic issues alone continues to perpetuate the problematization and marginalization of ethnic minority communities. Problems experienced by ethnic minority communities remain 'invisibilized', except in rare instances (for example, NACAB 1991; Amin and Oppenheim 1992). We noted above how these studies highlighted structural discrimination in the social security system, and the discriminatory treatment of ethnic minority communities by Benefits Agency staff, providing some explanations for the low take-up of benefit among these communities. Two other recent studies (Sadiq-Sangster 1991; Law *et al.* 1993) that investigate attitudes to claiming social security benefits among ethnic minority communities fall into the 'visible' approach category, whereas Bloch's (1993) study tackles the 'race' dimension with a 'partially visible' approach. We can now briefly re-evaluate these three studies.

An assessment of some recent studies

Law *et al.* (1993) selected five different ethnic minority communities to examine their attitudes to claiming social security benefits. The findings identify key factors contributing to low benefits take-up. These were: the administrative complexity of the benefit system; the inaccessibility of the Benefits Agency (e.g. perceived difficulties of communication with Benefits Agency staff); and religious and cultural factors, such as a sense of stigma attached to claiming, based on a belief that those who claimed would be looked down on in the community. The study illustrates the importance of the simultaneous impact of these dimensions on low benefits take-up among the respondents.

Among the Bangladeshi community, Law *et al.* found that the sense of stigma, particularly among young people, was based on reasons perceived to be enshrined in the Islamic traditions of self-sufficiency and autonomy achieved through work. Consequently, many Bangladeshi young people interviewed for the study only claimed benefit after exhausting all alternative avenues. This factor was not prevalent among the older people who had a work history in this country. They reconciled claiming benefit, which is based on a contributory system, with the Islamic model of contributing to collective funds to help the poor and needy.

Late claiming was also noted by Sadiq-Sangster (1991), in her study of Pakistani Mirpuri families. She examined not only the impact of religious beliefs, but also the lack of adequate help in making claims, finding that some families had accumulated serious debts as a result. Her study showed stereotyped assumptions about close Asian family support systems. This kind of support was on occasions not available to some families, not necessarily because of the lack of willingness to care, but because either there was no extended family nearby or members of the extended family were also in similar difficult situations (see Chapter 4, this volume, for related discussion). Sadiq-Sangster provides a deeper understanding of the family support and reliance system, which is based on a complex system of *lena-dena* (literally 'give and take'), providing direct material goods or indirect support (e.g. visiting and caring for sick relatives, attendance at sibling weddings). Inability to fulfil these functions can seriously affect family relationships and the perceived and expected dependency on family support. Sadiq-Sangster's study also notes the ways in which the actual experiences of individual claimants at Benefits Agency offices affect take-up of benefits among ethnic minority communities.

These findings are important, as they highlight specific problem areas which are generally submerged in research studies focusing on linguistic and cultural differences, and which sometimes inadvertently contribute to common perceptions of 'ignorant' ethnic minority communities. In fact, it is the limitations of such studies themselves that provide us with an incomplete picture. The emphasis within them remains on looking for the source of problems among the ethnic minority communities, and structural factors largely remain buried.

Bloch's (1993) study constitutes an interesting example of the limitations of the 'partially visible' approach. While exemplary for its findings of communication-related issues, Bloch does not bring out some of the underlying problems that the study sample perceives or experiences. The

Afro-Caribbean sample, who could all read and write English, 'tended to focus on the more personal interactions and their perceptions of discrimination and prejudice against them' (p. 48). Some of these experiences and perceptions are reported, but the report summary does not take up the implications of these experiences, save for specific comments, such as the need for the benefits system to take account of sickle cell disease among Afro-Caribbean populations. The recommendation that the Benefits Agency should give high priority to a strategy of recruitment of more staff from ethnic minority communities thus again provides only a partial view of the findings. Further, the more general recommendation, presumably to address the many issues of racism highlighted by the respondents, that 'the Benefits Agency should set up a process of regular consultation with campaigning groups . . . with the aim of improving service delivery to the black community and challenging racism within the welfare benefits system' (pp. 54–5), not only is vague but disappears altogether from the summary of the report.

Conclusion

In reviewing the limitations of recent research, we are not arguing that any identifiable information needs of ethnic minority communities should be disregarded. However, we have attempted to illustrate that the focus on the issues of language and information alone, which appears to be prevalent in what continues to be a very limited range of 'race'-related social security research, is problematic. Additionally, without an adequate national system of ethnic monitoring of social security customers, we cannot effectively examine the extent, nature and consequences of the low take-up of benefit among ethnic minority communities, although all the evidence from small-scale studies, as we have shown, points to the very great scope of this problem on a national scale. Without a critical approach to addressing the 'race' dimension in social policy research along the lines outlined above, the value of most studies will continue to be partial, obscuring some of the real causes of social problems among ethnic minority communities, and problematizing the members of those communities themselves.

Consequently, much social security and community care policy will continue to be seriously flawed and the financial and social costs will continue to be borne by the marginalized groups, especially minority ethnic communities. Transactions around social security and other cash benefits are playing an increasingly central role in underpinning the care 'packages' theoretically available under the new care regime, and the relevance of the community care regime to ethnic minority communities is growing as the latter age. The evidence drawn together in this chapter suggests both that members of black and ethnic minorities are not receiving levels of income to which they are entitled, which impacts on their prospects for receiving and purchasing care, and that much current research is unable to demonstrate the structural reasons for this.

Notes

1 This section draws on the work of Amin and Oppenheim (1992), to whom the present authors are indebted.
2 A fuller consideration of this issue can be found in Craig (1992a). See also Glendinning and Craig (1993).

Annotated bibliography

Rai, D. K. (1995) *In the Margins: Current Practices in Qualitative Social Research with Asian Communities*. Hull: University of Humberside, Social Research Papers No. 2.
Reviews current social research practices (especially qualitative research) of researchers, funders, research institutes, government and voluntary sector organizations in relation to the dimension of 'race'. The report concludes that the 'race' dimension remains, with few exceptions, 'in the margins'.

Law, I., Karmani, I., Hylton, C. and Deacon, A. (1993) *Racial Equality and Social Security Service Delivery*. Leeds: University of Leeds School of Sociology and Social Policy, Research Working Paper No. 10.
A report of a research project which explores the experience of a number of minority ethnic communities (especially Chinese, Bangladeshi and Pakistani), living in Leeds, of social security service delivery, particularly in relation to means-tested benefits. It provides a summary of key findings and outlines policy implications.

Sadiq-Sangster, A. (1991) *Living on Income Support: an Asian Experience*. London: Family Service Units.
Reports the findings of a small qualitative research study, conducted by a researcher of Asian origin, with South Asian families living on income support, as part of a wider study of poverty among Family Support Unit families. The report explores differing cultural understandings of some key social security policy areas, such as indebtedness, loans and the structural limitations of the social fund.

9

An opportunity for change: voluntary sector provision in a mixed economy of care

Karl Atkin

Introduction

After many years of neglect, recent debates on community care have begun to recognize the potential significance of ethnicity in formulating policy. For example, the White Paper *Caring for People*, which preceded the NHS and Community Care Act, identified people from ethnic minorities as having 'particular care needs'. *Caring for People* concluded that 'good community care' must take account of 'the circumstances' of minority communities, be sensitive to their needs and planned in consultation with them (Cmnd 849). The policy guidance associated with the NHS and Community Care Act, and the reviews of practice published by the Social Service Inspectorate, further support this policy (Department of Health 1990; Audit Commission 1994).

Recognition of the 'particular needs' of minority groups at the highest level of policy-making has been described as 'something of a breakthrough' (Walker and Ahmad 1994), especially since empirical evidence demonstrates that community services fail to recognize and respond to the needs of people from black and ethnic minorities (Atkin and Rollings 1993a). More significantly, however, acknowledgment of the 'particular needs' of 'minorities' comes as health and social services are undergoing the most substantial changes since the origins of the welfare state (Wistow *et al.* 1994). The principles informing this restructuring provide the general framework in which the rhetoric of 'good community care' for minority groups will be realized.

The mixed economy of care and voluntary provision

Two concerns – one financial and the other organizational – inform these general changes. First, the UK government, under pressure to control growing public spending on health and social care, was concerned with using existing budgets more 'efficiently' (Midwinter 1994). Consequently, 'value for money' and preventing the waste and inappropriate targeting of resources, identified by various reports (see Audit Commission 1986), emerge as central aspects of government policy. Second, government policy has questioned the responsiveness and accessibility of community care services. Griffiths's agenda for action on community care, for example, argued that community service delivery was poorly related to need (Griffiths 1988). This echoed the concerns of an earlier Audit Commission report, which emphasized the importance of 'a flexible service response' that offered a wider range of options. The report concluded by calling for 'the adjustment of services to meet the needs of people rather than the adjustment of people to meet the needs of services' (Audit Commission 1986). Ensuring that provision was tailored to more systematically assessed needs and preferences of individual users and their carers became a fundamental policy goal for future community care services. 'Citizenship', 'consumerism', 'participation' and 'choice' have emerged as key ideals in attempts to empower recipients of health and social services (Cmnd 849; Cmnd 1599).

A mixed economy of care is a practical attempt by government policy to realize these political ideals and ensure an individualized service response in social care. Social service departments are allocated the strategic tasks of mobilizing new sources of care and coordinating their delivery. In this respect they are to become *enabling* authorities that make 'maximum possible use of private and voluntary providers' (Cmnd 849). The statutory sector has never had a monopoly on social care provision and a mixed economy of care which includes private, voluntary and social services is not entirely new (Wistow *et al.* 1994). It would, however, be a mistake to over-state the degree of continuity in the responsibilities of social service departments and the expected role of voluntary organizations following the community care legislation. The important difference is the application of 'market principles' to the mixed economy of care. This 'quasi-market' transforms the previous relationship between social services and voluntary sector providers.

The idea that market efficacy rather than collective planning is the best way of ensuring efficiency, accountability and choice in health and social services is at the heart of government health care policy. To achieve this the 1990 NHS and Community Care Act separated purchasing and providing functions in public health and social care agencies – a fundamental prerequisite to ensuring market efficacy (Enthoven 1985). *Caring for People*, for example, described the responsibilities of social service departments as 'securing the delivery of services, not simply by acting as direct providers but by developing the purchasing and contracting role to become enabling authorities' (Cmnd 849). Social service departments, therefore, would no longer provide services but become purchasers and care managers, with responsibility for preparing community care plans for the locality, assessing individual needs and arranging packages of care. This was to be achieved through the principles of market competition. Voluntary sector and private organizations – the independent sector – would compete to provide these services.

Government policy recognizes that the emerging market orientation requires a 'cultural' revolution that radically alters the traditional relationship between social services and voluntary organizations (Audit Commission 1992b). An enabling role based on market principles is far less compatible with the traditional and established values of local authority social service departments (Wistow *et al.* 1994). None the less, the 'contract economy' and the changes it implies provide the context in which the 'particular care needs' of black and ethnic minorities will be met. An understanding of the delivery and organization of voluntary services to black and ethnic minorities is, therefore, fundamental to the debate on the future of community care, especially since the purpose of stimulating the development of the non-statutory sector was expressed in terms of benefits to the consumer (Cmnd 849). These included: a wider range of choice; more flexible and innovatory ways of meeting individual needs; and better value for money resulting from competition between providers (Wistow *et al.* 1994). The increased importance of voluntary sector provision, therefore, seems to offer a potential solution to the inaccessibility and inappropriateness of mainstream service delivery.

This chapter, by critically evaluating the operation of voluntary services in multiracial Britain, will examine the extent to which voluntary provision is able to meet the social care needs of people from black and ethnic minorities (see Chapter 7, this volume, for a discussion of the voluntary sector in relation to mental health). First, it considers the role of so-called 'mainstream' voluntary provision and its ability to provide accessible and appropriate service support to people from black and ethnic minorities. Second, it explores the specific role of voluntary sector provision provided by minority groups and the difficulties these organizations face. Third, it examines the extent to which the enabling and purchasing roles of social services departments can ensure a mixed economy of care that meets the needs of people from black and ethnic minorities.

Established voluntary sector provision

As we shall see, the provision of specialist voluntary services by minorities for minorities is sparse (Field and Jackson 1989; Walker and Ahmad 1994). Consequently, 'mainstream' or 'established' voluntary provision represents the more likely form of provision available to black people through a mixed economy of care. There is no systematic examination of how voluntary sector organizations have responded to the needs of ethnic minorities since the introduction of the 1990 NHS and Community Care Act. Evidence suggests, however, that 'mainstream' voluntary agencies are ill-equipped to meet the needs of ethnic minority users.

The general unsuitability and inaccessibility of community service provision to people from ethnic minorities is well established (Connelly 1990; Atkin and Rollings 1993a). The voluntary sector is no exception and experiences similar problems of ethnocentric and discriminatory service provision to those of health and social services (Sedley 1989; Phaure 1991; Bowling 1990; Rooney and McKain 1990; Patel 1990). Norman (1985), for example, describes 'a long established voluntary sector' which has done little to recognize that we live in a multiracial society – whether in employment policy, staff and volunteer training, committee membership, relationships with ethnic minority voluntary organizations or provision of services to individuals in minority groups. Voluntary organizations seem unclear about what an equal opportunities policy is, and many have no awareness of the detailed monitoring and follow-up procedures such policies would involve (Dungate 1984). Not surprisingly, low take-up of voluntary sector services by ethnic minorities is common, despite a demonstrated demand for these services (Field and Jackson 1989).

Voluntary organizations, for example, adopt the same socio-cultural explanations as statutory organizations to account for the behaviour of minority groups (Dungate 1984; Atkin and Rollings 1993a). Stereotypes and myths are evident in the activities of voluntary sector providers. These serve to disadvantage people from ethnic minorities. For example, the assumption that Asian people, and to a lesser extent African-Caribbean people, live in self-supporting families is often used as an excuse for not making necessary changes to the existing services or expanding the level of service provision to black and ethnic minorities (Dungate 1984; Atkin and Rollings 1992). This view is unjustified for two reasons. First, although the extended family is more common among Asian families (Barker 1984), there are still a significant proportion of Asian people who live alone, with few relatives in this country (Cameron et al. 1989). The extended Afro-Caribbean family has always been rare in the UK (Baxter 1989a). In addition, socio-economic and demographic factors may influence the willingness and ability of families to provide care (Owen 1993). The size of Hindu and Sikh families is beginning to resemble that of 'white' families (Ahmad and Atkin 1996). Second, and perhaps more importantly, living in an extended family does not mean that service support is unnecessary. Life in an extended family, for example, can be a source of stress and marginalization. Further, the extended family may not have the material and emotional resources to meet the needs of family members. The imagined extended family represents a convenient excuse for not providing service support (Atkin and Rollings 1992) (see also Chapters 4 and 5).

Voluntary sector providers also follow the tendency of health and social services in identifying health and social 'problems' of minority ethnic communities as arising from cultural practices (Field and Jackson 1989; Atkin and Rollings 1993b). Black people are often characterized as being in some way to blame for their own needs because of deviant and unsatisfactory lifestyles (Cameron et al. 1989; see also Chapters 2 and 3, this volume).

These ideas about the 'difference' of black people are extended to their understanding of voluntary sector provision. The tradition of formal voluntary provision is seen as 'alien' to many black people and they are criticized for this 'ignorance' (Dungate 1984). Consequently, many voluntary organizations blame the potential client group for either experiencing specific problems or failing to understand an organization's aims, rather than examine the relevance of the services being provided (Dungate 1984; Field and Jackson 1989; Sedley 1989).

These assumptions, myths and stereotypes ignore the fact that racial inequalities and poverty create additional needs for support. The average income of Afro-Caribbean and Asian, and particularly Pakistani and Bangladeshi, families living in the UK, for example, is well below that of 'white' families. The significance of the additional barriers faced by black people in having their care needs recognized is reflected in another assumption voluntary sector providers share with statutory services. Many voluntary sector organizations claim that their services are 'open to all' or 'everyone is treated the same' (Dungate 1984; Field and Jackson 1989; Atkin and Rollings 1993b), as this response, from a national survey examining the role of voluntary sector provision to black and ethnic minorities, illustrates:

> The sad fact is that we have practically no clients in any ethnic minority group. Our charity is open to all regardless of race, sex, colour or creed and yet out of many thousands of members we can only think of two or three people who come into the category of ethnic minorities. Frankly, we don't know why this is.
>
> (Dungate 1984)

The assumption that *same service for all*, irrespective of needs, equates with *equal service to all* legitimates non-recognition of the service needs of minority ethnic communities. Such responses, by default, privilege the white population by ignoring the obstacles faced by people from ethnic minorities in gaining access to services (Dungate 1984; National Association for Health Authorities 1988). The consequences of these responses have been described as 'sins of omission' (Field and Jackson 1989). Black people do not have the same opportunities as the white population; they experience greater disadvantage and suffer more barriers to service receipt (Glendinning and Pearson 1988). An 'open to all' or 'colour blind' approach is used as an excuse by voluntary sector providers for disregarding the potential needs of people from ethnic minorities and avoiding making the necessary changes to existing provision.

The culture of change

There is no indication that voluntary sector provision is likely to undergo the 'cultural' revolution required to meet the social care needs of ethnic minorities. Evidence suggests, for example, that despite their willingness to change and adapt to a multiracial society, national voluntary organizations do not know how to make their services more widely available and relevant (Dungate 1984; Field and Jackson 1989). For example, a review of four national voluntary organizations – The Down's Syndrome Association, National Council for One Parent Families, Maternity Alliance and Family Service Units – suggested that none was fully prepared for the challenge of an anti-racist strategy in either employment procedures or service delivery (Sedley 1989). The Health and Race Project at the University of Liverpool surveyed seventy voluntary organizations in Liverpool and came to similar conclusions (Rooney and McKain 1990). The sample included a broad range of organizations: self-help organizations which focused on a particular illness; bodies like the St John Ambulance Brigade, Red Cross and various hospital Leagues of Friends; and large, relatively well funded agencies like Barnardo's and Liverpool Personal Service Society. The project reported that, in an area with large black communities, 98 per cent of management committees were white, 99 per cent of the users were white, 98 per cent of the employees were white and 99 per cent of the volunteers were white. Only 8 per cent of the organizations had a written policy which addressed the issue of race. The issue of racial inequality was not yet on the agenda of the substantial majority of organizations and the report concluded that voluntary sector organizations were 'organised by, with and for the white community'. Connelly (1990), in examining the changes taking place within voluntary services during the 1980s, described two polarized approaches to change. Some national voluntary organizations show little recognition that the multiracial, multicultural, multilingual nature of British society has any significant implications for their roles and responsibilities. At the other extreme, some organizations are so overwhelmed by a sense of outrage at the position of black people and the amount that has to be done, that they become disabled (Connelly 1990).

Ethnic minority voluntary organizations

The importance of black voluntary organizations, although small in number, in meeting the social care needs of black people is well established (Lalljie 1983; Blakemore 1985; Norman 1985; Glendinning and Pearson 1988; Farleigh 1990; Butt *et al.* 1991; Eribo 1991). The literature, for example, describes an increasing number of community projects designed to meet the needs of, and provide support for, members of ethnic minority communities (Hardingham 1988; Bowling 1990; Pharoah and Redmond 1991). The diversity of these organizations is acknowledged and these so-called 'specialist' voluntary organizations do not experience the problems of ethnocentric and discriminatory service provision evident in the activities of statutory and 'mainstream' voluntary services (Farleigh 1990; Eribo 1991; Butt 1994). Indeed, the lack of appropriate and adequate statutory and voluntary service provision for black communities is given as one of the main reasons for the growth of these organizations (Ahmad 1988a). Black voluntary organizations subsidize and complement other forms of provision by providing services to communities where statutory and 'mainstream' voluntary provision are unable or unwilling to do so (Bhaduri 1988; Ahmad 1989). Glendenning and Pearson (1988), for example, argue that the black and ethnic minority voluntary sector has clearly filled 'a major and appalling gap' in service provision for older people in their communities. Lalljie remarked that black self-help organizations provided support geared to the needs of black people, as well as making these needs visible (Lalljie 1983).

Voluntary organizations where services are provided by minorities for minorities would seem to meet one of the main requirements of present government policy on community care – their 'closeness' to the user. These providers, because they are locally based, small-scale organizations, seem in a better position to tailor their services to individual needs and be sensitive to the needs of people from black and ethnic minorities than either statutory or 'mainstream' voluntary providers (Atkin and Rollings 1993b). There is no systematic evidence evaluating the role of black voluntary organizations in the 'contract economy'. None the less, despite its importance in providing support to black and ethnic minorities, other evidence suggests that the black voluntary sector is vulnerable and may find it difficult to function in a mixed economy of care (Ahmad 1988b; Glendinning and Pearson 1988; Mirza 1991).

There is no inevitability about the existence of such voluntary organizations, and even if they did exist they might not have the time or organizational skills to initiate and operate a wide range of community services (Lalljie 1983; Ahmad 1988a, b). A conference on service response to the needs of older people from black communities, organized by Bradford Social Services Department and Bradford University, concluded that in terms of providing what people wanted and needed, voluntary agencies had a better record than statutory agencies, but were generally felt to be doing their work on 'a shoestring' and with little support (Jolley 1988). In general, black voluntary organizations face two major problems in providing community care: limited resources and establishing a working relationship with statutory services.

Limited resources

Although most voluntary organizations, black and white, face the problem of limited resources, black voluntary organizations seem particularly disadvantaged (Norman 1985; Ahmad 1988b; Jolley 1988; Ahmad 1989; Jarrett 1990; Mitchell 1990; Rooney and McKain 1990; Mirza 1991). An open forum on care in the community, organized by the Standing Conference of Ethnic Minority Senior Citizens (SCEMSC), painted a picture of cutbacks, grants withdrawn, transport difficulties and inadequate and inaccessible premises (May 1989). Daniel (1988) describes similar problems for some black voluntary sector day centres and contrasts these with the conditions in local authority day centres, which are mainstream funded, adequately staffed and held in premises which conform to health, safety and fire regulations.

Since most black voluntary care initiatives are dependent on temporary or short-term funding from 'special' or 'soft' budgets, such as inner-cities monies or Section 11 funding, they are vulnerable to funding crises (Norman 1985; Ball 1988; Fryer 1989; Butt 1994). Access to funding is related to access to the political structure, and to the knowledge and information within which bids can be framed to fit the ideas that are currently in favour. National or local forums, which allocate resources for community services, rarely have representations from black organizations and are not involved in the decision-making process. Consequently, funding tends to go to those who are already organized within the mainstream (Rooney and McKain 1990).

Relationship with statutory services

A major problem faced by black voluntary organizations is the unequal power relationship between the statutory sector and the black voluntary sector (Atkin and Rollings 1993b). Social services departments increasingly define the context in which voluntary services operate. This provides the basis for potential exploitation, often ruling out the possibility of partnership and joint work, since the terms and conditions of the partnership have usually been defined by the statutory agencies. The relationship between black voluntary organizations and statutory services reflects similar assumptions and stereotypes to those that disadvantage black service users. Black users, for example, often characterize community service provision as being difficult to communicate with, slow to respond, unwilling to understand, narrow in perspective and resistant to pressure. Comparable experience suggests that such feelings characterize the relationship between statutory services and minority voluntary organizations (Ahmad 1988a, b; Daniel 1988; May 1989; Farleigh 1990; Rooney and McKain 1990; Mirza 1991; Jeyasingham 1992).

In practical terms there is a general reluctance on the part of statutory and 'mainstream' voluntary agencies to initiate any mechanism for consultation with the black voluntary sector (May 1989; Farleigh 1990). A seminar organized for black organizations by the National Institute of Social Work (cited in Ahmad 1988b) concluded that the black communities and their organizations cannot form effective partnerships with the statutory sector unless, and until, 'their voices are heard and their proposals are included in the restructuring of the partnership arrangements'. In the absence of a constructive working relationship with statutory services, black and voluntary organizations often find themselves in 'constrained predicaments' and 'end up with more frustration, further disappointment, reinforced mistrust and increased disparity' (Ahmad 1988b).

The difficulties statutory services have in establishing a partnership with black voluntary organizations is further compounded by their expectations of these voluntary organizations. Statutory provision often expects the black voluntary sector to parallel the provision offered by its own services (Jolley 1988; Field and Jackson 1989; Patel 1990; Walker and Ahmad 1994). Glendenning and Pearson (1988) argue, for example, that although community-based projects and self-help organizations provide invaluable support for black and ethnic minority older people, few provide the coverage needed by their communities. Moreover, there is an inherent danger that statutory service provision assumes that the existence of a black voluntary sector somehow solves 'the problem' and absolves it of any responsibility for the social care needs of black minorities. Pointing to this 'special provision', statutory provision has remained relatively static and inaccessible (Ahmad 1993; Atkin and Rollings 1993b).

Funding black community groups is the most popular means by which social services departments feel they are implementing equal opportunity policies (Butt 1994). This is seen, however, as a reactive rather than proactive response. For example, in evaluating the implementation and development of equal opportunity policies in social service provision, Butt (1994) notes a lack of clear objectives that went beyond bland statements that this funding would allow the department to implement its equal opportunity policy. None the less, the existence of a black voluntary sector, although important in responding to the needs of black communities in the absence of appropriate statutory services, does not imply that the needs of black people are being met adequately (Patel 1990; Dourado 1991), particularly since most projects are small-scale and 'experimental' (Patel 1990).

Further, the culture of 'special provision' among social service departments does little to help in developing a partnership with black voluntary services. Although separate provision can be beneficial, too often it is a euphemism for short-term, inadequately funded and marginal provision (Walker and Ahmad 1994). In many cases it has led to internal divisions within the minority ethnic communities as they compete with each other on the basis of 'culturally distinctive needs' (Ahmad 1993: Chapter 11). Moreover, the approach to 'culturally distinctive needs', adopted by many social services departments, paradoxically fails to recognize the diversity of Britain's black minority populations. The 'special provisions' provided by black voluntary organizations are often considered together as 'other' when funding is allocated. They are perceived as 'black' voluntary sector providers meeting 'special' needs, rather than separate organizations meeting distinct needs. In effect, the diversity of Britain's black populations is ignored (see also Chapters 3 and 7, this volume).

While this review of the many challenges and obstacles faced by the specialist voluntary sector servicing minority ethnic communities has indicated the cumulative difficulties it faces, this should not be allowed to obscure the very real contribution and success of individual agencies. In the field of mental health there are many exemplars of innovatory provision and in relation to, for example, sickle cell anaemia, community mobilization in relation to specific forms of support and care has been critical to ensuring formal service provision (e.g. Francis *et al.* 1989).

The enabling and purchasing role of social services

It is generally recognized that the lack of a flourishing independent sector in social care will make it difficult for social services to establish a mixed economy of care (Hoyles and Le Grand 1990). Optimists argue that the current changes will encourage the emergence of an independent providing sector (Green 1990), particularly given the expected success of the 'enterprise culture' in the NHS (Robinson 1988). Flynn (1990b), for example, sets out a range of interventions which social service departments can deploy to stimulate alternative suppliers of services. On the supply side this includes help with business and development grants, subsidies and credit for start-up and working capital, training, licensing and regulation. On the demand side he advocates that case managers need to operate as 'brokers' and 'advisers' rather than as agents making all the decisions (Flynn 1990a). Others, however, suggest that a voluntary sector grounded in market principles will never emerge because voluntary organizations have social rather than market objectives (Leibenstein 1966). To some extent government policy recognized some of these difficulties and introduced the idea of the 'enabling authority' (Wistow *et al.* 1994). As we have seen, the NHS and Community Care Act charges social services departments with strategic tasks of mobilizing new sources of care and coordinating their delivery according to market principles (Wistow *et al.* 1994). The mixed economy of care, however, is unlikely to solve the inability of social services to meet the needs of black minorities.

Disadvantage and the mixed economy of care

Theoretically, the ability of 'market principles' to rectify the difficulties faced by statutory services in meeting the needs of black people has been questioned: choice does not necessarily follow from 'market' competition. For example, the supposed neutrality of the market and the principles of the 'hidden hand' implicit in the works of the New Right (Hayek 1952) and assumed by government policy could be used to depoliticize allocative decisions. Disadvantage is supposedly mediated though the 'market' rather than being the consequence of 'political' decisions. Decisions about priorities, however, cannot be divorced from the political and social context. Inequalities in health and social care have begun to be seen as inevitable and consequently decision-making is based on 'priorities' rather than 'need' (Klein 1988). Policy-makers have to form a judgement about the relative 'pay offs' to be gained from spending money one way or another (Culyer 1988). Deciding what priorities will be put on the agenda is a political decision and not a market one. These political decisions are likely to reflect the inequalities that exist in society and, therefore, to perpetuate the structural disadvantage faced by certain social groups (Papadakis and Taylor-Gooby 1987). Consequently, critics have questioned the extent to which the application of market principles empowers users (Winkler 1987; Barnes and Wistow 1992). Some of these arguments relate to the limited account of consumerism offered by government policy. The 'supermarket' model of health and social care, as it has been called, offers individual rights to 'customers' rather than wider political or social rights (Winkler 1987; Pollit 1988). The Citizen's Charter, for instance, focuses on reducing waiting lists and delays in outpatients rather than more fundamental issues concerning equity. Moreover, it redefines structural problems as problems of communication and hence places strong emphasis on improving information systems rather than tackling the issues of inaccessible service provision. The established power relationship between those providing and those receiving services remains unchallenged (Hoyles and Le Grand 1990; Papadakis and Taylor-Gooby 1987; Hambleton 1988; Plant et al. 1989). The status quo is maintained and the disadvantage facing ethnic minorities will continue. The future role of social services departments is likely to reflect the practical consequences of this.

The future role of social service departments

Enabling and purchasing voluntary sector provision in a mixed economy of care is likely to reflect the structural disadvantages facing people from black and ethnic minorities. Community provision has not traditionally been responsive to the views of people from black and ethnic minorities (Atkin and Rollings 1993a) and the enabling role of social services is likely to reflect this (Walker and Ahmad 1994). There is widespread uncertainty, puzzlement and ignorance about what should be done to meet the needs of black minorities (Butt et al. 1991; Walker and Ahmad 1994). Policy thus remains undeveloped and rarely goes beyond bland statements supporting the principles of racial equality, while the mechanisms that might achieve race equality and the principles that underlie them remain unexplored (Atkin and Rollings 1993a). Moreover, the consequences of institutional racism and in particular the racist assumptions, stereotypes and myths evident in the activities of practitioners, planners and policy-makers will continue to disadvantage people from black and ethnic minorities. Local authorities, for example, often list black people as 'high risk' clients, 'uncooperative' and 'difficult to work with' (Cameron et al. 1989; Williams 1990). Similarly, evidence suggests that racism within the NHS affects virtually all black people, with common stereotypes portraying black people as 'calling out doctors unnecessarily', 'being trivial complainers' and 'time wasters' (Ahmad et al. 1989).

On the supply side, a fundamental problem facing social service purchasers is that mainstream voluntary providers are not in a position to meet the social care needs of people from ethnic minorities. These services remain ethnocentric, and although there is an expressed willingness to change, the rhetoric is not matched by reality. Even when there is a genuine desire to change, the know-how and resources may be lacking (Dungate 1984; Field and Jackson 1989; Sedley 1989; Connelly 1990; Atkin and Rollings 1993b). This is seen as symptomatic of a community care policy that subjects voluntary groups to 'intolerable strains and unrealistic expectations' (Walker and Ahmad 1994).

Social services cannot, however, hide behind the voluntary sector's inability to provide care for black and ethnic minorities. Their enabling role means they have a responsibility to ensure that people from black and ethnic minorities, like other populations, have access to appropriate services that meet their particular needs (Moledina 1988). The 'contract economy' encourages various strategies to ensure this. When drawing up the contract specifications and service level agreements, local authorities should, first, commit the voluntary agency to racial equality and equal opportunity, and, second, ensure that the agency provides evidence proving its competence to provide services effectively (Connelly 1990; Rooney and McKain 1990). This is especially important given that many mainstream voluntary organizations do not have the same commitment to, or experience of, equal opportunities as many statutory agencies. Evidence suggests, however, that social service departments, even when able to introduce contract specifications to ensure equal opportunities and equitable service provision, do not have either the ability or the resources to enforce them (Walker and Ahmad 1994). Moreover, devolving its responsibility for equal opportunities policy to individual voluntary sector organizations, which have had little previous success in ensuring its successful operation, creates the additional problem of maintaining a coherent and sustainable commitment to an equal opportunities policy. The difficulty of maintaining equitable service delivery would seem to rest with individual providers rather than as a more systemic problem facing welfare provision. Decisions about allocations that disadvantage people from ethnic minorities, therefore, become obscured and are seen as a consequence of an individual rather than a collective response. Responsibility for disadvantage becomes diffuse and fragmented, thus making it all the more difficult to tackle. The general effect of institutional racism, where the procedures and policies of an institution lead to racially discriminatory outcomes for minority ethnic communities, is ignored. It is replaced by an account that explains racism in terms of the dysfunction of individual organizations and the actions of the practitioners who work in that institution.

While we can acknowledge the very significant role played by specific specialist voluntary agencies, it remains the case that in general black voluntary provision, which offers a solution to inaccessible and appropriate service delivery, is under-developed and under-resourced (Jeyasingham

1992). The fact that voluntary services are threatened by under-resourcing indicates how hard it will be for black voluntary groups not only to survive but also to 'professionalize' to the degree needed to realize their potential in the new contract culture (Walker and Ahmad 1994). Social services' preference for consulting and negotiating with well established, professional, predominantly white voluntary sector organizations compounds the problem (Barnes and Wistow 1992; Walker and Ahmad 1994). Being smaller, less well resourced and less experienced, the black voluntary sector provider is ill-equipped to compete with the longer established and better resourced white organizations (Jeyasingham 1992). Community care policy assumes 'a level playing field' in competition for resources, yet, as we have seen, specialist black voluntary organizations experience greater disadvantage than mainstream voluntary organizations. In effect, they have to negotiate more barriers with fewer resources (Daniel 1988; Rooney and McKain 1990; Walker and Ahmad 1994).

Moreover, increased efficiency, for instance, may be obtained at the expense of accessibility and quality (Robinson 1988). For example, positive reasons for funding black voluntary providers, such as their expertise, their existing links with black communities and the willingness of black people to use services that these groups provide, are often not reflected in service level agreements (Mirza 1991; Butt 1994). Much of the time spent in drawing up contract specifications is used to ensure that social services departments can measure success or failure, rather than to decide what success or failure mean (Butt 1994). This emphasis, according to Butt (1994), will mean 'success' being measured in financial terms rather than in terms of the quality of service being provided. Further, the pressures on local authorities to achieve low unit costs will force them into block contracts with large-scale service providers (Local Government Information Unit 1990). Potentially the black voluntary sector could become 'squeezed out' by large private or national voluntary care agencies (Williams 1990; Mirza 1991; Phaure 1991), resulting in standardized community services which are insensitive to the needs of ethnic minorities. An alternative approach involving collaboration with larger 'white' purchaser organizations could result in the relative loss of autonomy (Jeyasingham 1992). In effect, black voluntary organizations would have to enter into relationships with the same organizations whose inability to develop accessible and acceptable provision to people from minority ethnic groups led to the emergence of the black voluntary sector in the first place.

Discussion

Recent government policy promoting the contracting out of community services will result in the voluntary sector growing increasingly important as a provider of community services. This 'contract economy' provides the context in which the 'particular care needs' of ethnic minorities will be met.

The mixed economy of care, however, creates the problem that their needs may be swept aside and marginalized. The market and enabling principles implicit in the mixed economy of care reflect the racism and disadvantage faced by ethnic minorities. Indeed, it is questionable whether a mixed economy of care offers an appropriate means of enhancing choice for ethnic minorities. Community care policy presumes a level playing field and ignores the reality that black communities have never enjoyed equality of access to welfare services.

Specifically, social service provision has not been responsive to the views of people from black and ethnic minorities, and their 'enabling role' in relation to social services is likely to reflect this. There is uncertainty about what should be done to meet the needs of black minorities, compounded by the erroneous and unhelpful assumptions, stereotypes and myths evident in the activities of practitioners, planners and policy-makers. The application of 'market principles' is unlikely to rectify these difficulties. Choice does not necessarily follow from market competition. Such competition may result in less rather than more choice as the market reflects the inequalities that already exist in society and perpetuates the structural disadvantage faced by certain social groups. Mainstream voluntary services are not in a position to accommodate the social care needs of people from ethnic minorities. The black voluntary sector, which offers a partial solution to inaccessible and appropriate service delivery, is under-developed and under-resourced, and forced to operate within a racist and ethnocentric framework.

This, however, is not an inevitable consequence of a mixed economy of care. Levick (1992), for example, points to the 'janus face' of community care legislation. He castigates 'counsels of despair' who do little to advance 'transformative thinking and practice'. Adopting a Gramscian approach, he argues that legislation is made up of contradictory and changeable elements that create the possibility of 'radical possibilities'. A similar belief is held by Harrison (1993) in his review of the black voluntary housing movement. He argues that the 'much excellent work' that stresses the negative consequences of racism in housing policy needs to be supplemented by accounts acknowledging the significance of struggles to improve conditions and highlight successes.

Writings on 'race' and social care tend to focus on the problems of accessibility and appropriateness, as well as general disadvantage in the provision of services (Atkin and Rollings 1993a). The evaluation offered by this chapter draws on such material and highlights the unfair structuring of opportunities. The critical emphasis of the literature on 'race' and social care is perhaps understandable and has successfully highlighted the negative consequences of racism, marginalization and unequal treatment. By focusing on disadvantage there is a danger, however, of adopting a 'victim-oriented' perspective that undervalues the significance and contributions of the struggle of black-led organizations. This victim-oriented approach advocates a paternalist solution to the problems faced by black people, while neglecting the possibility of empowerment. Moreover, high-lighting the negative consequences of service provision leads to a danger that little is done to advance thinking and practice. Maulana Karenga describes the dilemma:

> How does one prove strength in opposition without overstating the case, diluting criticisms of the system and absolving the oppressor in the process? How does one criticise the system and state of things without contributing to the victimology school which thrives on lit-anies of lost battles and causality lists, while omitting victories and strengths and the possibilities for change inherent in both black peo-ple and society.
>
> (Cited in Jeyasingham 1992)

In response to this dilemma, Malcolm Harrison's account of the black voluntary housing movement provides a particularly good case study high-lighting both the threats and opportunities faced by ethnic minority vol-untary organizations (Harrison 1990, 1993). Despite a constraining and sometimes hostile external environment, Harrison argues that the black voluntary housing movement provides a case study of positive achievement and offers a reminder of what can be accomplished through struggle and emancipatory activity. Further, the movement recognizes the diversity among Britain's black and ethnic minorities, as housing associations often offered housing support to specific groups such as Afro-Caribbean people or Muslim people. Harrison's account begins in the late 1980s, with what he describes as 'a startling development towards ethnic pluralism in official social policy in England' (Harrison 1993: 23). The Housing Corporation embarked on a programme to encourage, create and sustain separate black-run organ-izations as a channel for delivering social rented housing. The establish-ment of this programme seemed to be in response to reports from the National Federation of Housing Associations and other bodies, which indicated that the housing needs of black and minority ethnic people were substantially worse than for other groups and that such people were also under-represented in every area of housing association work. Establish-ing the programme meant housing corporations 'enabling' minority ethnic housing associations. Harrison judges the programme a success, although acknowledging that the gains achieved by the programme remain precar-ious. Specifically, he points to increasing financial pressures that are likely to threaten smaller organizations and the national political forces pressing for a more commercially oriented arrangement in social housing provision: issues, as we have seen, of concern to voluntary organizations meeting the health and social care needs of people from black and ethnic minorities. None the less, Harrison notes that the emergence of the black housing voluntary movement had exerted pressure in the housing field through a range of channels. Further, the programme initiated by the Housing Cor-poration ensured wider acceptance of good practice among larger housing associations and raised awareness of the desire for self-management and community involvement among black-run associations. Harrison feels that the emergence of a black voluntary housing movement demonstrates that resistance, dissent and grass roots pressure can produce responses and empower people from black and ethnic minorities.

The emergence of voluntary organizations that meet the neglected social care needs of minority groups reflects the potential of empowerment and struggle by focusing on strategies, resources and forms of support that black people find helpful. The current restructuring of the welfare state represents a particular site of praxis offering the opportunity of empowerment, albeit within a context established by current government policy. None the less these changes symbolize what Harrison would describe as managed or organized consumption that creates 'the ground on which solidarities are forged and mobilisation takes place' (Harrison 1990). Despite the overwhelming power of established institutions in Britain, there is frequently scope for successful pressure from the 'grass roots' (Farrar 1992; Harrison 1993). Government policy on social care raises the danger that needs of minorities may be swept aside and marginalized while also presenting the opportunity for need-led care planning, the opening of consultation and planning processes to direct local influence, a new awareness of carers' needs and a recognition of the particular circumstances of black and ethnic minorities (Walker and Ahmad 1994).

The critical analysis of voluntary sector provision in a mixed economy of care offered by this chapter demonstrates the importance of black people being aware of their rights and taking subsequent action to secure them. Priorities rather than 'objective' need are likely to inform the mixed economy of care. Consequently, the importance of informed emancipatory struggle grounded in critical analysis is fundamental in ensuring that the social care needs of black people are reflected in these priorities. Following the conclusions of Walker and Ahmad (1994), linking a critical analysis of health and social care needs, a realistic assessment of the capacity and limitations of community care and an insistence on the statutory obligations being honoured is essential in ensuring that a mixed economy of care will meet the 'particular care needs' of black people.

Annotated bibliography

Bowes, A. and Sim, D. (eds) (1991) *Demands and Constraints: Ethnic Minorities and Social Services in Scotland*. Edinburgh: The Scottish Council for Voluntary Organisations.
This collection of papers, by presenting a wide range of research findings and practical experience, explores the organization of housing and social care in Scotland. The eleven chapters discuss the work of local authorities and voluntary agencies in meeting the needs of Scotland's ethnic minority population.

Harrison, M. (1993) The Black Voluntary Housing Movement: pioneering plural-
    istic social policy in a difficult climate, *Critical Social Policy*, 13(3), 21–35.
This paper describes the problems as well as successes of the black voluntary
housing movement. The author, by describing the successes, reminds us that change
is possible and that black and ethnic minorities are not simply the passive victims
of racism.

Bibliography

Abberley, P. (1987) The concept of oppression and the development of a social theory of disability, *Disability, Handicap and Society*, 2, 5–19.

Abbott, P. and Sapsford, R. (1987) *Community Care for Mentally Handicapped Children*. Milton Keynes: The Open University.

ABSWAP (Association of Black Social Workers and Allied Professionals) (1983) *Black Children in Care: Evidence to House of Commons Social Services Committee*. London: ABSWAP.

ADAPT (Asian Disabilities Advisory Project Team) (1993) *Asian and Disabled*. Bradford: Spastics Society/Barnardo's.

Adler, M. and Asquith, S. (1981) *The Politics of Discretion*. London: Heinemann.

Afshar, H. (1994) Muslim women in West Yorkshire: growing up with real and imaginary values amidst conflicting views of self and society, in H. Afshar, and M. Maynard (eds) *The Dynamics of 'Race' and Gender: Some Feminist Interventions*. London: Taylor and Francis.

Afshar, H. and Maynard, M. (1994) *The Dynamics of 'Race' and Gender*. London: Taylor and Francis.

Ahmad, A. (1989) Contracting out of equal opportunities, *Social Work Today*, 21(8), 26.

Ahmad, B. (1988a) Community social work: sharing the experience of ethnic groups, *Social Work Today*, 19(45), 13.

Ahmad, B. (1988b) When sharing assumptions can pave the way to partnership, *Social Work Today*, 20(15), 12.

Ahmad, R. (1991) *We Sinful Women: Contemporary Urdu Feminist Poetry*. London: Women's Press.

Ahmad, W. I. U. (ed.) (1993) *'Race' and Health in Contemporary Britain*. Buckingham: Open University Press.

Ahmad, W. I. U. (1996) Consanguinity and related demons: science and racism in the debate on consanguinity and birth outcome, in C. Samson and N. South (eds) *The Social Construction of Social Policy*. Basingstoke: Macmillan.

Ahmad, W. I. U. (1996) The trouble with culture, in D. Kelleher and S. Hillier (eds) *Researching Cultural Difference in Health*. London: Routledge.

Ahmad, W. I. U. and Atkin, K. (forthcoming) Ethnicity and caring for a disabled child: the case of children and sickle cell or thalassaemia, *British Journal of Social Work*.

Ahmad, W. I. U., Baker, M. R. and Kernohan, E. E. M. (1991) General practitioners' perceptions of Asian and non-Asian patients, *Family Practice*, 8(1), 52–6.

Ahmad, W. I. U. and Husband, C. (1993) Religious identity, citizenship and welfare: the case of Muslims in Britain, *American Journal of Islamic Social Science*, 10(2), 217–33.

Ahmad, W. I. U., Kernohan, E. E. M. and Baker, M. R. (1989) Health of British Asians: a research review, *Community Medicine*, 11, 49–56.

Ahmad, W. I. U. and Sheldon, T. (1993) Race and statistics, in M. Hammersley (ed.) *Social Research: Philosophy, Politics and Practice*. London: Sage.

Ahmad, W. I. U. and Walker, R. (forthcoming) Asian older people: housing, health and access to services, *Ageing and Society*.

Ahmed, A. S. (1988) *Discovering Islam: Making Sense of Muslim History and Society*. London: Routledge.

Ahmed, L. (1992) *Women and Gender in Islam: Historical Roots of a Modern Debate*. New Haven, CT and London: Yale University Press.

Alibhai-Brown, Y. (1993) Marriage of minds not hearts, *New Statesman and Society*, 12 February, 28–9.

Allsop, J. (1984) *Health Policy and the National Health Service*. London: Longman.

AMA/LGIU (1991) *Too High a Price?* London: Association of Metropolitan Authorities/Local Government Information Unit.

AMA/LGIU (1992) *A Review of Issues Relating to Charging for Community Care Services*. London: Association of Metropolitan Authorities/Local Government Information Unit, mimeo.

Amin, K. and Oppenheim, C. (1992) *Poverty in Black and White*. London: Child Poverty Action Group/Runnymede Trust.

Andersen, H. (1993) *Ethnicity and Gender in the West Midlands Labour Force*. Birmingham: West Midlands Low Pay Unit.

Anderson, B. (1991) *Imagined Communities*. London: Verso.

Anderson, R. (1971) *Family Structure in Nineteenth-century Lancashire*. Cambridge: Cambridge University Press.

Anionwu, E. N. (1993) Sickle cell and thalassaemia: community experiences and official response, in W. I. U. Ahmad (ed.) *'Race' and Health in Contemporary Britain*. Buckingham: Open University Press.

Anthias, F. (1992) *Ethnicity, Class, Gender and Migration: Greek Cypriots in Britain*. Aldershot: Avebury.

Anthias, F. and Yuval-Davis, N. (1993) *Racialized Boundaries*. London: Routledge.

Anwar, M. (1979) *The Myth of Return: Pakistanis in Britain*. London: Heinemann.

Arber, S. and Ginn, J. (1990) Men the forgotten carers, *Sociology*, 23(1), 111–18.

Atkin, K. (1992) Similarities and differences between informal carers, in J. Twigg (ed.) *Carers: Research and Practice*. London: HMSO.

Atkin, K. and Rollings, J. (1992) Informal care in Asian and Afro/Caribbean communities: a literature review, *British Journal of Social Work*, 22, 405–18.

Atkin, K. and Rollings, J. (1993a) *Community Care in a Multi-racial Britain: a Critical Review of the Literature*. London: HMSO.

Atkin, K. and Rollings, J. (1993b) Community care and voluntary provision: a review of the literature, *New Community*, 19(4), 659–67.

Atkinson, F. I. (1992) Experiences of informal carers providing nursing support for disabled dependants, *Journal of Advanced Nursing*, 17, 835–40.

Audit Commission (1986) *Making a Reality of Community Care*. London: HMSO.

Audit Commission (1992a) *Community Care: Managing the Cascade of Change*. London: HMSO.

Audit Commission (1992b) *The Community Revolution: Personal Social Services and Community Care*. London: HMSO.

Audit Commission (1994) *The Community Revolution: Personal Social Services and Community Care*. London: HMSO.

Baldwin, S. (1985) *The Cost of Caring: Families with Disabled Children*. London: Routledge.

Ball, H. (1988) The limits of influence: ethnic minorities and the partnership programme, *New Community*, 15(1), 7–22.

Ballard, R. (1979) Social work with ethnic minorities, in V. Khan (ed.) *Minority Families in Britain*. Basingstoke: Macmillan.

Ballard, R. (1990) Migration and kinship: the differential effect of marriage rules on the processes of Punjabi migration to Britain, in C. Clarke, C. Peach, and S. Vertovec (eds) *South Asians Overseas: Migration and Ethnicity*. Cambridge: Cambridge University Press.

Ballard, R. (1994) *Desh Pardesh: the South Asian Presence in Britain*. London: Hurst and Company.

Ballard, R. and Ballard, C. (1977) The Sikhs: the development of South Asian settlements in Britain, in J. L. Watson (ed.) *Between Two Cultures*. Oxford: Blackwell.

Banton, M. (1979) Gender roles and ethnic relations, *New Community*, 7(3), 323–32.

Barclay Report (1982) *Social Workers: Their Role and Tasks*. London: Bedford Square Press.

Barker, J. (1984) *Black and Asian Old People in Britain*. Mitcham: Age Concern Research Unit.

Barnes, C. (1991) *Disabled People in Britain and Discrimination: a Case for Anti-discrimination Legislation*. London: BCODP Hurst.

Barnes, C. (1995) Community participation and disability, in G. Craig and M. Mayo (eds) *Community Empowerment*. London: Zed Books.

Barnes, M. and Wistow, G. (eds) (1992) *Researching User Involvement*. Leeds: Nuffield Institute for Health Services Studies.

Barth, F. (1969) *Ethnic Groups and Boundaries*. London: Allen and Unwin.

Baxter, C. (1988) Black carers in focus, *Cancerlink*, 4, 4–5.

Baxter, C. (1989a) Cancer support and ethnic minority and migrant work communities. A summary of a research report commissioned by Cancerlink.

Baxter, C. (1989b) Parallels between the social role perception of people with learning difficulties and black and ethnic minority people, in A. Brechin and J. E. Walmsley (eds) *Making Connections: Reflecting on the Lives and Experiences of People with Learning Difficulties*. Sevenoaks: Hodder and Stoughton.

Baxter, C., Poonia, K., Ward, L. and Nadirshaw, Z. (1990) *Double Discrimination*. London: King's Fund.

Bayley, M. (1973) *Mental Handicap and Community Care*. London: Routledge and Kegan Paul.

Bebbington, P., Feeney, S., Flannigan, C., Glover, G., Lewis, S. and Wing, J. (1994)

Inner London collaborative audit of admissions in two health districts. II: Ethnicity and the use of the Mental Health Act, *British Journal of Psychiatry*, 165, 743–9.

Becker, S. and Silburn, R. (1990) *The New Poor Clients*. Nottingham: Nottingham University Benefits Research Unit/Community Care.

Begum, N. (1992) Doubly disabled, *Community Care*, September.

Begum, N. (1994) Optimism, pessimism and care management: the impact of community care policies, in N. Begum, M. Hill and A. Stevens (eds) *Reflections: Views of Black Disabled People on Their Lives and Community Care*. London: CCETSW.

Benefits Editorial (1994) Race, racism and social security, *Benefits*, 9 January, 1.

Ben-Tovim, G., Gabriel, J., Law, I. and Stredder, K. (1986) A political analysis of local struggles, in J. Rex and D. Mason (eds) *Theories of Race and Ethnic Relations*. Cambridge: Cambridge University Press.

Beresford, B. (1994) Resources and strategies: how parents cope with the care of a disabled child, *Journal of Child Psychology and Psychiatry*, 35(1), 171–209.

Bernal, M. (1987) *Black Athena*. London: Vintage Books.

Berry, S., Lee, M., and Griffiths, S. (1981) *Report on a Survey of West Indian Pensioners in Nottingham*. Nottingham: Social Services Department.

Bhachu, P. (1985) *Twice Migrants: East African Sikh Settlers in Britain*. London: Tavistock.

Bhachu, P. (1988) *Apni marzi kardhi*: home and work. Sikh women in Britain, in S. Westwood, and P. Bhachu (eds) *Enterprising Women: Ethnicity, Economy and Gender Relations*. London: Routledge.

Bhachu, P. (1991) Culture, ethnicity and class among Punjabi Sikh women in 1990s Britain, *New Community*, 17(3), 401–12.

Bhaduri, R. (1988) Coming in from the cold, *Insight*, 3(8), 12–14.

Bhalla, A. and Blakemore, K. (1981) *Elderly of the Minority Ethnic Groups*. Birmingham: All Faiths for One Race.

Bhavnani, K. K. and Coulson, M. (1986) Transforming socialist feminism: the challenge of racism, *Feminist Review*, 23, 81–92.

Bhavnani, K. and Phoenix, A. (1994) *Shifting Identities, Shifting Racisms*. London: Sage.

Blakemore, K. (1985) The state, the voluntary sector and new developments in provision for old minority racial groups, *Ageing and Society*, 5, 175–99.

Blakemore, K. and Boneham, M. (1994) *Age, Race and Ethnicity*. Buckingham: Open University Press.

Bloch, A. (1993) *Access to Benefits*. London: Policy Studies Institute.

Bottomore, T. (1992) Citizenship and social class, forty years on, in T. H. Marshall and T. Bottomore (eds) *Citizenship and Social Class*. London: Pluto Press.

Bould, M. (1990) Trapped within four walls, *Community Care*, 8(10), 17–19.

Bourne, J. (1980) Cheerleaders and ombudsmen: the sociology of race relations in Britain, *Race and Class*, 21(4), 331–52.

Bowler, I. (1993) 'They're not the same as us?' Midwives' stereotypes of South Asian maternity patients, *Sociology of Health and Illness*, 15(2), 157–78.

Bowling, B. (1990) *Elderly People from Ethnic Minorities: a Report on Four Projects*. London: Age Concern Institute of Gerontology.

Bradford Social Services Department (1989) *Survey of Carers*. Report for Social Services Committee, City of Bradford Metropolitan Council.

Brah, A. (1978) South Asian teenagers in Southall: their perceptions of marriage, family and ethnic identity, *New Community*, 6(3), 197–206.

Brah, A. (1992) Women of South Asian origin in Britain, in P. Braham, A. Rattansi and R. Skellington, (eds) *Racism and Antiracism: Inequalities, Opportunities and Policies*. London: Sage.

Braham, P., Rattansi, A. and Skellington, R. (eds) (1992) *Racism and Anti-Racism*. London: Sage/The Open University.

Brass, P. R. (1985) Ethnic groups and the state, in P. R. Brass (ed.) *Ethnic Groups and the State*. Beckenham: Croom Helm.

Brisenden, S. (1986) Independent living and the medical model of disability, *Disability, Handicap and Society*, 1(2), 173–8.

British Refugee Council (1985) *The Social Security Reforms*. London: British Refugee Council.

Brown, C. (1985) *Black and White Britain*. London: Policy Studies Institute.

Bryan, B., Dadzie, S. and Scafe, S. (1985) *The Heart of the Race: Black Women's Lives in Britain*. London: Virago.

Bulmer, M. (1987) *The Social Basis of Community Care*. London: Allen and Unwin.

Burghart, R. (1987) Conclusion: the perpetuation of Hinduism in an alien cultural milieu, in R. Burghart, (ed.) *Hinduism in Great Britain*. London: Tavistock.

Busfield, J. (1992) Managing madness, in J. Bornat, C. Pereira, D. Pilgrim and F. Williams (eds) *Community Care: a Reader*. London: Macmillan.

Butcher, H. (1993) Introduction: some examples and definitions, in Butcher *et al.* (eds) *Community and Public Policy*. London: Pluto Press.

Butcher, H., Glen, A., Henderson, P. and Smith, J. (eds) (1993) *Community and Public Policy*. London: Pluto Press.

Butt, J. (1994) *Same Service or Equal Service?* London: HMSO.

Butt, J., Gorbach, P. and Ahmad, B. (1991) *Equally Fair?* London: Race Equality Unit, National Institute for Social Work.

Cameron, E., Badger, F., Evers, H. and Atkin, K. (1989) Black old women, disability and health carers, in M. Jeffreys (ed.) *Growing Old in the Twentieth Century*. London: Routledge.

Carby, H. (1982) Black feminism and the boundaries of sisterhood, in CCCS, *The Empire Strikes Back: Race and Racism in 70s Britain*. London: Hutchinson.

Carey, S. and Shukur, A. (1985) A profile of the Bangladeshi community in East London, *New Community*, 12(2), 405–15.

CCETSW (1991a) *One Small Step towards Racial Justice*. London: CCETSW.

CCETSW (1991b) *Setting the Context for Change: Anti-racist Social Work Education*. London: CCETSW.

Chauhan, B. (1989) Keeping in touch with the Asian community, *Community Care*, 764, supplement, vi, vii.

Cmnd 169 (1957) *Report of the Royal Commission on Mental Illness and Mental Deficiency*. London: HMSO.

Cmnd 849 (1989) *Caring for People*. London: HMSO.

Cmnd 1599 (1991) *The Citizen's Charter: Raising the Standard*. London: HMSO.

Cochrane, R. and Sashidharan, S. (1996) Mental health and ethnic minorities: review of literature and implications for services, in W. Ahmad, T. Sheldon and O. Stuart (eds) NHS Centre for Reviews and Dissemination and Social Policy Research Unit, *Reviews of Ethnicity and Health*. York: NHS Centre for Reviews and Dissemination.

Cocking, I. and Athwal, S. (1990) A special case for treatment, *Social Work Today*, 21(22), 12–13.

Cohen, R. (1994) *Frontiers of Identity*. London: Longman.

Cohen, R., Coxall, J., Craig, G. and Sadiq-Sangster, A. (1992) *Hardship Britain*. London: Child Poverty Action Group.

Cohen, S. (1985) Anti-semitism, immigration controls and the welfare state, *Critical Social Policy*, Issue 13.

Cole, M. (1993) 'Black and ethnic minority' or 'Asian, black and other minority ethnic': a further note on nomenclature, *Sociology*, 27(4), 671–4.

Colley, L. (1992) *Britons: Forging the Nation*. New Haven, CT: Yale University Press.

Commission for Racial Equality (1988) *Homelessness and Discrimination: Report of a Formal Investigation into the London Borough of Tower Hamlets*. London: CRE.

Confederation of Indian Organisations (1987) *Double Bind: to Be Disabled and Asian*. London: Confederation of Indian Organisations.

Connelly, N. (1990) *Between Apathy and Outrage: Voluntary Organisations in Multiracial Britain*. London: Policy Studies Institute.

Cook, J. and Watt, S. (1992) Racism, women and poverty, in C. Glendinning and J. Millar (eds) *Women and Poverty in Britain: the 1990s*. Brighton: Harvester Press.

Coombe, V. (1981) Britain's other elderly, in J. Cheetham (ed.) *Social and Community Work in a Multi-racial Society*. London: Harper & Row.

Cooper, S. (1984) *Observations in Supplementary Benefit Offices*. London: Policy Studies Institute.

Cope, R. (1989) The compulsory detention of Afro-Caribbeans under the Mental Health Act, *New Community*, 15(3), 343–56.

Cowell, R. and Owen, S. (1985) *Ethnic Minorities and the CAB Service*. London: National Association of Citizens Advice Bureaux.

Craig, G. (1989) *Your Flexible Friend?* London: Social Security Consortium/Association of Metropolitan Authorities.

Craig, G. (1991) *Fit for Nothing?* London: Children's Society.

Craig, G. (1992a) *Cash or Care: a Question of Choice?* York: Joseph Rowntree Foundation/University of York.

Craig, G. (1992b) Managing the poorest, in T. Jeffs, P. Carter and M. Smith (eds) *Changing Social Work and Welfare*. Buckingham: Open University Press.

Craig, G. (1993) *The Community Care Reforms and Local Government Change*. Hull: University of Humberside Social Research Paper No. 1.

Craig, P. (1991) Costs and Benefits, *Journal of Social Policy*, 20(4), 537–66.

Centre for Reviews and Dissemination and Social Policy Research Unit (1996) *Reviews of Ethnicity and Health*, edited by W. Ahmad, T. Sheldon and O. Stuart. York: NHS Centre for Reviews and Dissemination.

Culyer, A. J. (1988) Inequality of health services is, in general, desirable, in D. G. Green (ed.) *Acceptable Inequalities? Essays in the Pursuit of Equality in Health Care*. London: IEA Health Unit.

Currer, C. (1986) Concepts of mental well- and ill-being: the case of Pathan mothers in Britain, in C. Currer and M. Stacey (eds) *Concepts of Health, Illness and Disease*. Leamington Spa: Berg.

Dalley, G. (1988) *Ideologies of Caring: Rethinking Community and Collectivism*. Basingstoke: Macmillan.

Daniel, S. (1988) A code to care for the elders, *Social Work Today*, 19(50), 9.

Department of Health (1989) *Caring for People, Community Care in the Next Decade and Beyond*. Cmnd 849. London: HMSO.

Department of Health (1990) *Community Care in the Next Decade and Beyond: Policy Guidance*. London: HMSO.

Department of Health (1991) *Purchase of Service*. London: HMSO.

Department of Health (1992) *Key Indicators of Local Authority Social Services*. London: HMSO.

Department of Health (1993) *Health of the Nation: Key Area Handbook – Mental Health*. London: Department of Health.

Department of Health (1994) *Mental Health Task Force: Black Mental Health – a Dialogue for Change*. Heywood: BAPS Health Publications Unit.

Dhruvarajan, V. (1993) Ethnic cultural retention and transmission among first generation Hindu Asian Indians in a Canadian prairie city, *Journal of Comparative Family Studies*, 24(1), 63–79.

Ditch, J. (1993) Next steps: restructuring the Department of Social Security, in R. Page and N. Deakin (eds) *The Costs of Welfare*. Aldershot: Avebury.

Dominelli, L. (1989) An uncaring profession? An examination of racism in social work, *New Community*, 15(3), 391–403.

Dominelli, L. (1992) An uncaring profession? An examination of racism in social work, in P. Braham, A. Rattansi and R. Skellington (eds) *Racism and Anti-racism*. London: Sage/The Open University.

Donald, J. and Rattansi, A. (eds) (1992) *'Race', Culture and Difference*. London: Sage/The Open University.

Donaldson, L. J. and Odell, A. (1986) Aspects of the health and social service needs of elderly Asians in Leicester: a community survey, *British Medical Journal*, 293, 1079–82.

Donovan, J. (1986) *We Don't Buy Sickness, It Just Comes*. Aldershot, Gower.

Dorn, A. and Troyna, B. (1982) Multiracial education and the politics of decision-making, *Oxford Review of Education*, 8(2), 175–85.

Dourado, P. (1991) Getting the message across, *Community Care*, 856, 22–3.

Doyle, E., Moffatt, P. and Corlett, S. (1994) Coping with disabilities: the perspective of young adults from different ethnic backgrounds in Inner London, *Social Science and Medicine*, 38(11), 1491–8.

Driedger, D. (1989) *The Last Civil Rights Movement: Disabled People's International*. London: Hurst.

Drury, B. (1991) Sikh girls and the maintenance of an ethnic culture, *New Community*, 17(3), 387–99.

DSS (1993a) *Households Below Average Income*. London: HMSO.

DSS (1993b) *Social Security Statistics 1993*. London: HMSO.

Dungate, M. (1984) *A Multiracial Society: the Role of National Voluntary Organisations*. London: Bedford Square Press.

Durrant, J. (1989) Moving forward in a multiracial society, *Community Care*, 792, iii–iv.

Dutt, R. and Ahmad, A. (1990) Griffiths and the black perspective, *Social Work and Social Sciences Review*, 2(1), 37–44.

Ehrenreich, B. and English, D. (1976) *Complaints and Disorders: the Sexual Politics of Sickness*. London: Readers and Writers Publishing Co-operative.

Ellis, K. (1993) *Squaring the Circle: User and Carer Participation in Needs Assessment*. York: Joseph Rowntree Foundation.

Enthoven, A. C. (1985) *Reflections on Management of the National Health Services*. London: Nuffield Provincial Hospitals Trust.

Eribo, L. (1991) *The Support You Need: Information for Carers of Afro-Caribbean Elderly People*. London: Bedford Square Press.

Etzioni, A. (1995) *The Spirit of Community*. London: Fontana.

Evandrou, M. (1990) The personal social services, in J. Hills (ed.) *The State of Welfare: the Welfare State in Britain Since 1974*. Oxford: Clarendon Press.

Farleigh, A. (1990) Invisible communities, *Community Care*, 806, 30–1.

Farrah, M. (1986) Black elders in Leicester: an action research report on the needs of black elderly people of African descent from the Caribbean, *Social Services Research*, 1, 47–9.

Farrar, M. (1992) Racism, education and black self-organisation, *Critical Social Policy*, 36, 53–72.

Featherstone, M. (1990) *Global Culture*. London: Sage.

Fenton, S. (1987) *Ageing Minorities: Black People as They Grow Old in Britain*. London: Commission for Racial Equality.

Fernando, S. (1988) *Race and Culture in Psychiatry*. London: Croom Helm.

Fernando, S. (1991) *Mental Health, Race and Culture*. London: MIND.

Field, S. and Jackson, H. (1989) *Race, Community Groups and Service Delivery*. London: HMSO.

Figgess, S., Daly, M., Noble, M. and Smith, G. (1993) *Information Survey Report*. Oldham: Oldham Disability Alliance/University of Oxford.

Finch, H. (1990) *Perspectives on Financial Support for the Elderly*. London: SCPR.

Finch, J. (1989) *Family Obligations and Social Change*. Cambridge: Polity.

Finch, J. and Groves, D. (1980) Community care and the family: a case for equal opportunities, *Journal of Social Policy*, 9(4), 487–511.

Finch, J. and Groves, D. (1983) *A Labour of Love: Women, Work and Caring*. London: Routledge and Kegan Paul.

Finch, J. and Mason, J. (1993) *Negotiating Family Responsibilities*. London: Routledge.

Finkelstein, V. (1993) The commonality of disability, in J. Swain, V. Finkelstein, S. French and M. Oliver (eds) *Disabling Barriers – Enabling Environments*. London: Sage.

Flew, A. (1984) *Education, Race and Revolution*. London: Centre for Policy Studies.

Flynn, N. (1990a) Maintaining the monopoly, *Insight*, 11 April, 8–9.

Flynn, N. (1990b) Stirring up the supply, *Insight*, 23 May, 12–13.

FPSC (1991) *An Ageing Population*. London: Family Policy Studies Centre.

Francis, E., David, J., Johnson, N. and Sashidharan, S. (1989) Black people and psychiatry in the UK, *Psychiatric Bulletin*, 13, 482–5.

Francis, J. (1993) Pressure group, *Community Care*, 24 June.

Fryer, P. (1984) *Staying Power: the History of Black People in Britain*. London: Pluto Press.

Fryer, R. G. (1989) *Conference on Services for Black Elders, Social Services Inspectorate, East Midlands Region*. London: Department of Health.

Gilroy, P. (1987) *'There Ain't No Black in the Union Jack': the Cultural Politics of Race and Nation*. London: Hutchinson.

Gilroy, P. (1990) The end of anti-racism, *New Community*, 17(1), 71–83.

Gilroy, P. (1992) The end of antiracism, in J. Donald and A. Rattansi (eds) *'Race', Culture and Difference*. London: Sage/The Open University.

Gilroy, P. (1993a) *Black Atlantic*. London: Verso.

Gilroy, P. (1993b) *Small Acts: Thoughts on the Politics of Black Cultures*. London: Serpent's Tail.

GLAD (1987) *Disability and Ethnic Minority Communities – a Study in Three London Boroughs*. London: Greater London Association for Disabled People.

GLCAB (1986) *Out of Service*. London: Greater London Citizens Advice Bureaux.

Glen, A. (1993) Methods and themes in community practice, in Butcher *et al.* (eds) *Community and Public Policy*. London: Pluto Press.

Glendinning, C. (1983) *Unshared Care*. London: Routledge.

Glendinning, C. and Craig, G. (1993) Rationing versus choice, in R. Page and N. Deakin (eds) *The Costs of Welfare*. Aldershot: Avebury.

Glendinning, F. and Pearson, M. (1988) *The Black and Ethnic Minority Elders in Britain: Health Needs and Access to Services*. London: Health Education Authority.

Goldberg, D. and Huxley, P. (1980) *Mental Illness in the Community: the Pathway to Psychiatric Care*. London: Tavistock.

Goldberg, D. and Huxley, P. (1992) *Common Mental Disorders: a Bio-social Model*. London: Routledge.

Gordon, P. and Klug, A. (1984) *Racism and Discrimination in Britain*. London: Runnymede Trust.

Gordon, P. and Newnham, N. (1985) *Passports to Benefits? Racism in Social Security*. London: Child Poverty Action Group and Runnymede Trust.

Gore, M. S. (1977) Family and social change, in M. N. Srinivas, S. Seshaiah and V. S. Parthasarathy (eds) *Dimensions of Social Change in India*. New Delhi: Allied Publishers.

Gottlieb, B. (1981) *Social Networks and Social Support*. London: Sage.

Gould, S. (1984) *The Mismeasurement of Man*. Harmondsworth: Penguin.

Graham, H. (1991) The concept of caring in feminist research: the case of domestic service, *Sociology*, 25(1), 61–78.

Gray, J. (1995) Hollowing out the core, *The Guardian*, 8 March, 26.

Green. D. G. (1990) *Medical Care: Is It a Consumer Good?* London: IEA Health Unit.

Green, H. (1988) *Informal Carers*. London: HMSO.

Grewal, S., Kay, J., Landor, L., Lewis, G. and Parmar, P. (1988) *Charting the Journey*. London: Sheba Feminist Publishers.

Griffiths, R. (1988) *Community Care: an Agenda for Action*. London: HMSO.

Guilliford, F. (1984) A comparison study of the experiences and service needs of Bangladeshi and white families with severely handicapped children. Unpublished dissertation for the Diploma of Clinical Psychology, Leicester, British Psychology Society.

Gunaratnum, Y. (1990) Asian carers, *Carelink*, 11, 6.

Guthch, R. (1990) *The Contract Culture: the Challenge for Voluntary Organisations*. London: National Council for Voluntary Organisations.

Hadley, R., Sills, P. and Dale, P. (1984) *Decentralising Social Services: a Model for Change*. London: Bedford Square Press.

Hall, S. (1992) New ethnicities, in J. Donald and A. Rattansi (eds) *Race Culture and Difference*. London: Sage.

Hall, S., Critcher, C., Jefferson, T., Clarke, J. and Roberts, B. (1978) *Policing the Crisis*. London: Macmillan.

Hambleton, R. (1988) Consumerism, decentralisation and local democracy, *Public Adminstration*, 66, 125–47.

Hardingham, S. (1988) Striving for equal opportunity, *Social Services Insight*, 3(32), 15–17.

Harris, A. (1971) *Handicapped and Impaired in Great Britain*. London: HMSO.

Harrison, M. (1990) Welfare state struggles, consumption and the politics of rights, *Capital and Class*, 42, 107–30.

Harrison, M. (1993) The Black Voluntary Housing Movement: pioneering pluralistic social policy in a difficult climate, *Critical Social Policy*, 39, 21–35.

Hayek, F. A. (1952) *The Road to Serfdom*. London: Ark Paperbacks.

Hellman, C. (1990) *Culture, Health and Illness*. Oxford: Butterworth Heinemann.

Henwood, K. and Phoenix, A. (forthcoming) 'Race' in psychology: teaching the subject, *Ethnic and Racial Studies*.

Hesse, B. (1993) Black to front and black again: racialization through contested times and spaces' in M. Keith and S. Pile (eds) *Place and the Politics of Identity*. London: Routledge.

Hicks, C. (1988) *Who Cares: Looking After People at Home*. London: Virago.

Hill, M. (1994) They are not our brothers: the disability movement and the black disability movement, in N. Begum, M. Hill and A. Stevens (eds) *Reflections: Views of Black Disabled People on Their Lives and Community Care*. London: CCETSW.

Hill, M. J. and Issacharoff, R. M. (1971) *Community Action and Race Relations*. London: Oxford University Press.

Hirst, M. (1992) Employment patterns of mothers with a disabled young person, *Work, Employment and Society*, 6(1), 87–101.

Hobsbawm, E. J. and Ranger, T. (1983) *The Invention of Tradition*. Cambridge: Cambridge University Press.

Holland, B. and Lewando-Hundt, G. (1987) *Coventry Ethnic Minorities Elderly Survey: Method and Data and Applied Action*. Coventry: City of Coventry Ethnic Development Unit.

hooks, b. (1991) *Yearning*. London: Turnaround Press.

House of Commons Social Services Committee (1985) *Community Care with Reference to Adult Mentally Ill and Mentally Handicapped People*. London: HMSO.

Howe, D. (1994) Modernity, post modernity and social work, *British Journal of Social Work*, 25(5), 513–32.

Hoyles, L. and Le Grand, J. (1990) *Markets in Social Care Services*. Bristol: School for Advanced Urban Studies, University of Bristol.

Huby, M. and Dix, G. (1992) *Evaluating the Social Fund*. Department of Social Security Research Report No. 9. London: HMSO.

Husband, C. (1987) *'Race' in Britain: Continuity and Change*. London: Hutchinson.

Husband, C. (1991) 'Race', conflictual politics and anti-racist social work, in CCETSW, *Setting the Context for Change: Antiracist Social Work Education*. London: CCETSW.

Husband, C. (1992) A policy against racism, *The Psychologist*, 5(9), 414–17.

Husband, C. (1994) *'Race' and Nation: the British Experience*. Perth, Australia: Paradigm Books.

Husband, C. (1995) The morally active practitioner and the ethics of anti-racist social work, in R. Hugman and D. B. Smith (eds) *Ethical Issues in Social Work*. London: Routledge.

Ineichen, B. (1987) The mental health of Asians in Britain: a research note, *New Community*, 4, 1–2.

Ineichen, B., Harrison, G. and Morgan, H. S. (1984) Psychiatric hospital admissions in Bristol, *British Journal of Psychiatry*, 145, 600–11.

IRR (1993) *Community Care: the Black Experience*. London: Institute of Race Relations.

Jackson, P. and Penrose, J. (1993) *Constructions of Race, Place and Nation*. London: UCL Press.

Jadeja, S. and Singh, J. (1993) Life in a cold climate, *Community Care*, 22, April, 12–13.

Jarrett, M. (1990) The black voluntary sector, *NCVO Newsletter*, 19, 7–8.

Jeffrey, P. (1976) *Migrants and Refugees: Muslim and Christian Pakistani Families in Bristol*. Cambridge: Cambridge University Press.

Jenkins, R. and Solomos, J. (eds) (1987) *Racism and Equal Opportunities in the 1980s*. Cambridge: Cambridge University Press.

Jenkins, S. (1994) *Winners and Losers*. York: University of Swansea/Joseph Rowntree Foundation.

Jessop, B., Bonnett, K., Bromley, S., and Ling, T. (1988) *Thatcherism*. Cambridge: Polity Press.

Jeyasingham, M. (1992) Acting for health: ethnic minorities and the community health movement, in W. I. U. Ahmad (ed.) *The Politics of 'Race' and Health*. Bradford: Race Relations Research Unit, Bradford University.

Jolley, J. (1988) Ethnic minority elders want more sensitive services, *Social Work Today*, 8(19), 19.

Joly, D. (1987) Associations amongst the Pakistani population in Britain, in J. Rex, D. Joly and C. Wilpert (eds) *Immigrant Associations in Europe*. Aldershot: Gower.

Jones, G. (1986) *Social Hygiene in Twentieth Century Britain*. Beckenham: Croom Helm.

Jones, K. (1960) *Mental Health and Social Policy*. London: Routledge and Kegan Paul.

Jones, T. (1993) *Britain's Ethnic Minorities*. London: Policy Studies Institute.

Keith, M. and Pile, S. (eds) (1993) *Place and the Politics of Identity*. London: Routledge.

Kestenbaum, A. (1992) *Cash for Care*. Nottingham: Independent Living Fund.

Kirp, D. (1979) *Doing Good by Doing Little*. London: University of California Press.

Klein, R. (1988) Acceptable inequalities, in D. G. Green (ed.) *Acceptable Inequalities? Essays on the Pursuit of Equality in Health Care*. London: IEA Health Unit.

Knapp, M. (1989) Private and voluntary welfare, in M. McCarthy (ed.) *New Politics of Welfare*. Basingstoke: Macmillan.

Knowles, C. and Mercer, S. (1992) Feminism and antiracism: an exploration of the political possibilities, in J. Donald and A. Rattansi (eds) *'Race', Culture and Difference*. London: Sage/The Open University.

Krause, I. B. (1990) Sinking heart: a Punjabi communication of distress, *Social Science and Medicine*, 29(4), 563–75.

Lalljie, R. (1983) *Black Elders: a Discussion Paper*. Nottinghamshire County Council SSD.

Lam, T. and Green, J. (1995) Primary health care and the Vietnamese community, *Health and Social Care in the Community*, 2(5), 293–9.

Land, H. and Rose, H. (1985) Compulsory altruism for some or an altruistic society for all, in P. Bean, J. Ferris and D. Whynes (eds) *In Defence of Welfare*. London: Tavistock.

LASA (1985) Black claimants target for cuts, *Review*, August.

Law, I., Hylton, C., Karmani, A. and Deacon, A. (1993) *Racial Equality and Social Security Service Delivery*. Leeds: University of Leeds School of Sociology and Social Policy, Research Working Paper No. 10.

Law, I., Karmani, I., Hylton, C. and Deacon, A. (1994) The effect of ethnicity on claiming benefits: some evidence from Chinese and Bangladeshi communities, *Benefits*, 9.

Lawrence, E. (1982a) In the abundance of water the fool is thirsty: sociology and black pathology, in Centre for Contemporary Cultural Studies, *The Empire Strikes Back*. London: Hutchinson.

Lawrence, E. (1982b) Just plain common sense: the 'roots' of racism, in Centre for Contemporary Cultural Studies, *The Empire Strikes Back*. London: Hutchinson.

Lee, M. (1987) *Sample Study of Black Families with a Mentally Handicapped Member*. Nottinghamshire County Council Social Services Department Research Unit.

Leff, J. (1973) Culture and the differentiation of emotional states, *British Journal of Psychiatry*, 125, 336–40.

Leibenstein, H. (1966) Allocative efficiency vs X-efficiency, *American Economic Review*, 56.

Levick, P. (1992) The janus face of community care legislation: an opportunity for radical possibilities?, *Critical Social Policy*, 12(1), 75–92.

Lewis, J. and Meredith, B. (1988) *Daughters Who Care: Daughters Caring for Mothers at Home*. London: Routledge and Kegan Paul.

Lister, R. (1992) *Women's Economic Dependency and Social Security*. Manchester: Equal Opportunities Commission.

Littlewood, R. and Lipsedge, M. (1989) *Aliens and Alienists: Ethnic Minorities and Psychiatry*. London: Unwin Hyman.

Local Government Information Unit (1990) The black community and community care, *Equalities News*, 10, 1–2.

London Borough of Camden (1990) *The Needs of Women Carers Whose First Language Is Not English*. Report of the Director of Law and Administration (Women's Unit), London Borough of Camden.

Lorde, A. (1984) *Sister Outsider*. New York: Crossing Press.

Lustgarten, L. (1987) Racial inequality and the limits of the law, in R. Jenkins and J. Solomos (eds) *Racism and Equal Opportunities in the 1980s*. Cambridge: Cambridge University Press.

McAvoy, B. R. (1990) Women's health, in B. R. McAvoy and L. J. Donaldson (eds) *Health Care for Asians*. Oxford: Oxford University Press.

McAvoy, B. R. and Donaldson, L. J. (eds) (1990) *Health Care for Asians*. Oxford: Oxford University Press.

McCalman, J. A. (1990) *The Forgotten People*. London: King's Fund Centre.

MacFarland, E., Dalton, M. and Walsh, D. (1989) Ethnic minority needs and service delivery, *New Community*, 15(3), 405–15.

McLaughlin, E. (1991) *Social Security and Community Care*. DSS Research Report No. 4. London: HMSO.

Mahtani, A. (1992) *Poverty, Debt and Indifference*. Sheffield: Sheffield City Polytechnic.

Malin, N. (ed.) (1994) *Implementing Community Care*. Buckingham: Open University Press.

Marks, L. (1990) *Dear Old Mother Levy's: the Jewish Maternity Home and Sick Room Helps Society 1895–1939*. Oxford: Oxford University Press.

Marsh, A. and McKay, S. (1993) *Families, Work and Benefits*. London: Policy Studies Institute.

Mason, D. (1990) 'A rose by any other name . . . ?' Categorisation, identity and social science, *New Community*, 17(1), 123–33.

Mason, D. (1994) On the dangers of disconnecting race and racism, *Sociology*, 28, 4.

May, A. (1989) The minority voice in search of an audience, *Health Service Journal*, 99, (5148), 4.

Meekosha, H. (1993) The bodies politic – equality, difference and community practice, in H. Butcher, A. Glen, P. Henderson and J. Smith (eds) *Community and Public Policy*. London: Pluto Press.

Midence, K. and Elander, J. (1994) *Sickle Cell Disease: a Psychological Approach*. Oxford: Radcliffe.

Midwinter, E. (1994) *The Development of Social Welfare in Britain*. Buckingham: Open University Press.

Miles, R. (1989) *Racism*. London: Routledge.

Miles, R. (1992) Migration, racism and the Nation State in contemporary Europe, in V. Satzewich (ed.) *Deconstructing a Nation: Immigration, Multiculturalism and Racism in 90s Canada*. Halifax: Fernwood Publishing.

Miller, E. and Gwynne, G. (1972) *A Life Apart*. London: Tavistock.

Minford, P. (1987) The role of social services: a view of the New Right, in M. Loney (ed.) *The State or the Market: Politics and Welfare in Contemporary Britain*. London: Sage/The Open University.

Mirza, K. (1991) Community care for the black community – waiting for guidance, in Central Council for Education and Training, *One Small Step for Racial Equality*. London: CCETSW.

Mitchell, D. (1990) Contracts for equality, *Insight*, 5(21), 15.

Modood, M. (1988) 'Black', racial equality and Asian identity, *New Community*, 14(3), 397-404.

Modood, T. (1992) *Not Easy Being British*. Stoke-on-Trent: Trentham Books.

Modood, T., Beishon, S. and Virdee, S. (1994) *Changing Ethnic Identities*. London: Policy Studies Institute.

Mohanty, C. T., Russo, A. and Torres, L. (1991) *Third World Women and the Politics of Feminism*. Bloomington: Indiana University Press.

Moledina, S. (1988) *Great Expectations: a Review of Services for Asian Elders in Brent*. London: Age Concern Brent.

Morris, J. (1991) *Pride against Prejudice: Transforming Attitudes to Disability*. London: The Women's Press.

Morris, J. (1993) *Community Care or Independent Living?* York: Joseph Rowntree Foundation.

Mumtaz, K. and Shaheed, F. (1987) *Women of Pakistan: Two Steps Forward, One Step Back?* London: Zed.

Murray, N. and Searle, C. (1989) *Racism and the Press in Thatcher's Britain*. London: Institute of Race Relations.

NACAB (1984) *The Kirklees Ethnic Minorities Advice Project*. London: National Association of Citizens Advice Bureaux.

NACAB (1991) *Barriers to Benefit*. London: National Association of Citizens Advice Bureaux.

National Association for Health Authorities (1988) *Action Not Words: a Strategy to Improve Health Services for Black and Ethnic Minority Groups*. Birmingham: National Association of Health Authorities.

Nissel, M. and Bonnerjea, L. (1982) *Family Care of the Handicapped Elderly: Who Pays?* London: Policy Studies Institute.

NISW (1991) *Ethnic Monitoring in Social Services Departments*. London: Race Equality Unit, National Institute for Social Work.

Norman, A. (1985) *Triple Jeopardy: Growing Old in a Second Homeland*. Policy Studies in Ageing No. 3. London: Centre for Policy on Ageing.

Nowikowski, S. and Ward, R. (1978) Middle class and British? An analysis of South Asians in suburbia, *New Community*, 7(1), 1–10.

Oldman, C. (1990) *Moving in Old Age: New Directions in Housing Policy*. London: HMSO.

Oliver, M. (1990) *The Politics of Disablement*. Basingstoke: Macmillan.

Oliver, M. (1993) Re-defining disability: a challenge to research, in J. Swain, V. Finkelstein, S. French and M. Oliver (eds) *Disabling Barriers – Enabling Environments*. London: Sage.

Oliver, M. (1995) Understanding the discourses of care in the community. Paper presented to the British Sociological Association Conference, Contested Cities, Leicester.

OPCS (Office of Population Censuses and Statistics) (1988) *The Prevalence of Disability among Adults*. OPCS Survey of Disability in Great Britain. London: HMSO.

Open University (1993) Oral history: Butetown. *Community Care Audio-cassette* 2, Side 2. Milton Keynes: The Open University.

Ouseley, H. (1995) Talent spotting, *The Guardian*, 25 February.

Owen, D. (1993) *Ethnic Minorities in Britain (1991 Census Papers 1–4)*. Warwick University Centre for Research in Ethnic Relations.

Pai, S. and Kapur, R. L. (1981) The burden on the family of a psychiatric patient: development of an interview schedule, *British Journal of Psychiatry*, 138, 332–5.

Papadakis, E. and Taylor-Gooby, P. (1987) Consumer attitudes and participation in state welfare, *Political Studies*, 35, 467–81.

Parker, G. (1990) *With Due Care and Attention: a Review of Research on Informal Care*, 2nd edn. London: Family Policy Studies Centre.

Parker, G. (1992) Counting care: numbers and types of carers, in J. Twigg (ed.) *Carers: Research and Practice*. London: HMSO.

Parker, G. (1993) A four-way stretch? The politics of disability and caring, in J. Swain, V. Finkelstein, S. French and M. Oliver (eds) *Disabling Barriers – Enabling Environments*. London: Sage.

Parker, G. and Lawton, D. (1994) *Different Types of Care, Different Types of Carer: Evidence from the General Household Survey*. London: HMSO.

Parmar, P. (1982) Gender, race and class: Asian women in resistance, in Centre for Contemporary Cultural Studies, *The Empire Strikes Back*. London: Hutchinson.

Patel, N. (1990) *A 'Race' against Time: Social Service Provision to Black Elders*. London: Runnymede Trust.

Peach, C. (1984) The force of West Indian island identity, in C. Clarke, D. Ley, and C. Peach (eds) *Geography and Ethnic Pluralism*. London: Allen & Unwin.

Peach, C. (1986) Pattern of Afro-Caribbean migration and settlement in Great Britain: 1945–1981, in C. Brock (ed.) *The Caribbean in Europe*. London: Frank Cass.

Petch, H. (1994) *The Bare Necessities*. London: CHAR/London Homelessness Forum.

Pettman, J. (1992) *Living in the Margins*. North Sydney: Allen & Unwin.

Pharoah, C. and Redmond, E. (1991) Care for ethnic elders, *Health Service Journal*, 101(5252), 20–22.

Phaure, S. (1991) *Who Really Cares: Models of Voluntary Sector Community Care and Black Communities*. London: London Voluntary Service Council.

Pieterse, J. N. (1991) Fiction of Europe, *Race and Class*, 32, 3–10.

Pillsbury, B. L. K. (1978) Doing the month: confinement and convalescence of Chinese women after childbirth, *Social Science and Medicine*, 12, 11–22.

Plant, P., Lesser, H. and Taylor-Gooby, P. (1989) *Political Philosophy and Social Welfare: Essays on the Normative Basis of Welfare Provision*. London: Routledge.

Pollit, C. (1988) Bringing consumers into performance measurement: concepts, consequences and constraints, *Policy and Politics*, 16(2), 77–88.

Potts, M. and Fido, R. (1990) *A Fit Person to Be Removed*. Plymouth: Northcote Press.

Powell, M. and Perkins, E. (1984) Asian families with a pre-school handicapped child – a study, *Mental Handicap*, 12, 50–2.

Quine, L. and Pahl, J. (1985) Examining the causes of stress in families with severely mentally handicapped children, *British Journal of Social Work*, 15, 501–17.

Qureshi, H. (1996) Family obligations and support, in A. Walker (ed.) *The New Generational Contract*. London: UCL.

Qureshi, H. and Walker, A. (1989) *The Caring Relationship*. Basingstoke: Macmillan.

Rack, P. (1982) *Race, Culture and Mental Disorder*. London: Tavistock.

Rack, P. (1990) Psychological and psychiatric disorders, in B. R. McAvoy and L. Donaldson (eds) *Health Care for Asians*. Oxford: Oxford University Press.

RADAR (Royal Association for Disability and Rehabilitation) (1984) *Disability and Minority Ethnic Groups: a Factsheet of Issues and Initiatives*. London: Royal Association for Disability and Rehabilitation.

Rai, D. K. (1995) *Social Research amongst Asian Communities*. Social Research Papers No. 2. Hull: University of Humberside.

Rao, V. K. R. V. (1977) Some thoughts on social change in India, in M. N. Srinivas, S. Seshaiah and V. S. Parthasarathy (eds) *Dimensions of Social Change in India*. New Delhi: Allied Publishers.

Rattansi, A. (1992) Changing the subject? Racism, culture and education, in J. Donald and A. Rattansi (eds) *'Race', Culture and Difference*. London: Sage.

Rattansi, A. (1994) Western racisms, ethnicities and identities in a 'postmodern' France, in A. Rattansi and S. Westwood (eds) *Racism, Modernity and Identity*. Cambridge: Polity Press.

Rex, J. (1982) West Indian and Asian youth, in E. Cashmare and B. Troyna (eds) *Black Youth in Crisis*. London: Allen and Unwin.

Rex, J. (1991) *Ethnic Identity and Ethnic Mobilisation in Britain*. Warwick: Centre for Research in Ethnic Relations.

Rex, J. and Mason, D. (eds) (1986) *Theories of Race and Ethnic Relations*. Cambridge: Cambridge University Press.

Rex, J., Joly, D. and Wilpert, C. (eds) (1987) *Immigrant Associations in Europe*. Aldershot: Gower.

Ritchie, J. and England, J. (1985) *The Hackney Benefit Study*. London: SCPR.

Robinson, R. (1988) *Efficiency and the NHS: a Case for Internal Markets*. London: IEA.

Robinson, V. (1986) *Transients, Settlers and Refugees*. Oxford: Clarendon Press.

Rooney, B. (1987) *Racism and Resistance to Change*. Liverpool: Sociology Department, University of Liverpool.

Rooney, B. and McKain, J. (1990) *Voluntary Health Organisations and the Black Community in Liverpool*. Liverpool: Sociology Department, Liverpool University.

Rose, M. E. (1971) *The English Poor Law*. Newton Abbot: David and Charles.

Ryan, W. (1971) *Blaming the Victim*. New York: Pantheon.

Sadiq-Sangster, A. (1991) *Living on Income Support: an Asian Experience*. London: Family Service Units.

Saggar, S. (1993) The politics of 'race' policy in Britain, *Critical Social Policy*, 37, 32–51.

Saifullah Khan, V. (1977) The Pakistanis: Mirpuri villagers at home and in Bradford, in J. L. Watson (ed.) *Between Two Cultures*. Oxford: Blackwell.

Samad, Y. (1992) Book burning and race relations: political mobilisation of Bradford Muslims, *New Community*, 18(4), 507–20.

Scull, A. (1984) *Decarceration: Community Treatment and the Deviant: a Radical View*, 2nd edn. Cambridge: Polity Press.

Searle, C. (1989) *Your Daily Dose: Racism and The Sun*. London: Campaign for Press and Broadcasting Freedom.

Sedley, A. (1989) *The Challenge of Anti Racism: Lessons from a Voluntary Organisation*. London: Family Service Units.

Sharabi, H. (1990) *Theory, Politics and the Arab World*. London: Routledge.

Shaw, A. (1988) *A Pakistani Community in Britain*. Oxford: Blackwell.

Sheldon, T. and Parker, H. (1992) The use of 'ethnicity' and 'race' in health research: a cautionary note, in W. I. U. Ahmad (ed.) *The Politics of 'Race' and Health*. Bradford: Race Relations Unit, Bradford University.

Sinclair, I., Parker, R., Leat, D. and Williams, J. (1990) *The Kaleidoscope of Care: a Review of Welfare Provision for Elderly People*. London: HMSO.

Singh, R. (1992) *Immigrants to Citizens: the Sikh Community in Bradford*. Bradford: Race Relations Unit, Bradford University.

Skellington, R. (with Morris, P.) (1992) *'Race' in Britain Today*. London: Sage.

Sly, F. (1994) Ethnic groups and the labour market, *Employment Gazette*, May.

Smyth, M. and Robus, N. (1989) *The Financial Circumstances of Families with Disabled Children Living in Private Households*. London: HMSO.

Solomos, J. (1989) *Race and Racism in Contemporary Britain*. Basingstoke: Macmillan.

SSI (Social Services Inspectorate) (1991) *Care Management and Assessment: Manager's Guide*. Milton Keynes: HMSO.

Stuart, O. (1992) Race and disability: just a double oppression?, *Disability, Handicap and Society*, 7(2), 177–88.

Stuart, O. (1993) Double oppression: an appropriate starting-point?, in J. Swain, V. Finkelstein, S. French and M. Oliver (eds) *Disabling Barriers – Enabling Environments*. London: Sage.

Stubbs, P. (1993) 'Ethnically sensitive' or 'anti-racist'?, in W. I. U. Ahmad (ed.) *'Race' and Health in Contemporary Britain*. Buckingham: Open University Press.

Tarpey, M. (1984) *English Speakers Only*. London: Islington People's Rights.

Taylor-Gooby, P. (1994) Postmodernism and social policy: a great leap backwards?, *Journal of Social Policy*, 33(3), 385–404.

Thomas, R. (1992) Religion and ageing in the Indian tradition, *Ageing and Society*, 12, 105–13.

Torkington, N. P. K. (1991) *Black Health a Political Issue*. Liverpool: Liverpool Institute of Higher Education.

Troyna, B. and Williams, J. (1986) *Racism, Education and the State*. Beckenham: Croom Helm.

TUC (1994) *Black Workers in the Labour Market*. London: Trades Union Congress.

Turner, B. S. (1994) *Orientalism, Postmodernism and Globalism*. London: Routledge.
Turner, J. C. (1987) *Rediscovering the Social Group*. Oxford: Basil Blackwell.
Twigg, J. (1992) *Carers: Research and Practice*. London: HMSO.
Twigg, J. and Atkin, K. (1994) *Carers Perceived*. Buckingham: Open University Press.
Uppal, J. (1988) Helping Asian families in Smethwick, *Carelink*, 4, 3.
Wakil, P. A. (1970) Explorations into the kin-networks of the Punjabi society: a preliminary statement, *Journal of Marriage and the Family*, 30, 700–7.
Walker, C. (1987) How a survey led to providing more responsive help for Asian families, *Social Work Today*, 19(7), 12–13.
Walker, R. and Ahmad, W. I. U. (1994) Windows of opportunity in rotting frames: care providers' perspectives on community care and black communities, *Critical Social Policy*, 40, 46–69.
Wallman, S. (1986) Ethnicity and the boundary process in context, in J. Rex and D. Mason (eds) *Theories of Race and Ethnic Relations*. Cambridge: Cambridge University Press.
Warrier, S. (1988) Marriage, maternity, and female economic activity: Gujarati mothers in Britain, in S. Westwood and P. Bhachu (eds) *Enterprising Women: Ethnicity, Economy and Gender Relations*. London: Routledge.
Watson, E. (1984) Health of infants and use of health services by mothers of different ethnic groups in East London, *Community Medicine*, 6, 127–35.
Watters, C. (1994) Asians and psychiatric services in Britain: avenues of access and parameters of treatment. Unpublished PhD thesis, University of Sussex.
Watters, C. (1995) Representations of Asians in British psychiatry, in C. Samson and N. South (eds) *Social Construction of Social Policy*. Basingstoke: Macmillan.
Wenger, C. (1984) *The Supportive Networks*. London: Allen & Unwin.
Werbner, P. (1988) Taking and giving: working women and female bonds in a Pakistani immigrant neighbourhood, in Westwood, S. and Bhachu, P. (eds) *Enterprising Women: Ethnicity, Economy and Gender Relations*. London: Routledge.
Werbner, P. (1990a) Manchester Pakistanis: division and unity, in C. Clarke, C. Peach and S. Vertovec (eds) *South Asians Overseas: Migration and Ethnicity*. Cambridge: Cambridge University Press.
Werbner, P. (1990b) *The Migration Process: Capital, Gifts and Offerings among British Pakistanis*. London: Berg.
Werbner, P. (1991) The fiction of unity in ethnic politics – aspects of representation and the state among British Pakistanis, in P. Werbner and M. Anwar (eds) *Black and Ethnic Leaderships. The Cultural Dimensions of Political Action*. London: Routledge.
West, C. (1993) *Race Matters*. Boston: Beacon Press.
Westwood, S. (1988) Workers and wives: continuities and discontinuities in the lives of Gujarati women, in S. Westwood and P. Bhachu (eds) *Enterprising Women: Ethnicity, Economy and Gender Relations*. London: Routledge.
Westwood, S. and Bhachu, P. (eds) (1988) *Enterprising Women: Ethnicity, Economy and Gender Relations*. London: Routledge.
Williams, A. (1990) Contract friendly or contract deadly?, *Community Care Project Newsletter*, 17, 23–4.
Williams, F. (1989) *Social Policy: a Critical Introduction*. Cambridge: Polity Press.
Williams, F. (1992) Women with learning difficulties are women, too, in M. Langan and L. Day (eds) *Women, Oppression and Social Work*. London: Routledge.
Wilmott, P. (1986) *Social Networks, Informal Care and Public Policy*. London: Policy Studies Institute.

Wilson, A. (1979) *Finding a Voice: Asian Women in Britain*. London: Virago.

Winkler, F. (1987) Consumerism in health care: beyond the supermarket model, *Policy and Politics*, 15(1), 1–8.

Wistow, M., Knapp, M., Hardy, B. and Allen, C. (1994) *Social Care in a Mixed Economy*. Buckingham: Open University Press.

Wood, P. (1981) *International Classification of Impairment, Disabilities and Handicaps*. Geneva: World Health Organization.

Wright, P. (1985) *On Living in an Old Country*. London: Verso.

Young, K. (1986) Ethnic pluralism and the policy agenda in Britain, in N. Glazer and K. Young (eds) *Ethnic Pluralism and Public Policy*. London: Gower Press.

Young, M. and Wilmot, P. (1957) *Family and Kinship in East London*. London: Routledge.

Zamora, M. (1988) Black carers in Haringey, *Carelink*, 4, 2.

Zarit, S. H. (1989) Do we need another 'stress and caregiving' study?, *Gerontologist*, 29, 2.

Index

'RACE' AND HEALTH IN CONTEMPORARY BRITAIN

Waqar I. U. Ahmad (ed.)

This book is the first critical introduction to the subject of 'race' and health in contemporary Britain and fills a vital gap in the existing literature. Written by leading black and white academic researchers, policy analysts and service providers, committed to achieving anti-racist change, the book provides an analysis of the health and health care of Britain's black population within the context of political, economic and institutional structures and the ideology of racism. Contributions cover: politics of health research; areas of current health concern such as mental health, maternity services and care of the elderly; and health policy issues such as equality in service delivery, employment in the NHS, NHS reforms and health promotion. The book reviews and advances debates in health research and health care delivery in relation to black populations. It is vital reading for students and teachers in the social sciences (especially sociology of health, 'race' relations and social policy), public health and health promotion, nursing, and social work as well as for health service managers, policymakers and community organizations.

> There is much to recommend this coherently edited collection which may well become one of the defining texts . . . in ethnicity and health.
> (*Sociology of Health and Illness 1994*)

> A quite outstanding first critical introduction . . . The book is an absolute 'must' for *all* health workers whether in the policy, service or educational fields.
> (*Journal of the Institute of Health Education 1994*)

Contents
Introduction – Part 1: Politics of research – Making black people sick: 'race', ideology and health research – 'Ethnically sensitive' or 'anti-racist'? Models for health research and service delivery – Part 2: Current health issues: pregnancy, birth and maternity care – Sickle cell and thalassaemia: community experiences and official response – Epidemiology, ethnicity and schizophrenia – Health margins: black elders' care: models, policies and prospects – Part 3: Health policy: health promotion for ethnic minorities: past, present and future – Race equality and employment in the National Health Service – Equal opportunities in service delivery: responses to a changing population? – Conclusions: promoting equitable health and health care: a case for action – Bibliography – Index.

Contributors
Waqar I. U. Ahmad, Elizabeth N. Anionwu, Raj Bhopal, Errol Francis, Jennette Golding, Mark R. D. Johnson, Alison MacFarlane, Luise Parsons, Naina Patel, Sashi P. Sashidharan, Paul Stubbs, Laurence Ward, Martin White.

256pp   0 335 15697 5 (Paperback)   0 335 15698 3 (Hardback)

CARERS PERCEIVED
POLICY AND PRACTICE IN INFORMAL CARE

Julia Twigg and Karl Atkin

Carers are the bedrock of community care, and yet our understanding of how they do and do not fit into the care system is limited. Concern is often expressed about the need to support carers, but the best way to do this is not always clear.

This book breaks new ground in exploring the reality of how service providers like doctors, social workers, and community nurses respond to carers. It looks at which carers get help and why, analysing how age, relationship, class and gender structure the responses of service providers and carers. It examines the moral and policy issues posed by trying to incorporate carers' interests into service provision. What would services look like if they took the needs of carers seriously? How far can they afford to do so? Is this only achieved at the expense of disabled people? What is the proper relationship between carers and services? Carers pose in acute form many of the central dilemmas of social welfare, and the account presented here has the widest significance for the analysis of community care.

Focusing on the views of carers as well as service providers, the book looks at caring across a variety of relationships and conditions, including people with mental health problems and learning disabilities.

Contents
Informal care – Carers in the service system – The carers' experience   Social services – The health sector – Services in a mixed setting – Carers of people with learning disabilities – Carers of adults with mental health problems – Mediating – Structuring – Carers in the policy arena – Appendix – References – Index.

192pp   0 335 19111 8 (Paperback)   0 335 19112 6 (Hardback)

IMPLEMENTING COMMUNITY CARE

Nigel Malin (ed.)

This introductory text provides a unique overview of the implementation of community care policy and the process of managing changes in the field. The central thesis is an expansion of the theme of integrating policy and professional practice in order to assess the requirements for providing models of care based upon a user and care management perspective. The book analyses the impact of changes for community nurses, social workers, those employed in residential and home-based care and discusses anticipated new roles and functions. Its examination of changes in policy and planning both at national and local level makes it a valuable sourcebook for health care, social work practitioners and planners, but the volume is designed for use by students and professionals alike. The emphasis throughout is on the design and delivery of services and providing an overview of research findings, particularly in relation to measuring service effectiveness.

Contents
Preface – Section 1: The policy context – Development of community care – Management and finance – Community care planning – Care management – Section 2: Staff and users – The caring professions – The family and informal care – Measuring service quality – The consumer role – Section 3: Models of care – Residential services – Day services – Domiciliary services – Index.

Contributors
Andy Alaszewski, Michael Beazley, John Brown, David Challis, Brian Hardy, Bob Hudson, Aileen McIntosh, Steve McNally, Nigel Malin, Jill Manthorpe, Jim Monarch, John Rose, Len Spriggs, Gerald Wistow, Wai-Ling Wun.

224pp   0 335 15738 6 (Paperback)